International Political Economy Series

The global political economy is in flux as a series of cumulative crises impacts its organization and governance. The IPE series has tracked its development in both analysis and structure over the last three decades. It has always had a concentration on the global South. Now the South increasingly challenges the North as the centre of development, also reflected in a growing number of submissions and publications on indebted Eurozone economies in Southern Europe. An indispensable resource for scholars and researchers, the series examines a variety of capitalisms and connections by focusing on emerging economies, companies and sectors, debates and policies. It informs diverse policy communities as the established trans-Atlantic North declines and 'the rest', especially the BRICS, rise.

More information about this series at
http://www.springer.com/series/13996

Simone Raudino

Development Aid and Sustainable Economic Growth in Africa

The Limits of Western and Chinese Engagements

palgrave
macmillan

Simone Raudino
GAP Consultants
Hong Kong

International Political Economy Series
ISBN 978-3-319-38935-6 ISBN 978-3-319-38936-3 (eBook)
DOI 10.1007/978-3-319-38936-3

Library of Congress Control Number: 2016953825

Printed on acid-free paper

This Palgrave Macmillan imprint is published by Springer Nature
The registered company is Springer International Publishing AG
The registered company address is: Gewerbestrasse 11, 6330 Cham, Switzerland

To Coco,
For what lies ahead is far better than anything we leave behind

Preface

The core ideas developed in this book matured during professional stints with the United Nations (Angola, 2005–2006) and the European Union (South Africa, 2006–2008). Institutional field work allowed first-hand access to analyses, databases, reports and other sources of structured information from the Italian government, the United Nations and the European Union.[9] References to government and international organizations' information which are not properly referenced in the text should be understood as being elaborated or accessed in the exercise of past professional duties.

These ideas have been further elaborated during my doctoral research at The University of Hong Kong (2010–2013), which has run parallel to the experience of founder and director of GAP Consultants Ltd, a Hong Kong registered limited company providing business advisory services and engaging in commodity trade between China, Europe and Africa. The private sector has proven fertile ground to develop ideas contained in this book, since it provided real-life exposure to a number of economic variables—including commercial regulations; local administrative policies; fiscal, financial and banking provisions; company rules; informal business practices; and local socio-anthropological features—that have played a key role in the Asian economic miracle. Many of these variables would have easily slipped under my academic radar had I not been obliged to face (and sometimes fight against) them in daily business practices—including the Chinese government control over the currency exchange market or Chinese standard business practices in dealing with foreign competitors.

Since September 2013, research for this book has also been complemented with new field experience as a project officer at the European Union Delegation to Afghanistan. Although Afghanistan is not touched by many of the dynamics discussed here—including massive Chinese investments from the early 2000s onwards and large export volumes of natural resources—, it nonetheless maintains a number of similarities with most Sub-Saharan African countries. As a Least Developed Country, Afghanistan and the average Sub-Saharan country have a high percentage of their populations depending upon subsistence agriculture, little to no manufacturing capacity, a virtually useless right of industrial access to OECD markets at zero import duties, high official development assistance levels, limited amounts of inward foreign direct investments and large capital flight outflows.

In this respect, it is interesting to notice how Ashraf Ghani replied to a question on the risk of Chinese involvement in Afghanistan and the meaning of his Beijing trip right after being sworn in as President of Afghanistan: "[…] we are not going to be an African country, because we are going to determine our fate […]", while also pointing out that "[…] mining companies in the West did horrors everywhere in the world and we are learning from those". President Ghani concluded that "ODA has not made a single country rich—it's investment and trade and getting the institutions right that [entail] change"—a line that could also represent the summa of this book.[10]

Simone Raudino
GAP Consultants, Hong Kong

Acknowledgements

This book is the result of multidisciplinary work carried out at the crossroads of academia, government and business. People from different walks of life have contributed to it—it is an honour and a pleasure acknowledging their influence and assistance.

There are persons to be thanked for this remarkable journey even before it started. I am grateful to Julia Strauss from School of Oriental and African Studies (SOAS) and Barry Sautman from Hong Kong University of Science and Technology (HKUST) for pointing me to the European Study Department at the University of Hong Kong (HKU), which provided the perfect combination of multidisciplinary expertise and flexibility needed for this research.

My major debt of gratitude goes to Wayne Cristaudo from Charles Darwin University and Roland Vogt from HKU for having believed in an unorthodox project. Useful ideas and generous words of advice came from HKU academic staff and researchers. I would like to particularly thank Ian Holliday, Stephan Auer, Andreas Leutzsch, Tim Gruenewald, Denis Meyer, Üner Daglier, Martin Chung, Uzma Ashraf, Kristina Tolinsson and Erick Komolo for their availability to engage in discussions on topics relating to politics, national cultures and international relations. I am indebted to Xianming Zhou and Larry Qiu at the HKU Faculty of Business and Economics for discussion on macroeconomic and international trade issues.

The original project proposal benefited from exchanges with authors, diplomats and civil servants working on development, including Robert

Calderisi, David Sogge, Carlo Cibó, Pier Forlano, Tembi Tambo and Eunice Rendón Cárdenas. Heartfelt thanks for earlier draft revisions and comments also go to Adams Bodomo, Arlo Poletti, Emily Winterbotham, Shraddha Mahapatra and Kenichi Masamoto.

Former and present EU colleagues have added valuable criticisms and insightful perspectives to original ideas relating to Europe's interests, belief systems and political vision in its work with developing countries; they include Patrick Simonnet, Andrea Rossi, Milko van Gool, Martina Spernbauer, Gabriel Moyano Vital and Gaël Griette.

A number of ideas contained in this book are the result of creative discussions and business initiatives that owe much to the entrepreneurial communities in Hong Kong and the Guangdong region. In economics as in other fields, there is nothing that can impress learning processes as much as hands-on experience—not the seduction of sophisticated narrative, nor the elegance of theories or the solidity of water-tight logic. For their availability in sharing entrepreneurial experiences, their passion and their resoluteness to engage in the never-ending trial-and-error reality of business life, I thank, among others, Zumin Luo, Sidney Yankson, Andrew Kwok, Ron Hevey, Connie Han and Juan Carlos Sanchez.

I must extend many thanks to my editors and Proofreader at Springer—Timothy Shaw, Judith Allan and Baghyalakshmi Jagannathan—for their generous support, useful advises and patient work in the long revision process that made this book eventually see the light of day.

Last but not least, I am grateful to all those who made this book possible through their emotional and logistic support, with special gratitude to Jill and Maya for their unfaltering welcoming presence even during the rainy days of this long journey.

Contents

1 A Practitioner's Perspective on Development Aid 1

2 The Theory of Economic Development 43

3 The Praxis of Economic Growth: Lessons from History 79

4 A Quantitative Assessment of Africa's International Economic Relations 129

5 A Qualitative Analysis of Africa–West Economic Relations 165

6 A Qualitative Analysis of Africa–China Economic Relations 209

Conclusions 245

Index 257

Abbreviations

ACP	African Caribbean Pacific
AD	Anti-Dumping
AfDB	African Development Bank
AGOA	African Growth and Opportunity Act
AIS	African Investor Survey
ASEAN	Association of South-East Asian Nations
AU	African Union
BENELUX	Belgium, the Netherlands and Luxemburg
BIT	Bilateral Investment Treaties
BOP	Balance of Payments
BRICS	Brazil, Russia, India, China and South Africa
CA	Current Account
CABC	China Africa Business Council
CADF	China Africa Development Fund
CARICOM	Caribbean Community
CCP	China Communist Party
CDB	China Development Bank
CEMAC	Economic and Monetary Community of Central Africa
CEPGL	Economic Community of the Great Lakes Countries
CIC	China Investment Corporation
COMESA	Common Market for Eastern and Southern Africa
CPC	Communist Party of China
CSP	Country Strategy Papers
CSR	Corporate Social Responsibility
DAC	Development Aid Committee
DC	Domestic Company
DDA	Doha Development Agenda

DE	Domestic Entrepreneur
DG	Director General
DRC	Democratic Republic of Congo
EAC	East African Community
EBA	Everything But Arms
EC	European Commission
ECA	Economic Commission for Africa
ECCAS	Economic Community of Central African States
ECOWAS	Economic Community of West African States
EDF	European Development Fund
EIB	European Investment Bank
EP	European Parliament
EPA	Economic Partnership Agreements
EU	European Union
ExIm	China Export Import Bank
FA	Financial Account
FAO	Food and Agriculture Organization
FDI	Foreign Direct Investment
FE	Foreign Entrepreneur
FOCAC	Forum on China-Africa Cooperation
FTA	Free Trade Agreement
GATT	General Agreement on Tariff and Trade
GDE	Gross Domestic Expense
GDP	Gross Domestic Product
GNI	Gross National Income
GNP	Gross National Product
GVC	Global Value Chain
HDI	Human Development Index
HIPC	Highly Indebted Poor Countries
H-O	Heckscher-Ohlin
IBRD	International Bank for Reconstruction and Development
IBSA	India, Brazil and South Africa
ICT	Information and Communication Technology
IDA	International Development Association
IFC	International Finance Corporation
IFI	International Financial Institutions
IMF	International Monetary Fund
IMP	Investment Monitoring Platform
IO	International Organization
IOM	International Organization for Migration
IPA	Investment Promotion Agency
ISI	Import Substitution Industrialization

ISIC	International Standard Industrial Classification
JV	Joint Venture
LAD	Least Absolute Deviations
LDC	Least Developed Countries
M&A	Merger and Acquisition
MAI	Multilateral Agreement for Investment
MDG	Millennium Development Goals
MENA	Middle East and North Africa
MERCOSUR	Mercado Común del Sur
MIGA	Multilateral Investment Guarantee Agency
MIP	Multiannual Indicative Programme
MOFA	Chinese Ministry of Foreign Affairs
MOFCOM	Chinese Ministry of Commerce
NAFTA	North America Free Trade Association
NAMA	Non-Agricultural Market Access
NAO	National Authorizing Officer
NDRC	National Development and Reform Commission
NGO	Non-Governmental Organization
NIE	Newly Industrialized Economies
OCT	Overseas Countries and Territories
ODA	Official Development Assistance
OECD	Organisation for Economic Co-operation and Development
O&M	Operations and Maintenance
OOF	Other Official Flows
OPEC	Organization of the Petroleum Exporting Countries
PF	Private Flows
PISA	Program for International Study Assessment
PRSP	Poverty Reduction Strategy Papers
PTA	Preferential Trade Agreement
R&D	Research and Development
REC	Regional Economic Community
RMC	Regional Member Countries
RTA	Regional Trade Agreement
SADC	Southern African Development Community
SAP	Structural Adjustment Program
SASAC	State-Owned Assets Supervision and Administration Commission
SDR	Special Drawing Rights
SG	Secretary General
SME	Small- and Medium-Sized Enterprises
SOE	State-Owned Enterprise
SPX	Subcontracting and Partnership Exchange
SSA	Sub-Saharan Africa

TFP	Total Factor Productivity
TIFA	Trade and Investment Framework Agreement
TNC	Transnational Corporation
TRIPS	Trade-Related Aspects of Intellectual Property Rights
UAE	United Arab Emirates
UK	United Kingdom
UN	United Nations
UNDP	United Nations Development Programme
UNIDO	United Nations Industrial Development Organization
USA	United States of America
VC	Venture Capital
WB	World Bank
WDI	World Development Indicators
WFOE	Wholly Foreign Owned Enterprise
WOE	Wholly Owned Enterprise
WTO	World Trade Organization

List of Figures

Fig. 1.1	Conceptual box of Western development aid: how institutional discourse presents ODA	10
Fig. 1.2	Institutional view of development aid's production cycle	12
Fig. 1.3	Stock of ODA inflows to Africa (1960–2010) compared to the cost of major USA financial operations, 2011 constant prices, billion USD (Source: OECD)	23
Fig. 1.4	Inward ODA (billion USD) and GDP growth per capita (constant prices 2005, constant exchange rate 2005) in India, China, Brazil and Africa, over the period 1970–2010 (Source: OECD, UNCTAD)	25
Fig. 1.5	GDP per capita of Sub-Saharan Africa excluding South Africa, constant prices (2000) and constant exchange rate (2000), USD, 1970–2012 (Source: UNCTAD)	27
Fig. 1.6	Total ODA to Sub-Saharan Africa, constant prices (2000) and constant exchange rate (2000), million USD, 1970–2012 (Source: OECD)	27
Fig. 1.7	Africa's economic relations with the EU, USA and China: relative proportions of ODA, trade FDI, and capital flight (estimate) (Source: European Commission, OECD, Global Trade, USA Census Bureau)	29
Fig. 4.1	Sum of current accounts of non-oil exporting, non-mineral exporting Sub-Saharan African countries except South Africa, 1980–2014, million USD at current prices and current exchange rate (Source: UNCTAD)	133
Fig. 4.2	Sum of current accounts of all Sub-Saharan African countries except South Africa, 1980–2014, million USD at current prices and current exchange rate (Source: UNCTAD)	133

Fig. 4.3 EU–African ACP countries trade structure: EU imports (red), 2011 (Source: European Commission). 135
Fig. 4.4 EU–African ACP countries trade structure: EU exports (blue), 2011 (Source: European Commission). 136
Fig. 4.5 EU–African ACP countries trade balance by industry, 2011 (Source: European Commission) 137
Fig. 4.6 FDI towards Sub-Saharan Africa excluding South Africa: countries having received more than 5 billion USD in FDI stock + rest of Sub-Saharan Africa, excluding South Africa (Source: UNCTAD) 152

List of Tables

Table 1.1 Key economic and financial indicators in Africa–EU, Africa–USA and Africa–China relations, current prices (2011) and current exchange rate (2011), billion USD (Source: European Commission, OECD, Global Trade, USA Census Bureau) 30

Table 1.2 USA–Africa, EU–Africa and PRC–Africa 2010 trade balances, current exchange rates, billion USD (Source: European Commission, Global Trade, USA Census Bureau) 31

Introduction

What do we know about Africa's economic relations with its international partners? Can these relations be audited—in the same way we audit, for example, business relations between two companies—to determine what the involved parties are, respectively, gaining from their relation? If so, what shall be the yardstick of measurement to determine the "costs" and "benefits" of each party? Once we have chosen such yardstick, can we resolve whether one of the parties is benefiting more than the others?

"Development Aid and Sustainable Growth in Africa" strives to answer these questions by investigating economic relations between Africa and its most important politico-economic partners: the European Union and the USA (as a proxy for the West)[1] and China. It provides a bird's-eye view of these relations and their role—if any—in Africa's traditional economic backwardness. It answers fairly neat research questions, thus renouncing a comprehensive inquiry into the reasons and responsibilities for today's division of wealth between "haves" and "have-nots" nations. To draw a metaphor, if the object of inquiry was cancer (poverty), the book does not try establishing a comprehensive list of cancer's causes or prioritizing these causes by order of importance; what it does instead is studying one specific variable—say diet (international economic relations)—to understand whether it can be correlated to cancer. The study remains acutely aware of the fact that many other variables have already been positively correlated to cancer: smoke (corruption), genetic predisposition (geography), air pollution (population density) and electromagnetic exposure (culture), to name but a few.

Out of metaphor, this book does not suggest that Africa's international relations can be taken as the only reason for the socio-economic situation of African countries, nor does it try establishing a hierarchy between the different mechanisms behind poverty. Similarly, it does not seek a comprehensive explanation of Africa's socio-economic standing, nor does it propose a general theory of what Thomas Malthus considered "the grand object of all inquiries in political economy"[2]: the causes of the wealth and poverty of nations. Instead, it tries establishing a positive correlation between Africa's international economic relations and the continent's lack of endogenous development mechanisms, to subsequently provide an interpretative analysis of the mechanisms linking the two phenomena.

Scope, Epistemology and Key Sources

The book engages with wide conceptual geographical units, including "Africa", "West" and "China". Over and beyond the issue of a neat operationalization of these concepts,[3] it is legitimate to question whether these areas have enough in common to be part of single conceptual units. Many an international scholar question the meaningfulness of putting under the same conceptual umbrella geopolitical regions as fragmented and heterogeneous as Africa's multiple subregions, or even countries pertaining to different continents as those grouped under the concept of "West". Africa is a geographically, culturally, ethnically and, even, economically fragmented continent: grouping these realities under a single conceptual unit, the argument goes, is an oversimplification of a more complex reality. Similarly, the concept of "West" is blurred: from a cultural perspective, we can neither say that countries such as Turkey, post-Apartheid South Africa or Brazil outright pertain to the West—nor can we say the contrary. From a geopolitical and military perspective, even the clear-cut demarcation operated by the Cold War—which understood the West as an area of homogeneous political, military and economic interests, stretching across countries pertaining to the North Atlantic Treaty Organization (NATO) and its key allies—has, since 1989, expanded to include areas of Central and Eastern Europe that were formerly under the influence of the Soviet Union, as well as countries hitherto pertaining to the Non-Aligned Movement. From an economic perspective, borders are even more blurred: the traditional conceptualization of the West as a wealthy centre (including non-Western cultural realities such as Japan) plus a few client states on the one hand and the rest of the world—the so-called "underdeveloped" periphery—on the other, has come under multiple challenges by the reality of international economics, with "old rich clubs", such as the Organization for Economic Cooperation and Development (OECD), progressively accepting members from the periphery and "new rich clubs", such as the Organization of the Petroleum Exporting Countries (OPEC) or the BRICS (Brazil, Russia, India, China and South Africa) group of countries, being in constant formation.

Borders between neatly organized clusters of countries are artificial and naturally imply some form of oversimplification. In fact, any generalization entails an oversimplification. Yet, as this book argues, history does show a number of recurrent patterns laying common ground beneath regions that could otherwise be superficially read as significantly different. Why a desertic, land-locked, sparsely populated, poor in natural resources and prone to drought country such as Niger knows today similar economic fundamentals and social figures to a coastal, green, rich-in-commodity country such as Sierra Leone is something that can be explained on different levels. It would reasonably be possible to delve into the peculiarities of each country's climate, history, social traditions, agricultural systems, access to commercial routes and more, to eventually establish that all these factors contributed in pushing both countries towards independent but similar economic fates. Conversely, it would be possible engaging a similar analytical process by beginning from these countries' similarities first, including the political role that colonialism and globalization originally assigned them between the eighteenth and the nineteenth century, to conclude that such analogies might have contributed in shaping their current politico-economic role within the world order. Similar considerations could be replicated when it comes to identify the common variables that shaped these countries' economic histories.

In his seminal work, "Theory of International Politics", Kenneth Waltz famously distinguished between "reductionist" and "systemic" theories, defining the former as theories dealing with the behaviour of parts and explaining "[…] international outcomes through elements located at national or subnational level" (Waltz 1979: 60), and the latter as theories conceiving of causes operating at the international level, including an anarchical structure affecting behaviour through socialization and competition among its actors. The difference between the two theories is not only in the object of analysis, if not in the way of arranging their materials and causes. Kenneth Waltz's landmark distinction is not only important for defining two levels of customary analysis in international relations (national and subnational vs. international), but also for introducing the idea that states' behavioural patterns can be studied either by beginning from their differences (specific features of each state) or by beginning from their commonalities (the most important being their embeddedness in an international anarchical system rewarding specific behaviours while punishing others).

Every theory claims its own domain and the one used in this book is no exception, being inspired by Waltz's understanding of systemic theory. A study on the impact of international economic relations upon the African continent alone will not explain the role of domestic corruption upon widespread poverty in the continent, or why Botswana, contrary to some of its neighbours, has managed to engage in a successful expansion of its middle class from the 1980s onwards. It will not, for a number of reasons, including the fact that it is not intended to do so. Any study has to accept the physiological limitations that epistemology imposes upon social research, including the depth versus breadth; qualitative versus quantitative; and inductive versus deductive trade-offs. This book wilfully renounces to explain variables that either lie outside its research question or impact the research object in the way Waltz describes as "reductionist". Nonetheless, by shedding light on the centrality of some structural economic variables in international relations, the study invites scrutiny on the role of these same variables also at national and subnational level.[4]

This work is interested in showing structural patterns of economic engagement rather than explaining how specific economic variables have worked in specific countries within specific periods. The research dissects Africa's economic dynamics to analyse that particular bit which relates to its international economic relations and their effects upon domestic dynamics. It ignores domestic variables such as domestically nurtured corruption, autochthon cultures, local diseases, traditional social structures, religions and more. Because of this, the phenomena under scrutiny cannot represent the whole set of variables that contributed in shaping the situation in which African economies are today. In line with a number of theories in political science, international economics and law, this book assigns to the "international component" a fundamental weight in determining the politico-economic path that many formerly colonized countries have eventually undertaken.

Within the "international component", variables considered having logical and ontological priority in determining Africa's economic relations have been given priority. These variables are, by and large, captured by the balance of payments (BoP) items of the analysed regions, plus capital flight and migration. In the interest of avoiding a wild proliferation of variables, other international factors—which no doubt contributed to the situation being analysed—have not being considered. Throughout the text, examples are provided to show how historical instances fit within the general patterns described by the theory—yet, these examples represent exemplificatory cases with explanatory purposes rather than rigorously analysed datasets.[5]

A second epistemological assumption is based on the idea that the theory of political economy is shaped by a different set of goals and assessment criteria than its praxis.[6] This difference reflects a cleavage existing between academia on the one hand and political or business institutions on the other hand. Whereas theoretical contributions in academia need to abide by scholarly standards of novelty and originality of thought, political and business practices are guided by rather contingent factors, including pragmatic interests and power relations between the involved social actors. What is contingent is not necessarily novel and what is novel is not necessarily contingent. International economic policies serving the interests of specific social actors are unlikely to be dismissed on the argument of having been implemented for "too long" or for failing to say anything new. Institutions such as serfdom, indenture and economic monopolies have not been challenged because they had been used for "too long"; they have been challenged—and reversed—because of a change of power relations between different social classes: under new circumstances, formerly disadvantaged socio-economic actors have muscled up and took on the privileges of a minority. The difference with the life cycle of social theories is stark: academic theories, as other intellectual products, operate under the constant requirement of innovation for innovation's sake—the self-justifying need for originality of thought being a legitimate propeller of change across academic theories.

Mainstream economic circles consider a number of charges against neoliberal policies as out of fashion, because they have long been discussed with little results in mainstream thinking or policy praxis. In the Western world, normative perceptions on the democracy-liberal nexus are deeply engrained in the public opinion, to such an extent that in many intellectual environments it is considered in between the tedious and the intellectually shabby to point out that Europe has regularly sustained gruesome dictators in Africa and the Middle East—Muammar Gheddafi, Ben Ali and Hosni Mubarak being the most recent examples, the list including however dozens of other cases—in exchange for their geopolitical alliances and open market policies. Considerations on Latin American authoritarian regimes propped by the USA are typically met with similar attitudes. This research assumes that development theory can contribute towards public policy only by avoiding a detachment from economic and political praxes, something that necessarily entails posing old questions that have already elicited a wealth of theoretical answers. Although many would see structural economic theories as thoroughly refuted, the econometric analysis offered in this book suggests that many aspects of these theories still hold their relevance in describing West–Africa and China–Africa policy praxes and that to explore these praxes does not mean to exclude or downplay other explanations of poverty.

The discussion developed in the book remains mindful of the fact that in ontological reality there is little separation between the analytical and the normative spheres. A "benign reading" of current international political relations necessarily implies a problem with the domestic management, culture or institutional setting of underdeveloped countries. An approach that places the locus of Africa's problems upon the lack of domestic reforms takes attention away from the international structure, suggests that the international economic system needs no fundamental reform and shifts the locus of responsibility towards the people and governments of African countries. Conversely, an approach positing West–Africa–China international relations as a key element in determining a disparity of wealth distribution among these regions necessarily suggests a revisiting of international rules—something that has been claimed in international development circles since the 1970s at least.

Structure and Sources

Chapter 1 offers some anecdotal evidence on official development assistance (ODA) which invites scrutiny on its inconsistencies and questions whether Western aid—and the broader politico-economic cooperation framework it is embedded in—is really assisting Africa in achieving sustainable economic growth. Following an unsuccessful hunt for consistent answers in the academic literature (Chap. 2), the quest moves into the history of political praxes in OECD countries and Newly Industrialized Economies (NIEs) (Chap. 3), in an effort to find a common policy denominator among graduated economies. The underpinning idea is that, beyond the different developmental paths followed by different countries at different times in history, there might be a track record of public policies that have proved to work throughout history.

Chapter 4 retrieves the economic data being analysed: BoP indicators reflecting relations between Africa–European Union, Africa–USA and Africa–China. Data presented here integrate preliminary data provided in Chap. 1, while introducing two variables not included in standard BoP analysis: capital flight and migration.

Chapter 5 subsequently makes use of the "yardstick" based on successful historical praxes to assess the extent, value and impact of Western policies in Africa. The analysis is historical and interpretative, while building upon data presented in Chap. 4. The assessment starts from an analysis of the actors involved to move towards the interests and governance systems behind these actors' policies. In so doing, the research poses straightforward questions on the origin and interests behind Western policies in Africa. Chapter 6 carries out a similar exercise with Chinese policies in Africa.

The analysis shows that, beyond the institutional narrative on the differences between Western and Chinese economic activities in Africa, the two relations rest on similar policy goals and economic mechanisms. Both the West and China entertain economic relations with Africa, mainly finalized at extracting raw material, accessing market outlets for their manufactured goods, promoting a normative environment guaranteeing high and safe returns on their foreign direct investment (FDI), and, at times, creating manufacturing zones relying on low-skilled local labour. It is suggested that the main differences are likely determined by the strong influence of the Chinese government on its national economy, as well as by the large number of Chinese nationals migrating to Africa and aligning their personal interests with the African quest for more industrialized, value-adding and self-relying local economies.

Some words of caution should be expressed on the sources of the book. This work accesses multiple sources—including government and international organizations' public and non-public primary sources, official datasets, and academic literature. Most statistics are updated to 2011, with only spot updates in 2013 and 2016; although development in China-Africa relations has happened at breakneck speed, the core arguments of the book are built upon the structural economic relations that China (and the West) have built and continue building with Africa, over the medium to long term. There are no explanations of yearly variations in BoP payments exchanges or even short-term trends, as these do not contribute in explaining the structural features defining West–Africa and China–Africa economic relations. China and Africa will likely continue expanding their trade, investment and migratory ties in the years to come, till eventually levelling off. Such trends will unlikely entail fundamental changes in the structure of the relationship, which is, by and large, shaped by the mid- to long-term features of the involved actors, including their respective economies, demographics, capital and technology stocks.

The primary sources accessed during the research were in English, French, Spanish, Portuguese or Italian—not Chinese, as relevant Chinese scholarship has only been accessed in English. Similarly, references made to Chinese government positions throughout the book are either coming from secondary sources or were picked from the information that Chinese government sources—including the Ministry of Foreign Affairs and the Ministry of Commerce—have selectively made available in English. It should also be acknowledged that, contrary to Western governmental sources, the author did not have preferential access to Chinese governmental analyses or reports.

The absence of primary Chinese sources contributes to difficulties in verifying their authenticity. While Western official sources are mostly embedded in a network of multilateral institutions and independent observers offering expert checks and solid counter-factual information,[7] Chinese data are, by and large, insulated from international scrutiny. Beijing is highly secretive about its economic policies and has gained a reputation for inflating figures on its international economic ventures, particularly in Africa—yet, international observers are often incapable of agreeing on alternative and more realistic figures. Consequently, the use of averages resulting from multiple sources—a technique often used in the book—cannot fully shoulder the principal risk of having different primary sources "cookedup" by Chinese authorities.[8]

Notes

1. According to the source of data, different group of states from the European Union and USA (e.g. the Organization for Economic Cooperation and Development [OECD] group of countries) might be used as a proxy for the concept of "West". This is explicitly indicated in the text.
2. Thomas Malthus writing to David Ricardo on 26 January, 1817 (Landes 1998, p. 1).

3. The concept of "Africa" has generally been operationalized in the book as the fifty-four countries pertaining to the African Union plus Morocco, "West" as the European Union plus the USA, and China as the People's Republic of China (PRC). Different operationalizations of these concepts have sometimes been used and made explicit in the text.
4. For example, by underlying the importance of the nature of international trade in each country's capacity to produce and retain wealth, the study suggests that significant variations among African/G90 countries' gross domestic products (GDPs) can be explained not only by the fact that some countries have peacefully and effectively managed to exploit and trade in their natural resources, but also by the fact that some of these countries have managed to do it while overcoming typical investment rules and trading conditions offered by OECD countries.
5. One reason for this is that even the most rigorous quantitative studies on the impact of international economic variables, such as Official Development Aid (ODA) or foreign direct investment (FDI), upon national economies need accepting very restrictive assumptions and/or clear-cut frameworks, limiting their explanatory scope to specific time periods or geographical regions. Concerning ODA, these limitations are discussed in more depth in Chaps. 2 and 4.
6. The term "praxis" is often defined in philosophy as thoughtful practice or practice that is informed, purposeful and deliberate, thus representing, in simplified terms, the sum of theory and practice. Karl Marx suggested that the difference between bees and architects is that bees build marvellous structures based on practice, while architects build marvellous structures based on praxis, the difference lying in the fact that architects are involved in reflective practices, while bees behave following natural instincts: "[…] But what distinguishes the worst architect from the best of bees is this, that the architect raises his structure in imagination before he erects it in reality". Following Marx's reasoning, architects "think" about what they are doing and constantly re-evaluate their values, skills, theories and knowledge as they apply them to the structure they are building. Contrary to "practice", "praxis" also draws from the repertoire of past experiences, in order to understand situations and develop new possibilities for action. Because of their highly

reflective and thoughtful nature, political and economic actions are referred to as "praxes" rather than "practices".

7. With important limitations: as a matter of example, in January 2012, the government of Greece was condemned by the European Commission for falsifying data about its public finances and allowing political pressures to obstruct the collection of accurate statistics (Barber 2010).
8. It should, however, be noted that any data fabrication on the Chinese side is more likely to strengthen some of the analyses contained in the book: while the Chinese rhetoric on its engagement with Africa has been moulded on a revolutionary "win-win" concept (diversified trade; high FDI in non-commodity sectors; availability to leave value-adding activities in Africa; balanced migratory patterns, etc.), analyses contained here suggest that the interests and mechanisms underpinning Chinese economic ventures in Africa do not differ substantially from those underpinning Western economic ventures.
9. Access to non-public (confidential, restricted or unclassified) documents was organized in the respect of my employers' policies, standards and guidelines on information sensitivity, classification and handling of information.
10. Lecture by Ashraf Ghani, Chatham House, 4 December 2014.

References

Barber, T. (2010). Greece condemned for falsifying data. *Financial Times.*

Landes, D. S. (1998). *The wealth and poverty of nations: Why some are so rich and some so poor* (1st ed.). New York: W.W. Norton.

Waltz, K. N. (1979). *Theory of international politics* (1st ed.). New York: Addison-Wesley.

CHAPTER 1

A Practitioner's Perspective on Development Aid

1 Official Development Assistance to Africa

"We made it".[1] A colleague from the "finance and contract section" of the European Union (EU) Delegation to South Africa was riding joyfully through the corridors of our political unit, sharing with us his professional contentment at having met yet another budgetary deadline: few extra-million euros had been successfully disbursed that morning. The payment in case did not relate to any of the Delegation's internal expenses or external activities; it related, instead, to a transfer of funds from the EU Development Cooperation Instrument (DCI) to the South African government. Such operations are technically called "direct budget support" and have become common currency in the world of development aid; they consist in net transfers of cash from a governmental body (the European Union in this case) towards another governmental body (South African government in this case), usually against a more or less tight promise on how they will be used. They are not exactly peanuts—at least according to the laymen's understanding of money: in the EU–South Africa case, they represented the large bulk of a 980 million euros financial commitment made by Brussels over the 2008–2013 period for that country only.

The heavy red tape that entangles every tranche of these payments and the close sequence of disbursement deadlines certainly justified my colleague's euphoria. And yet, something pointed at an anthropological quiz I was not fully able to grasp. In which other real-life situation had I witnessed someone cheering at having managed to siphon off a few million

S. Raudino, *Development Aid and Sustainable Economic Growth in Africa*, DOI 10.1007/978-3-319-38936-3_1

euros on behalf of his employer, knowing little of where this money was going to? What type of organization could ask some of its employees to exclusively concern themselves with liquidating bulk payments devoid of any production or profitable logic, and under such a stringent time schedule? Of course, the financial departments of any private or public organization deal with payments and transfers, but these normally fit within a "production cycle" logic: payments go in salaries, commissions, trainings, raw materials, equipment purchases and whatever else is needed to produce what they produce, be it goods or services. But what was "direct budget support" producing?

The question is trickier than it might look. Development funds channelled towards direct budget support—as all other aid modalities discussed in this book—were not meant to be employed in life-threatening situations. Humanitarian aid and assistance in crisis prevention are among the budget lines that development agencies dedicate to natural or man-made disasters, financing the kind of activities that Western public opinions usually conjure up when thinking about foreign aid: disaster relief, food and water distribution, refugee assistance, response to epidemic outbreaks and the alike. Development aid deals with situations that still have a potential for threatening lives—including dire poverty and poor sanitary conditions—, but cannot be solved through short-term measures. These situations are little different from those that many parts of the developed world experienced until fairly recently and that are still to be seen in Roma camps and rundown areas of Western metropolis, where illiteracy, unemployment, family degradation, weak institutional presence and lack of service delivery are the rule rather than the exception. So, if direct budget support did not have the compelling goal of saving people from death, what was the logic of throwing money at problems in far away and little-known countries? What motivated Western people and governments to intervene and what were the expectations of these engagements?

By the time I joined the EU, I had ready-made answers for such questions. It was not, in fact, very difficult to provide answers, as a "Directorate General communication" was tasked with informing the public on the aims and modalities of development aid—and any other EU activity for that matter. The standard line of answer characterized aid as a moral obligation finalized at eradicating poverty and supporting rights and services that would not otherwise be available in low-income and mid-income countries, in the interest of a better world.[2] Other ready-made answers were based on more thought-provoking lines of argument: by helping low and mid-income countries standing on their own feet, the West is fostering its self-interest of having stable, prosperous and commercially thriving neighbours. The argument was sometimes also framed in terms of Europe's own interest in jump-starting the development of neighbouring Africa, similarly to the USA's own interest in assisting Latin American neighbours in becoming mature trade partners. In fact, the whole lot of countries pertaining to the Organization of Economic Cooperation and Development (OECD, the "rich") has an interest in assisting the Group of 90 countries (G90, the "poor") because peaceful and stable international environments are conducive to trade expansion and general economic growth.

They all seemed logical lines of argument and I also maintained for several years that development aid produces better lives for poor people in poor countries, while benefiting the international system at large. That line was not simply a matter of faith towards my employer, it was also consistent with academic knowledge and hands-on experience. Western Universities provide students of international relations and development economics with multiple readings on development aid. By no means are these readings uncritical or supine to institutional propaganda, but they still assume that aid agencies such as the United Nations or the European Union bring positive changes to people in developing countries. And rightfully so; was not I a witness to the building of schools, hospitals and roads; resettlement of internally displaced people and international refugees; distribution of basic commodities? Were not children vaccinated and elderly hospitalized in clinical facilities sponsored by Western donors? Were not youngsters given vocational training by those faith-based organizations that received funds from Western governments? Were not—in one sentence—the lives of those people better off after the intervention of aid organizations?

2 Given Directions

Of course they were! It seemed evident that development money was used to improve poor people's lives: activities were financed and some positive results were clearly under sight. But how exactly was development to happen? How were recipient countries to pass from a situation of inorganic, unbalanced and externally subsidized survival to one of self-sustaining growth? How would development aid help a least developed country (say

2005 Angola) transform into a lower-middle income country (say 2005 Egypt), into an upper-middle income country (say 2005 Thailand), and finally into a fully developed country (say 2005 Netherland)? Indeed, as the development economist Arthur Lewis put it, "[…] the economists' dream would be to have a single theory of growth that took an economy from the lowest level […] past the dividing line […] up to the level of Western Europe and beyond" (W.A. Lewis 1984, p. 4).

If that was the finality of development aid, it looked as an abysmal task. It would have entailed, *inter alia*, questions relating to the paths that had been followed by developed countries during their own development; national elites' capacities in leading their countries; inquiries into global economic, financial and trade flows. I could picture eyebrows raising everywhere in the academic and diplomatic communities as to the viability of these questions. Perhaps a more manageable starting point would have been to understand whether activities sponsored by development aid fitted into the developing process at all: was development aid helping beneficiary countries going through progressive stages of socio-economic development?

I did not have a ready-made answer for this question, but my organization did. It was a mild "yes", albeit formulated in somehow indirect terms. Several EU directorate generals (DGs), including DG Aid and DG Development, worked at a "range of modalities for implementing development aid […] [and for the] eradication of poverty in the context of sustainable development" (European Parliament 2005, p. 4). "Sustainability" stood here for a host of meanings, which also included the importance of "[…] investing in wealth creation—with emphasis on issues such as entrepreneurship, job creation, access to credit, property rights and infrastructures" (European Parliament 2005, p. 6).[3] Thus, among other things, Europe wanted its developing partners to engage in "sustainable wealth creation": getting rich, on their own. Aid policies were meant not only to improve poor people's lives in poor countries, if not to support these countries in acquiring self-sustainable means to improve their own peoples' living standards.[4] This is a concept on which developed countries have spared no ink: the European Consensus on Development openly acknowledges this finality—as also do, in more or less direct terms, the Paris Declaration on Aid Effectiveness, the United Nations Millennium Declaration, the United Nations Agenda 21, the OECD's Development Aid Committee (DAC) guidelines, the scores of World Bank's Poverty Reduction Strategy Papers (PRSPs) and roughly any other commitment, plan, strategy or declaration subscribed by major donors of development aid.[5]

If the statutory aim of Western development organizations includes the promotion of conditions for *self-sustainable* growth in beneficiary countries, it remained unclear how these aims could translate in pragmatic activities. Locating the link between development aid and the mechanisms promoting *self-sustainable* growth is not a straightforward exercise. Macro donor organizations such as the EU or the World Bank (WB) establish framework conditions to finance activities but seldom go in the nitty-gritty of the mechanisms that are supposed to contribute towards sustainable economic growth.

Framework conditions on development cooperation provide terms of reference on how funds are used—typically clustered around (1) principles; (2) modalities and (3) policy fields—but say little about their impact upon a country's capacity to produce wealth. The OECD Development Aid Committee has shaped a number of Official Development Assistance (ODA) *principles*, which have subsequently become the gold standard among major aid agencies.[6] Similarly, donor agencies' framework conditions set out *policy areas*[7] and *modalities* of intervention,[8] but say little on the *master plan*, the donor strategy that should identify priorities and pace the actions deemed necessary to create sustainable economic growth.[9]

The content and meaning of these framework conditions are clear to most observers: development agencies sponsor programmes and policies in line with the national priorities of developing countries, coordinated among them, coherent with other donors' policies, implemented through different modalities and involving different economic and institutional sectors. OECD donor agencies ensure their taxpayers as to the fact that development funds are spent conscientiously and in activities agreed with beneficiary countries. Yet, how did these activities contribute in promoting *sustainable* development—the process of autonomously and endogenously generating durable wealth—remained to me an unanswered question.

In particular, when looking at these assumptions and strategies, I spotted four interesting odd points: (1) development models were extremely general, often referring to "hub" concepts which eschewed key qualifications and avoided establishing logical or chronological priorities in their interventions.[10] These models either failed to specify the causal nexuses that linked ODA actions to economic growth mechanisms or assumed such nexuses to be in line with a set of neoclassic economic assumptions that were far from being uncontested in the economic discipline; (2) in an industry saturated with analyses and obsessed with the quantitative representation of its activities, development agencies could never produce conclusive and authoritative studies correlating aid activities to solid economic results in beneficiary countries; (3) development strategies seemed to be isolated from solid historical analyses: today, there are 74 sovereign countries classified as "high income" by the World Bank, but seldom if ever was the history of their economic, industrial and trade policies taken into account by ODA development strategies; (4) several ODA policies caused vehement protests in developing countries, an element that suggested a conflict of interests that did not show from the ODA institutional discourse.

First, donor organizations were always ready to go into technical details concerning the activities they financed—be they schools, hospitals, training hours delivered, kilometres of roads built, lunch packages distributed, medical and construction kits delivered, refugees airlifted and the like—but seemed to avoid explaining how these activities were contributing towards self-sustainable economic growth. Did roads, bridges, ports and airports built by foreign companies at no cost or at lower-than-market costs for beneficiary countries improve these countries' chances to kick-start self-sustainable growth? If that was the case, donors were failing to provide a thorough review of the mechanisms through which such economic growth was meant to happen.

Western ODA refrain was that infrastructures were necessary to attract foreign direct investments (FDI); but, were infrastructures necessary independently from, say, the nature, or even the existence, of the beneficiary country's national industrial texture, the expected rate of usage or the capacity to exploit these facilities and provide for their operating and maintenance (O&M) costs? If hospitals and schools were built, did that mean that the beneficiary country was moving towards sustainable development? What about the human and financial resources necessary to staff and run these hospitals? If money and expertise stopped coming from foreign donors, would the beneficiary Ministry of Health be in a position to maintain these hospitals? Could beneficiary governments afford them? Should those hospitals have gone private, were people in their catchment areas wealthy enough to pay for medical fees and drug bills? The issue is not whether these structures benefited people: the argument by which these interventions were justified by humanitarianism misses the point of explaining the causal link between normative, welfarist and externally funded policies, on the one hand, and economic growth dynamics, on the other.

Similar questions seemed to receive scant attention from donor organizations, aside from the all evident issue of O&M expenses. Even less attention could come from the implementing organizations or the contractors tasked with the operational aspects of the job: building, digging, training, teaching, decontaminating, curing, moving, distributing, consulting and the alike. It was not part of their job description to appraise the underpinning logic of these activities, and it was not in their interest to question the legitimacy of incoming business: they carried it out, glad to have a solid client and proud to serve a good cause.[11]

The consequence of this missing link was some detachment between theoretical objectives and pragmatic activities: donor agencies claimed to promote *sustainable development*, but mainly financed infrastructures, consumer goods and service delivery activities as opposed to investments in manufacturing facilities, capital goods or technology transfer.[12] Welfarist-like programmes clearly contributed in improving living conditions, but failed to create productive capacity, jobs and, ultimately, sustainable poverty reduction. Because there were immediate beneficiaries to testify as to the benefits of ODA activities, the question of how these activities exactly contributed in generating growth was largely neglected.

Second, ODA largely relied on quantitative data to justify, identify, formulate and appraise its activities. The whole aid industry had a strong quantitative drive: the Organization for Economic Cooperation and Development, United Nations and World Bank are among the most used and quoted secondary sources of socio-economic data worldwide.[13] Yet, the industry as a whole seemed to be avoiding positive methodologies in verifying the macroeconomic impact of its activities: not a single *institutional* study, to my knowledge, had tried putting in relation ODA levels with economic growth or economic sustainability levels. Concurrently, those academic studies that ventured into these research questions emerged with controversial results, as discussed in Chap. 2.

Third, evidence from the development patterns historically followed by mature economies—also referred to as today's developed countries (TDC)—did not seem to be taken into consideration. For example, there is little historical evidence that different groups of countries which successfully graduated from widespread poverty into mid or high income status—including China and part of South-East Asia as discussed in Chap. 3—have developed infrastructures before their industries. Britain, as a matter of example, went into an early industrialization phase (approximately 1790–1815, with the steam engine, mechanized textile production and improved iron production) before investing in major infrastructural works. Similarly, none of these countries had social welfare programmes before they attained an economic status strong enough to afford budget surpluses paying for poverty alleviation programmes.

Fourth, when it came to assisting developing countries in setting out their economic, financial and trade policies—an eventuality that arose through the principle of conditionality every time beneficiary countries negotiated a political or trade agreement with donor countries, rescheduled their debt with the Paris or London clubs or applied for a new loan or grant to international financial institutions (IFIs)—, donor countries adopted a set of stances that stirred controversy. The most contested of these stances were grounded in neoclassic economic assumptions, which pushed ODA beneficiary countries towards the adoption of neoliberal policies. Programmatic policies of international donor agencies typically promoted liberal economic reforms reposing, *inter alia*, on concepts such as "lifting impediment to service sector growth", "promoting decentralized wage bargaining", "removing indexation mechanisms", "relaxing labour market regulations", "reducing unemployment benefits", "opening markets" and "fostering competition".[14] These "medicines" were dispensed through a one-size-fits-it-all approach, as if they could indiscriminately cure all economic growth problems, independently from the where, when and how of their "patients".

Was such an assumption credible? Long before the "no global" manifestations of Seattle, Prague and Washington in the 1990s, there had already been strikes and popular protests across developing countries adopting liberal policies. Why were these people protesting against those very same organizations and policies that purportedly came to their help? Were all the dispossessed of developing countries victims of their governments' corruption and incapacity? Were they all entrenched leftists with ideological aversion towards the imperial Leviathans sitting in Washington, Brussels and Tokyo?

Economists' answers in this respect were contradicting. Mainstream economists suggest that liberal economic policies have served well the interests of Western societies since the nineteenth century at least. There is however little in the way of consistent proofs as to the impact of these policies upon the overall well-being of colonies first, and low and mid-income countries after decolonization or after the fall of the communist bloc. Till now, the academic debate remains open, and development experts' positions vary widely across economic schools, intellectual lineages and governmental organizations. Chapter 2 provides an overview of different economic schools' standpoints on the subject; suffice here to say that among development practitioners also, there were heated debates about the economic policy environment in which they worked.

Why, as a matter of example, should a twenty-first century developing country decide to embrace neoclassic economic measures for growth (as requested by IFIs) was one of such questions. Several objections to neoliberal reforms in developing countries made plain and straightforward sense from a social research perspective: how could the very same economic recipes realistically apply to the 145 different countries classified as low- and mid-income by the World Bank? How could these policies be the same that catered to the interests of high-income countries? Could Angola—an oil producing country with no manufacturing capacity at all—realistically follow the same economic and trade model of the European Union? Why market deregulation and trade liberalization were aprioristically considered essential conditions for development when Europe and the USA only adopted them gradually and fairly recently?

Most development agencies eschewed such questions: institutional discourse either ignored or swept them under the carpet of "hub" concepts, such as "integrated world economy", "private sector development" or "trade for aid". The whole ODA discourse was, in fact, built on trivialized economic principles portraying aid as aimed at "opening", "integrating" and "greening" the beneficiary countries' economies. Not much was said to specify, qualify and justify these concepts and their implementing provisions: as long as some people in beneficiary countries could access better roads, use hospitals and rely on better-trained public administrators, they were assumed to be in the process of "developing sustainably".

The key passage about this "sustainable growth" mechanism remained blurred: what *exactly* was the plan the West had for poor countries? Framework conditions for financing development activities did not say much about their underpinning rationale, if not professing a shallow and undeterred faith towards open economies and the necessity for foreign investments to flow in. But why and how would all neoclassic policies be deemed equally fit to meet developmental challenges in 145 economies classified as low- and mid-income by the WB?

Since there was little in the way of a strategy, it made sense that there were no specific tactics either: seldom, if ever, did development agencies detail how single pragmatic activities contributed towards the grand-plan

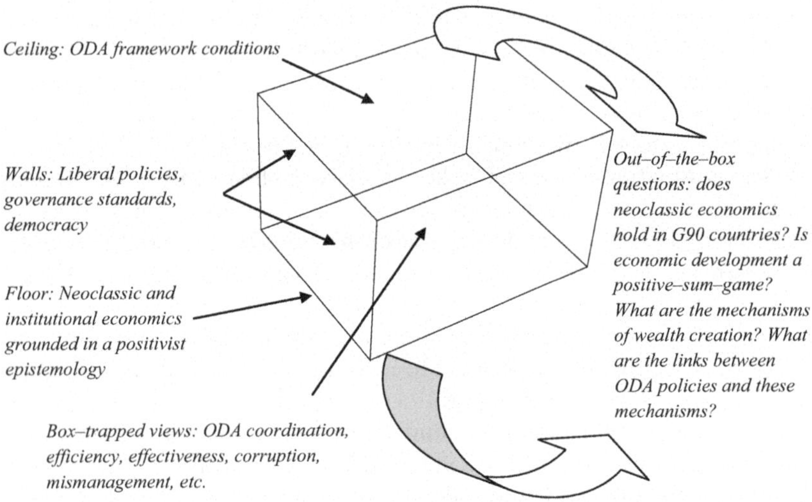

Fig. 1.1 Conceptual box of Western development aid: how institutional discourse presents ODA

of sustainable growth. Because hospitals, roads and trainings were good for the beneficiaries, the aid industry's discourse maintained that they were also good for the development of national economies. Since agricultural service delivery was good for farmers, the aid discourse assumed these activities to strategically contribute towards economic growth. Instead of singling out a developmental rationale, donor organizations produced mountains of technical data showcasing service delivery and transfer of consumable goods as their contribution towards sustainable development.

It seemed to me that such cosmetic information portrayed development aid through a conceptual box, where observers were only exposed to selected items (Fig. 1.1). Mainstream neoclassic economic assumptions constituted a solid floor, representing scientific confidence in the existence of a universal formula conducive towards growth. The neoliberal policies that relied on and emanated from such theoretical assumptions constituted the walls of the conceptual box. The framework conditions regulating ODA guaranteed that development aid activities abode to moral, deontological and good governance standards; this functioned as the ceiling of what development aid organizations presented as the legitimate boundaries of development activities. As long as money was spent in "do-good" activities, compatible with mainstream economic knowledge and properly audited, it was presented by the development aid industry as conducive towards "sustainable development".

Sitting inside the conceptual box created by ODA institutional discourse, it was difficult spotting issues lurking below the floor, beyond the walls or above the ceiling: most debates were instead located in the only accessible theoretical space left by mainstream discourse. There were little questions as to the solidity of foundational economic assumptions (the floor) or the working logic of the policies that ensued from them (the walls), and even less as to the relation between ODA framework conditions and the mechanisms of self-sustaining and endogenous growth (the ceiling). Instead, most questions dealt with subjects lying within the theoretical space created by mainstream economics and Western praxis in development aid: efficacy, efficiency, coordination, corruption, mismanagement, wastes and the alike.

When dealing with the obvious limits of ODA, it seemed to me that development agencies heaped energy and attention on the shortcomings happening within the box, while overlooking the broader picture. The ODA industry worked hard to keep down the *prevalence* of the disease they were fighting (absolute number of poor people), administering as many symptomatic drugs as possible (development projects), while asking few questions about the public health strategy in place to bring down the *incidence* of the disease (number of new poor people arising every year). Tackling the rate of new cases arising every year is the normal strategy used in epidemiology to deal with epidemic outbreaks; instead, development organizations had little in the way of an empirically proven economic growth strategy for their partner countries.

The ODA discourse portrayed a logical, workable and sustainable production cycle that was fully consistent with mainstream economic theory. The script ran as follows: international funds were invested in measures aimed at eradicating poverty by assisting developing countries in achieving self-sustaining economic growth. Experts drawn from different fields were designing the technical policies meant to take poor countries out of poverty, a goal that was in everyone's interest. Modalities designed by experts varied, including government-to-government budget support as well as direct and indirect project management. Views from civil society

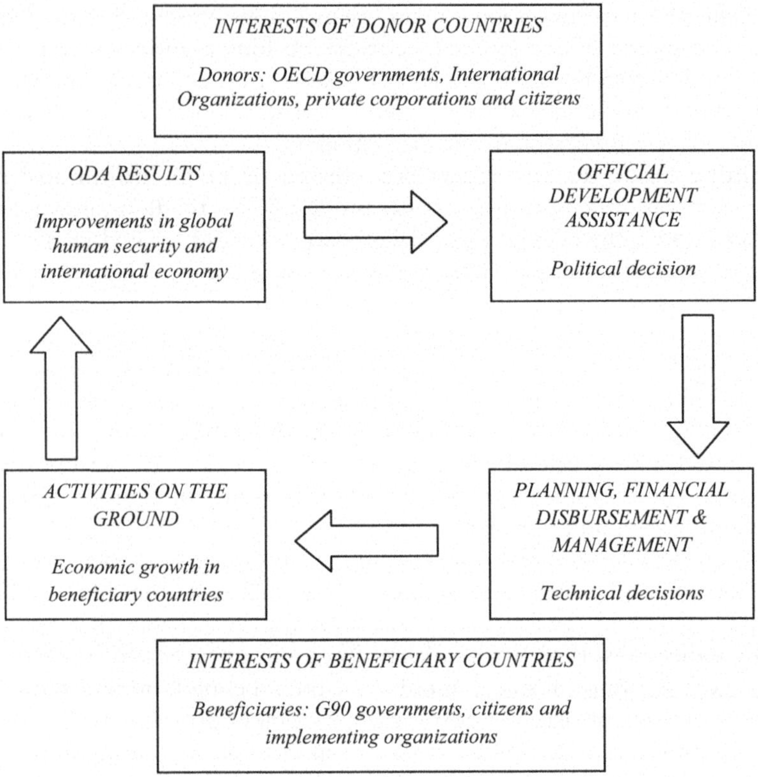

Fig. 1.2 Institutional view of development aid's production cycle

organizations and academia were taken into due consideration. Results were to be found in enhanced living conditions in beneficiary countries as well as compliance with humanitarian duties. Potential gains for aid donors included reduced costs from incoming refugees, illegal migrants and participation in international peacekeeping operations. The conceptual box showed iron logic (Fig. 1.2).

Like contracted labour, development practitioners were asked to drive following the route indicated by their employers. The political level of donor countries set the policy direction to achieve socio-economic development in beneficiary countries, and people working in the aid industry were trained, hired and paid to drive in that direction.

3 Bumpy Road

Even development activities within the "conceptual box" carried their own problems. The production cycle looked theoretically smooth but its mechanisms were far from perfect, giving headaches to people in the aid industry and obliging them to put up with inconsistencies here and there. These inconsistencies were of a varied nature, including (1) corruption and unethical practices; (2) policy, management and technical issues; and (3) system-inherent limits.

Corruption in Western aid is neither endemic nor overwhelming, but is nonetheless present, particularly among beneficiary organizations. In 2005, the international community in Angola had evidence that representatives of beneficiary ministries were taking personal advantage of funds channelled through their offices. Local implementing organizations used to embezzle or resell equipment that had been procured for development projects. Implementing organizations paid their own secretaries international study trips to "strengthen capacity" among administrative staff. In other cases, donor agencies were part of unethical practices, hand-in-hand with the beneficiary organizations they were financing. Implementing NGOs seldom underwent truly meritocratic and transparent procurement exercises: many contracts were instead granted through informal agreements between donors, beneficiaries and implementing agencies. Inefficient contractors continued receiving funds because of the special relationship their directors had established with the country director of sponsor agencies. The examples could easily pile up; in fact, libraries are already ridden with books written by disgruntled aid practitioners posing corruption and poor ODA administration as the main trouble with development aid.[15]

These practices were unfortunate and there were active efforts to keep distortions to a minimum. Development agencies were acutely aware of unethical practices and many initiatives bore testimony as to the political will to do something about it. Donor governments regularly engaged beneficiary governments on the need to keep their lines clean by improving their transparency, investigation, accountability and legal redress standards in the use of public funds. Donor agencies regularly financed seminars in an effort to foster best practices and deontological behaviour, both within their ranks and among partner organizations. Anti-fraud and internal auditing services in Western development organizations dealing with development funds were acquiring increasingly stringent standards over the years, while treaty articles dealing with anti-corruption measures were becoming regular features in international development partnerships.

Still, from a systemic perspective, corruption and unethical practices were hardly surprising in the aid industry. Every year, roughly 166 billion USD worth of ODA[16] were spent in partnership with some of the most ineffective bureaucracies on earth, throughout cultural contexts assigning a different understanding and significance to the Western concept of "corruption". Administrators on the donor side often had incentives in creating "cooperative relationships" with their beneficiary counterparts—be it for their own good or for the interests of the organization or government they represented. Assets channelled through ODA were typically fungible anyway—meaning that they could allow beneficiaries to free previously-committed resources, and use them for different finalities from those they were originally meant to; ensuring a fair and transparent allocation did not automatically provide guarantees as to how funds were eventually used.

Looking at the issue from a pragmatic perspective, it was legitimate asking what could have been *realistically* done to eliminate corruption from the system. Donor organizations pursued increasingly stringent steps, but there was also a general awareness that societal practices could not be changed overnight. Most practitioners tried keeping their own backyard clean, knowing nonetheless that real-world situations are way apart from what development projects' promotional leaflets publicized.[17] Faced with corruption cases, donor organizations often preferred having discreet chats with relevant ministries or implementing agencies rather than creating scandals. Although anti-corruption rules were clearly delineated on paper, real cases were dealt in a less clear-cut way: donors often asked partners to limit irregular practices rather than rigidly enforcing "no trespassing" lines.

Deeper, albeit less evident, problems related to shortcomings in aid management. These problems were taken extremely seriously by the aid industry: donor agencies organize every year hundreds of seminars and brain-storming exercises to improve the efficiency, effectiveness, impact and coherence of their programmes.[18] Why were there hundreds of different organizations operating uncoordinatedly, inefficiently and independently from the beneficiary government's priorities? Why donors did not fulfil the financial commitments they had undertaken? Why, on the other hand, millions of USD got decommissioned every year after implementing agencies had failed to meet budgetary deadlines and bureaucratic requirements set by donors? How to engage the international community in donating more and better aid? Questions of these sorts remain at the core of the debate in the aid industry; in fact, the attention coming from donor organizations on aid management issues has inspired—and financed—most of the literature on development aid, which is largely driven by its polity, policies and technical issues.[19]

The necessity to improve aid delivery quality was constantly on development agencies' agenda. The sheer number of international organizations, regional economic communities (RECs), ministries, national development agencies, NGOs, think tanks, programmes and initiatives operating in the world of development aid had multiplied to such an extent that the main players themselves felt it necessary to resort to some degree of self-restraint, capping the number of activities and agencies. Questions were naturally raised as to the need for such vast network of actors resulting in mazes of overlapping and cross-cutting activities, particularly in the light of the fact that little independent data existed as to the capabilities of these structures. Paradoxically, as new programmes were created to coordinate and establish some order within the many "spaghetti junctions" of development aid, more actors were added to the system. The obsession with "coordination"—an eternally sought-after chimera with little proof of ontological existence—brought many to question whether this was not a scapegoat to divert attention away from more substantial problems within the industry, including overcrowding and poor value for money.

Many practitioners also spotted a third set of problems that were inherent to the system—that is, problems that were not recognized as such by the system itself. These problems could be seen by adopting critical—or second-order cybernetics—analyses of the aid system, a technique that consists in stepping out of the internal observers' shoes (the aid practitioner) to look at the observer as part of the broader system being scrutinized.[20] These readings do not take the system's rules and structures as pre-given: existing institutions and social power relations are not taken for granted and are instead analysed on the basis of their contribution to the system's economy. If the appropriateness of having Western actors intervening upon African problems was not taken for granted (an assumption that is normally done—otherwise, there would not be any development aid budget in first instance), it would have been legitimate wondering on what bases these agencies could apply twenty-first century Western developing models to social, economic and cultural contexts that resembled nothing the West had recently been through.

Incentivizing endogenous development in foreign social and cultural contexts is a radically different undertaking than exporting businesses abroad: while in the latter case, it is possible to reproduce a standardized organizational model (to which employees are obliged to abide), in the former case, it is necessary to obtain the willingness, motivation, sense of ownership and participation of the people that need to adopt such a model. Just like exporting democracy does not simply relate to building national assemblies and organizing elections, there is also more to incentivizing economic development than simply assisting a country in setting up the manifestations of that growth, be they infrastructures, public services or modern governance standards. All in all, exporting social organizational models is a far more contentious and sophisticated venture than exporting internet access, chain restaurants or consultancy firms.

The list of system-inherent inconsistencies was quite long. The fact that most NGOs staff were coming from donor countries (rather than from beneficiary countries) and were paid salaries that bore little relation to their "no profit" status seemed inconsistent with ODA's finalities. Westerners worked on African development not because they were African experts (they were when fared against their fellow nationals; not when compared with Africans themselves), but because they were representative of the taxpayers' communities that sponsored those projects and because they carried a Western vision and approach with them. More generally, it seemed problematic that donor countries went to extreme lengths to recover the assets they had put into development aid: quota for their nationals to be hired by international organizations and NGOs, tied-aid practices in public procurement exercises, trade of votes in international fora against aid money, use of development agreements as a *tromp l'oeil* every time political, trade, financial, migration or military agreements were sealed between an aid donor and an aid beneficiary country and more. It also seemed inconsistent that development officers working for governmental agencies had little incentives by their organizations' code of conduct to publish or publicly discuss any issue lying below, beyond or above the aid conceptual box.[21]

System-inherent inconsistencies are nonetheless of a philosophical nature. Posing these questions was a helpful exercise in investigating the limits of ODA despite the amount of funds, energy and expertise that went into it. It was nonetheless difficult intervening upon them: being of a *systemic* nature, they could hardly be addressed until the *system* was redressed. Few isolated variables might be changed—Scandinavian countries, among others, have been successful in diminishing the percentage of their tied aid—but most problems pertaining to this level looked as intrinsic features of the aid industry. Without a return for the donor country, there would unlikely be an aid policy in first instance; questioning the legitimacy of such a return meant going into a Catch-22 situation. ODA was born with built-in inconsistencies: the British Colonial Development Act of 1929—the forefather of European development cooperation policies—was primarily meant to expand the British tropical colonies' demand for British goods and workforce rather than to serve the colonies.[22] From the onset, ODA was built around interests and goals that differed markedly from its statutory aims; reasoning on the gap between the reality and the rhetoric of these policies allowed putting things into perspective but could hardly provide a road map for action.

However ridden with problems, the aid system looked to me still sound and functioning. All in all, the development aid's production cycle made sense and the system looked solid enough to stand criticisms from the many observers pointing at its flaws. Money was disbursed, activities implemented and some results were under sight: if children got vaccinated and elderly hospitalized, it was thanks to aid donors. No one liked to tread on angels' toes and there was little reason to insist on the shortcomings of an industry that vowed to foster human well-being. The picture was one of cars travelling on an old, unpaved road: potholes and bumps everywhere made the trip slow and uncomfortable, but the direction towards development was assumed to be correct. Was it not so?

4 Doubts

It took some years before it came to my attention that a few other things did not quite add up—and these were not the usual bumps and potholes found on unpaved roads. Bad road conditions have an impact on the speed, quality and chances of success of a journey towards a given destination, but the nature of these questions related instead to the direction itself. Were we actually travelling in the right direction?

The first of these doubts related to expectations and feedbacks. The production cycle of ODA was different from those characterizing private businesses, where it is usually easier to directly correlate costs and benefits. If what the ODA industry was doing bore little resemblance to other businesses—whether public or private; in the first, secondary or tertiary sector—what results should have been expected? In other words, how realistic were development aid's expectations of achieving sustainable economic growth in beneficiary countries?

Answering this question meant verifying where development aid had gone so far—an exercise that required feedback from the field. Contrary to public resources invested in domestic policies—where they were under everyone's eyes and could be broadly assessed at face value—development activities were secluded from the scrutiny of most citizens in donor countries. Because taxpayers could not directly assess the impact of these policies, their judgments had to rely upon auditing exercises and technical feedback. But what kind of feedback had development aid produced along the years?

Unsurprisingly, ODA auditing—also known as monitoring & evaluation (M&E) or monitoring & reporting (M&R)—only covered activities carried out within the box-trapped aid mechanism. Project auditing was not tasked with assessing the mechanisms through which development projects contributed towards sustainable economic growth; rather, they were meant to "[...] assess the status of project implementation in relation to the approved work plan and budget". In other words, "[...] The overall purpose of monitoring is to ensure effectively managed results and outputs through measurement and assessment of performance" (UNEP 2005, p. 50). Technical feedback said nothing about the logic of the project itself; what it did instead was to verify that the project had been implemented according to the principal's specifications. Hundreds of millions of USD could go wasted in unused facilities or irrelevant trainings; if these facilities had been built and training had been executed according to the programme's (faulty) logical framework, no problem would be picked up by M&E/M&R exercises. Conversely, an innovative project with a strong potential to positively impact the economy of a beneficiary country was red-flagged by M&E/M&R if its implementation did not respect its own operational set-out.

Perhaps more surprising was the fact that auditing was almost done in-house: a selected number of companies were closely working with the same departments of those organizations that had set up the aid's framework conditions and operational modalities, operated financial transactions and shaped ODA communication strategies.[23] Auditing exercises provided results that seemed to be little related to the ultimate goal of ODA, which was to assist people in exiting poverty by giving them a role in processes of sustainable wealth creation. The activities of donor institutions and implementing organizations were instead assessed against the objectives they had set for themselves; since M&E/M&R exercises used the projects' own logical framework and envisaged activities as their only yardstick, they measured amount and quality of activities carried out rather than their results in creating sustainable economic growth.

Performance assessments of poverty reduction strategy papers, project appraisals and M&E/M&R audits typically provided figures showing activities being carried out—such as numbers of people trained, refugees repatriated and sheltered, pupils vaccinated, or kilometres of road built. These "activities" were meant to contribute towards "specific objectives" among their beneficiaries, indicated at times in terms of "strengthened capacity", "social empowerment", or "improved access to infrastructures". In the leap from these "specific objectives" towards the "general objective" of creating sustainable economic development something went obviously lost, as there was little proof that the strategy had the capacity—or even the intention—of assisting developing countries in setting up self-sustainable and value-adding economies.

M&E/M&R exercises typically produced statements referring to the projects' activities. Donor agencies received regular reports as to their projects' results in tackling the *prevalence* of the recipients' needs: number of needy people attended in a given period of time. However, these documents seldom addressed the question of their impact upon the *incidence* of the problems causing the need for intervention in first instance: what did these activities do to diminish the number of new needs arising down the road every year?

Why these challenges seldom surfaced in ODA reports was a question that lent itself to different classes of answers. The most evident was that most development projects did not posit the sustainable economic growth of beneficiary countries as an objective, or assumed that positive macroeconomic trends were to be automatically related to their activities, without elaborating methodologies to prove that. Activities were either exempted from evaluations against the economic growth criterion or automatically linked to positive macroeconomic developments, even when these were happening independently from any ODA strategy or result.[24] A second potential answer was that auditing exercises were not meant to provide extra-systemic feedback: only box-contained observations were sought, analyzed and discussed. A survey on the quality of a cigar brand is not interested in being told that cigars are bad for people's health; it is interested in knowing how customers like the product and how the product can be improved. Another possible reason was the fact that all actors involved in ODA projects had a logical interest in keeping the machine going: donor organizations' headquarters had taken political decisions and wanted them executed, country offices needed proving that headquarters' plans were carried out smoothly, implementing organizations needed business and, beneficiary governments were happy at receiving extra revenues. Those who could have given a negative feedback were the millions of poor who remained untouched by these policies—however, since the only people interviewed for auditing purposes were those who actually benefited from the programmes, these voices remained unheard. It was challenging to find a stakeholder in the whole auditing exercise that could have gained from discussing the extra-systemic shortcomings of development aid: none of the involved players had an interest in pointing the finger at out-of-the-box problems. As a consequence, M&E/M&R exercises typically provided technical recommendations for improving future projects along with a much more substantial message about the need to continue financing them.

The most plausible answer was that ODA agencies deemed the question irrelevant altogether. General macroeconomic, financial, trade and investment policies were defined at a political level above the designing of ODA programmes; the space in which the ODA box was embedded—the political space underneath, above and beyond its floor, ceiling and walls—was shaped and delimited by the high politics of donor countries, where decisions had the potential to directly impact their own domestic economic environment. ODA programmes were not meant to mingle with these issues and its actors avoided venturing in that direction.

If checks and balances were so weak and the auditing process fraud, it meant that we were receiving no substantial feedback about our journey. Some people naturally raised the kind of questions that Jonathan Starr pointedly set out in an African newspaper: "[…] what if Marriott Hotels operated without any revenue, room-rate or other meaningful customer-usage data from its individual hotels?" (Starr, 11 April 2011). Now, suppose aid cooperation was heading towards the wrong direction—how were people to realize it? If Marriott Hotels was to be run without any feedback, it would go bust in a matter of months: its shareholders, directors and staff would learn the lesson the hard way. Not the ODA industry, which did not depend on market results to pay its wages.

The aid industry bore instead a number of striking resemblances to a centrally planned economy where multi-year plans established the quantities of goods and services that needed being produced, independently from market inputs. Of course, state-owned enterprises were always willing to produce goods and services as long as their cadres and employees got remunerated, and, of course, it was always possible to find people willing to be assigned those goods and services for free—but were they contributing in creating growth? Were "beneficiary" economies improving their chances of becoming self-sustainable?[25]

The built-in auditing service was biased and could not be trusted; yet the aid industry's bureaucratic level relied on and drew legitimacy from it, continuing to drive steadily towards directions imparted by the political level. In such a situation, there were not many indicators available: practitioners on the ground developed an expertise on the basis of sectors and countries they worked in, but these experiences did not feed into historical, comparative or organic visions providing a meaningful picture. Field experience allowed putting things into perspective, gluing facts to ODA concepts and forcing theories to face undeniable realities, but it was of modest use in building a comprehensive understanding of social phenomena and a systematic view of the context these phenomena were embedded in. Field studies carried out by development agencies were based on the same assumptions, perspectives and methodologies used by auditing reports at project and country level, not to mention these agencies' conflict of interest in analysing the overall results of their own work.[26]

It seemed to me that other sources of analysis were obviously needed, including independent, comparative and long-term studies of the phenomenon.

5 Wrong Directions

The first necessary move was an effort to step back from the contingencies of development activities and particularly from the box-trapped debates and data typically discussed within the ODA industry. The first port of call in such a move is represented by the many academic studies questioning the impact of ODA upon beneficiary countries. A quick literature review of quantitative longitudinal studies showed no agreement on the nature and extent of such impact. These studies have the merit of quantifying the phenomenon and attempting to set positive benchmarks against which scientific analysis can be carried out. However, they artificially isolate and dissect the part (ODA) from the whole (overall economic relations between donors and beneficiaries), to such an extent that different micro-analyses of the same object (ODA flows to a given country in a given period) come to radically different conclusions. In a nutshell, positive statistical studies on ODA impact cannot agree on its capacity to stimulate economic and social development and cannot be taken as a consistent basis for its evaluation.

A second step was to contextualize ODA as a social phenomenon in order to measure its historical meaning, reach and significance. The forefathers of ODA were large-scale food assistance programmes commenced by the USA in 1896. These programmes, however, lacked continuity in time and political responsibility towards beneficiary countries, two elements that characterized British interventions following the adoption of the Colonial Development Act of 1929. The act recognized the UK government's responsibility for the development of its colonies on a continuing basis and established a Colonial Development Fund which provided limited resources for loans finalized to finance capital projects in the colonies. The French followed with the setting up of a *Fond d'investissement pour le Développement Economique et Social* (FIDES) in 1946; as its British counterpart, FIDES was also tasked with providing the colonies with direct grants, thus breaking away with the previous logic of overseas colonies having to self-finance their own infrastructures.

Econometric assessments of the ODA phenomenon can be carried out over relatively long periods of time and available statistics allow comparing post–World War II ODA flows to other grand-scale projects. Authoritative estimates suggest that ODA flows since 1960, worldwide and in Africa, correspond to 2537 billion USD and 711 billion USD respectively, constant prices. These figures do not account for public financial flows that do not meet the conditions for eligibility under OECD ODA criteria (and are therefore classified by the OECD as other official flows [OOF]), nor they include private financial flows.[27]

When compared to financial efforts devised in other historical projects, these amounts look rather impressive. The American administration invested less than 100 billion USD in the Marshall Plan, at constant prices[28]; from a time-comparable perspective, this means that in 2010, the international community has poured into Africa alone the double of the yearly budget that went into the Marshall Plan, which lasted four years in total. Similarly, the New Deal, Franklyn D. Roosevelt's set of policies credited with restoring the mightiness of the American economy after the 1929 crisis, cost an estimated 170 billion USD per year—roughly the

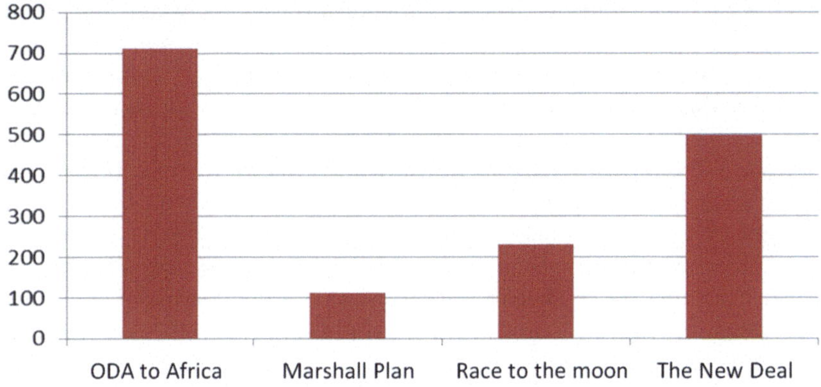

Fig. 1.3 Stock of ODA inflows to Africa (1960–2010) compared to the cost of major USA financial operations, 2011 constant prices, billion USD (*Source*: OECD)

same yearly ODA amount spent worldwide—over a three-year period only (Fig. 1.3).

However, while there is a widely shared scholarly agreement as to the success of these two operations, the same cannot be said of ODA results. Why, with comparable yearly financial efforts, had the Marshall Plan and the New Deal achieved concrete results in a matter of few years, while Western ODA policies in Africa have been trailing for more than 80 years with no safe result to speak of? And why western donors would continue pouring money in policies that are not providing clear results? Economists would point out that the above operations cannot be compared because the international economic system was much less competitive and interdependent in 1945 than it is today. In the case of the Marshall Plan, Europe had a number of assets—including capital and skilled labour—that Africa lacks today. Political scientists would likely remark that in Europe it was a matter of rebuilding a civil, institutional and industrial texture that was already there before the war, rather than setting it up from scratch as it is the case in most African countries. The same goes with the New Deal, which represented a set of heavily subsidized measures aimed at putting back on track a badly shaken—but still world leading—economy. These are all legitimate considerations and most ODA practitioners generally assumed that other long-term statistics could prove ODA's impact since the end of World War II.

One of these statistics looks at the relationship between long-term ODA flows deployed in specific countries and GDP growth in these same countries. GDP is a weak index of development, since it ignores all the variables that, since the publication of the first Human Development Report in 1990, have been considered key components of development indexes, including life expectancy, health and education levels. It also tells us nothing about the way resources are distributed within a given society. As weak as it is, GDP remains nonetheless a rough index of development: without economic growth, there can be no development sustainability because changes for the better need to be paid for and serviced along the years. Societies that have only undertaken a reshuffling of their assets without producing economic expansion (such as Cuba after the Castro revolution) have experienced an initial improvement of people's conditions but have subsequently failed to raise their general socio-economic standards. Societies that have improved their social indicators without expanding their economies (such as most Least Developed Countries engaged by the Millennium Development Goal initiative), have done so by relying on externally subsidized welfare systems, a model that runs against the very concept of *sustainable* development.

Looking at the countries that have received the highest amounts of ODA, African countries stand out as the largest beneficiaries: with aid transfers standing at 711 billion USD between 1971 and 2011, African countries have been, by far, the largest world beneficiaries of ODA. Brazil, China and India altogether have roughly received one-sixth of that amount: 121 billion USD over the same period, current prices. In per capita terms, this difference is even more remarkable: each African person has received 15 times more ODA contributions (715 USD) than his Brazilian, Chinese or Indian counterpart (their average being 40.8 USD). However, all these three countries have shown higher and more sustainable growth rates than any other Sub-Saharan country (Fig. 1.4).[29]

In 1960, both India and China had substantially lower GDP per capita than the average Sub-Saharan African country: India and China stood at roughly 180 USD a year, against roughly 500 USD a year for Sub-Saharan Africa. This was not simply due to the massive population of the two Asian giants: Thailand and Malaysia also had macroeconomic statistics fairly similar to those of 1960 Africa, but subsequently reached skyrocketing growth levels despite the negligible amounts of ODA they were receiving. Even an economy like Vietnam, kept in the grip of communism until today, managed to perform better than the average Sub-Saharan African

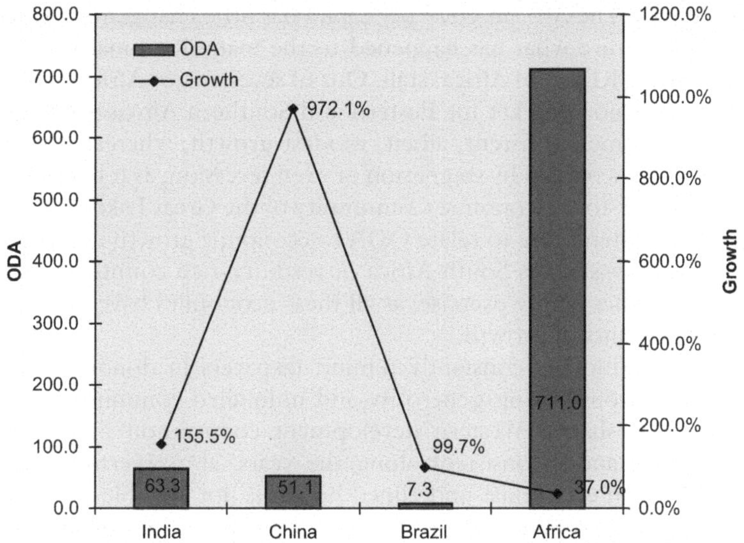

Fig. 1.4 Inward ODA (billion USD) and GDP growth per capita (constant prices 2005, constant exchange rate 2005) in India, China, Brazil and Africa, over the period 1970–2010 (*Source*: OECD, UNCTAD)

country, despite having started from a worse macroeconomic situation (150 USD per capita in 1960) and received substantially smaller amounts of ODA compared with Africa (372 USD for each person).

Comparisons are no easy exercise in international politics. The economic fates of African, Asian, Middle Eastern and Latin American countries might have been more influenced by their different political, economic, cultural and social structures than by the international support they received from donor countries. If that was the case—if ODA impact was somehow hidden behind the national specificities of each country or subregion—there should however be some track record of foreign aid's added value in absolute (rather than comparative) terms, showing that ODA had contributed towards the betterment of specific national or regional economies along the years. That is not the case: there is little macroeconomic proof of any such an impact along the years. The GDP per capita of 1970s Sub-Saharan Africa—the region with the highest amount of per-capita ODA in the world—was 380 USD, current prices. In 2010, it was 420 USD, up from 380 USD in 2005, current prices. The African GDP per capita has little changed in 40 years. These data picture what has happened to the many Regional Economic Communities (RECs) of Africa: stall. Out of seven major African RECs,[30] only the Common Market for Eastern and Southern Africa (COMESA) has showed some consistent, albeit, modest growth, whereas all others have been characterized by stagnation or even recession, as it has been the case for the war-torn Economic Community of the Great Lakes Countries (CEPGL).[31] Attempting to relate ODA to economic growth in more successful regions—such as South Africa or resource-rich countries—would represent a rather empty exercise, as all these economies have more plausible determinants of growth.

As aid practitioners constantly remind taxpayers in donor countries, ODA suffers from jerking generosity and unfulfilled commitments. The dynamics that shaped Western development cooperation policies have been complex and inconsistent along the years, also reverting existing trends. Many an economist underlined how it is not possible to compare macroeconomic progress from point A to point B without qualifying in-between trends and qualitative developments. The underlying assumption is that, if no link between absolute and relative amounts of ODA and economic growth can be established, development aid could at least show some correlation between periods of high ODA injections and periods of economic expansion. As it proves to be, this is a largely wrong assumption: during the aid industry's frenzy of the mid-1970s and 1980s, real GDP per capita in Sub-Saharan Africa actually fell of a good 20 % compared to 1975 levels. The 1990–2000 austerity in development aid, a down period in the aid profligacy–aid fatigue cycle, was met by a stabilization of African GDP. It is only since the early 2000s that we have witnessed some sort of correspondence between growth in ODA and growth in GDP. Overall, existing data over a 40-year time span do not allow establishing a positive and statistically relevant correlation between ODA and GDP growth (Figs. 1.5 and 1.6).[32]

The situation portrayed by macroeconomic data provided little proof as to the efficiency of ODA in dealing with the long-term problem of economic growth in Africa—and other developing economies for that matter. Conversely, ODA project assessments and M&E/M&R exercises provided indications of generally good developmental work being carried out. Empirical evidence on the ground showed that ODA operations were tackling some manifestations of poverty but ignoring its sources. How were these different insights to be reconciled?

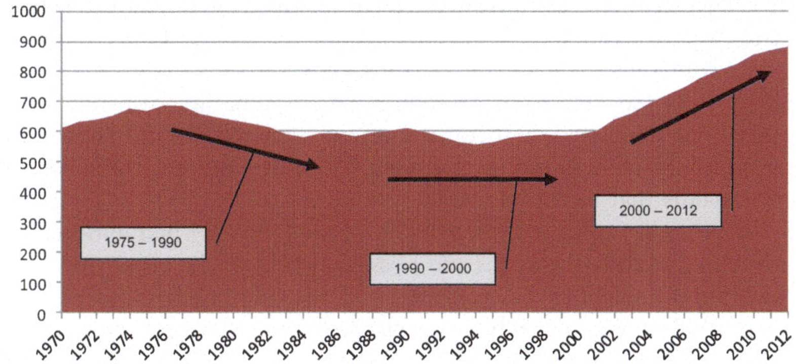

Fig. 1.5 GDP per capita of Sub-Saharan Africa excluding South Africa, constant prices (2000) and constant exchange rate (2000), USD, 1970–2012 (*Source*: UNCTAD)

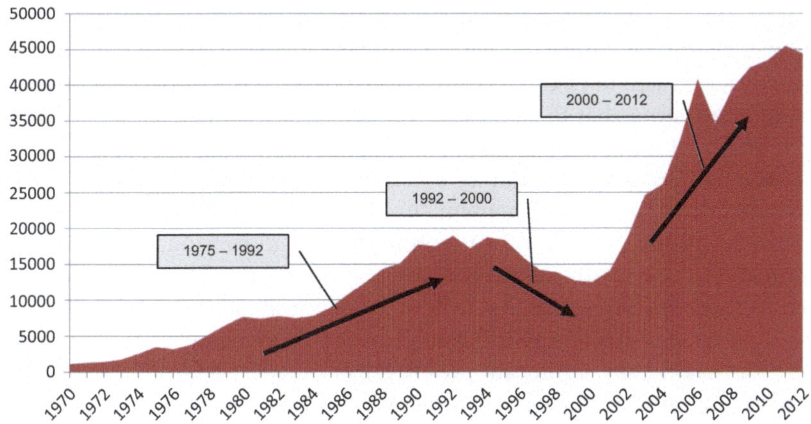

Fig. 1.6 Total ODA to Sub-Saharan Africa, constant prices (2000) and constant exchange rate (2000), million USD, 1970–2012 (*Source*: OECD)

A potential reading could have been a qualification of different typologies of aid: some ODA works and some ODA does not work. Seen from the macro-level, however, aid strategies are remarkably similar: ODA programmes have always been about service delivery, distribution of consumable goods, capacity building and infrastructure development. Differences in micro-management can justify different results in punctual projects or short-term periods in specific countries—not the overall ODA failure in justifying consistent, sustainable and long-term results.

The problem seemed to be more of a structural nature: available information rather suggested, in a consistent and organic fashion, that the car I was travelling on was going in circles. Travelling among the wild and spotting palms that looked remarkably similar to those I saw a few hours before, I became suspicious towards the whole journey I had undertaken. I started looking for landmarks and possible wheel tracks of previous passages. Until I came to *The* question: had the whole aid industry been going in circles? Was the whole development practitioners' community claiming to assist developing countries in creating wealth, while in fact it was redistributing a negligible portion of the wealth created in the West? In other words—was the ODA industry selling charity for sustainable development?

Suggesting that the Western model of development aid—a sector employing 60,000 government and international organization officers, giving jobs to a far larger non-governmental community and sitting on top of a "turnover" close to 160 billion USD a year[33]—pursued a substantially different agenda from its institutional mission is a rather contentious claim. Suggesting that the aid industry "sells charity for sustainable development" is a fundamentally different claim from pointing the finger at the box-trapped problems, including corruption, inefficiency, wastes, in-built inconsistencies, poor management, hidden interests and the alike. It is a statement about the lack of a theoretical basis addressing ODA policies towards their own official mission of creating sustainable economies—as well as the possibility that this is done consciously and purposefully. It is not a matter of signalling that the aid industry is travelling on too bumpy a road for making any significant progress towards destination; it is a matter of recognizing that it took a wrong direction all together. Is this possible—a 160 billion USD/year industry flourishing in an ambiguous environment without being sanctioned by markets, governments, academics or ordinary people?

To explore this possibility, it is necessary to change the usual level of analysis: the institutional portrayal of the ODA box should be transcended, while attention should be lent to elements lying outside the box. This exercise can be done by following a logical trail entailing few passages. First, ODA underlying economic assumptions—largely based on neoclassic tenets—and the policies stemming from them should be questioned.

Economic theories alone do not seem well-placed to represent a stable basis to inform macroeconomic policies. Second, these assumptions and policies should be compared with the real economic praxes through which developed countries have produced and continue producing their own wealth. Third, it should be asked whether Western ODA assumptions and policies are somehow compatible, or even linked, to these real economic praxes. Fourth, the broader relation between Western countries and Africa should be taken into consideration: Western aid policies do not float in a vacuum, being instead part of a much larger framework that shapes relations between societies, governments, economic factors and the international normative system. There is a whole world surrounding the conceptual box of aid practices—trade, investments, primary income, capital flight and more—whose impact and effects should be weighed against the effects of ODA policies.

6 The Larger Picture

A striking feature of Western accounts about the relationship between low and middle income countries, on the one side, and developed countries, on the other, is their consistent homogeneity. Surfing throughout policy papers or institutional messages of ministries dealing with security and foreign affairs in European countries, the visitor is introduced to the principles of developed countries' foreign policies, usually in terms of "global security", "mutual engagement", "burden sharing" and the alike. Skilfully polished diplomatic language leaves room for appreciable differences: certain governments underline their "atlanticism" rather than "europeism", "fight against terrorism" rather than "commitment towards international peace". However, when it comes to relationship with Africa, geopolitical terms usually give way to loftier and homogeneous wording, including "solidarity", "humanitarian assistance", "partnership for development" and "global responsibility".

The development practitioner that would exclusively rely on those sources, would have enough ground to believe that Africa—along with other least developed regions that are resource-scarce and devoid of geopolitical interest—is a training ground for Western countries' good international citizenry skills. Western public opinion seems, indeed, embedded within this mode of thinking, since it usually pictures Africa as a place where their countries have little to do but provide development assistance. Development debates engaged from such a perspective naturally lead towards box-trapped issues: the focus is on what works and what does not of ODA, leaving aside the general context in which ODA happens and from which ODA receives meaning and scope.

Were we to look at hard facts in Africa's international relations, these would however depict a different picture altogether. Let us take the relationship between Africa and its three main partners: the European Union, the People's Republic of China and the USA (1.7). Squeezing the meaning, value and weight of these three relationships (EU–Africa, PRC–Africa and USA–Africa) into a quantitative index is not fully feasible, but some aspects can be quantified in fairly precise terms. This is the case for some Balance of Payments (BoP) items—including trade, FDI and ODA—plus some other items off the BoP, which can be estimated through educated guessing techniques, as it is the case for capital flight, the outward flows of private and illegal assets. The rough picture that results from such an exercise is the following (Table 1.1)[34]:

Several elements are immediately evident and worthy of notice. The value of trade (goods and services) flows between Africa and these three regions far outweighs the value of ODA flows. In 2008, against incoming ODA from these three areas roughly valued at 33.7 billion USD, Africa exchanged goods and services worth 568 billion USD—more than 16 times the ODA value over. Raw data tell us little about the nature of these exchanges, but they do tell us that ODA value is but a tiny fraction (7 %) of the trade exchange value between Africa and the European Union plus the USA, and far a smaller fraction (1.3 %) of the trade exchange value between Africa and China. Africa is poor, but rich enough to be engaged business-wise. If we have to see the (partial) overlook of African economic relation-

Table 1.1 Key economic and financial indicators in Africa–EU, Africa–USA and Africa–China relations, current prices (2011) and current exchange rate (2011), billion USD (Source: European Commission, OECD, Global Trade, USA Census Bureau)

EU (EC + member states) ODA to Africa (2009)	USD 25
PRC ODA to Africa (Estimated 2009)	USD 1.5
USA ODA to Africa (2009)	USD 7.6
EU–Africa trade (2010)	USD 436
PRC–Africa trade (2010)	USD 102
USA–Africa trade (2010)	USD 104.5
Inward FDI flows in Africa (2010)	USD 55
Outward FDI flows from Africa (2010)	USD 6.6
Outward capital flight from Africa (estimated 2005)	USD 26.7

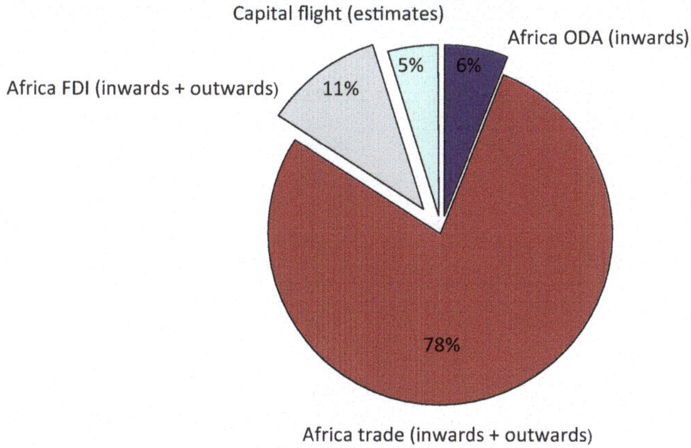

Fig. 1.7 Africa's economic relations with the EU, USA and China: relative proportions of ODA, trade, FDI and capital flight (estimate) (*Source*: European Commission, OECD, Global Trade, USA Census Bureau)

ship with its main international partners as a pie chart, then ODA would only represent a minor slice when compared to trade and FDI—and almost as big a portion as the outward flight of private and illegal capitals (Fig 1.7).

If 94 % of the financial exchanges between Africa and the developed world plus China are not related to development assistance, it is all too natural asking what these exchanges consist of and what impact they exert upon Africa, starting from the most important item—trade. The African trade balance looks at first sight quite healthy: in 2010, Africa had a positive balance with all the three partners (Table 1.2)[35]:

However, a quick look to the national level reveals that African trade surpluses are strongly concentrated among the "usual suspects": Gabon, Nigeria, Algeria, Libya, Equatorial Guinea, Zambia, Democratic Republic of Congo, Republic of Congo, Sudan and Angola.[36] These countries are heavy exporters of crude oil and raw minerals—about the only commodities the West and China are purchasing from them. Crude oil and raw minerals—as any other unprocessed product—lie at the low-end of the value-adding chain, having low profitability margins and suffering from all the disadvantages of the law of diminishing marginal returns. Engaging in trade with these countries likely means to purchase primary products in which little value has been added and sell manufactured products with a consistent portion of value added. On the contrary, South Africa, Namibia, Botswana

Table 1.2 USA–Africa, EU–Africa and PRC–Africa 2010 trade balances, current exchange rates, billion USD

	Import from Africa	*Export to Africa*	*Trade balance with Africa*
USA (2010)[a]	85	28.34	−56.66
EU (2010)[b]	172.18	157.08	−15.1
PRC (2010)[c]	48.52	53.44	−4.92

[a]Source: USA Census Bureau
[b]Source: European Commission, DG Trade, data retrieved in June 2011
[c]Source: Global Trade Information Services, data retrieved in June 2011

and Mauritius—the African countries with relatively diversified economies and the potential to export in sectors with higher profit margins and faster increases in productivity—are proportionally more engaged in intra-African trade than in intercontinental trade with the developed world plus China.

Under present circumstances, trade patterns between Africa and the West could not be much different anyway, since most African countries do not have competitive industries. Many of them do not have industries *tout court*. The few products in which African countries have a strong competitive advantage—raw agricultural products, textile and apparel—need to face heavily subsidized competition: both the USA and Europe allocate funds to the tune of 80 billion USD every year to their farmers, allowing them to survive competition coming from more efficient producers in the developing world. Similarly, the textile and apparel sectors in most OECD countries are protected by heavy import duties. To this extent, numbers do not justify the rhetoric that both the EU and the USA place on "trade development" agreements with Africa: the trading chapter of the EU Economic Partnership Agreements (EPAs) or the USA African Growth and Opportunity Act (AGOA) carries little but the promise to open dream markets to non-existing or stone-age era African manufacturers. Countless lists of items that are allowed into Western countries at zero import duties translate into a surreal message: African manufacturers could sell whatever industrial products they would like to if only they produced any of them in first instance. At the same time, African agricultural, textile and apparel products, in which African producers do have a competitive advantage, are effectively barred from most of the profitable OECD markets, because these are subject to subsidized competition or restricted market access.

The value of African FDI flows in 2008 was 83.1 billion USD—of this, 73.4 billion USD was inwards and 9.7 billion USD was outwards. Officially, Africa is receiving more capital than it is exporting. Albeit a tiny fraction (2.27 %) of the world's total FDI (3654 billion USD), African inward FDI has a considerably high FDI/GDP ratio, thus having the potential to command a real positive impact upon all economic sectors. Capital transfers into Africa suffer, however, from two major problems. The first, as noted by the UN Conference on Trade and Development (UNCTAD 2005), is that it is concentrated in countries with a strong oil and mineral exporting sector, thus contributing to an economic regime of low value added, limited reinvested earnings and periodic profit volatility. The second is that these injections of official capital are largely counteracted by a draining of private capital. Data on the phenomenon of capital flight are scarce and vary greatly, but analysts agree on the fact that it is of massive proportions. A 2008 study from the University of Massachusetts estimates the value of Sub-Saharan capital flight at an average of 17.5 billion USD per year in the first five years of the 2000s (Boyce and Ndikumana 2008); keeping the same GDP/Capital flight ratio for Maghreb countries would add an extra 9.2 billion USD for northern African countries—taking the total rough estimate to 26.7 billion USD a year. This means that out of every dollar of fresh investment capital that gets into Africa, roughly 36 Cents find their way back into foreign bank accounts through illegal means.

Measurable economic and financial flows are not the only variables accounting for today's relations between Africa, China and the West or, for that matter, between the whole lot of developing and developed countries. Some variables can only be artificially construed by attributing an economic value to hardly quantifiable phenomena, as is the case for migration-related economic consequences. The migration phenomenon brings mixed consequences, both for sending and receiving countries, who, in a free system, experience both advantages and disadvantages. However, OECD countries' ability to unilaterally screen incoming migrants from low-income countries on the basis of education and income normally translates in the capacity to bring in cheap brain and liquid assets while leaving outside unskilled labour—a system complemented by OECD companies delocalizing low-value adding operations to developing countries. Similarly, in the last few years, China has shown an extraordinary capacity to control and regulate the flow of immigrants while refusing to curb its flow of illegal emigrants. This is to be coupled with state policies purposefully aimed at incentivizing legal emigration.

The brain drain phenomenon, by which skilled people who have been educated in developing countries subsequently move to developed countries, hits the African continent particularly hard. Data are scarce and inconsistent; however, the UN Economic Commission for Africa (Goodrich 2011, p. 348) estimates that 127,000 African professionals have left the continent between 1960 and 1989, while the International Organization for Migration (Usher 2005, p. 15) places the number of skilled persons leaving the continent at 20,000 a year since 1990. These numbers have piled up over the years and current estimates of the total number of qualified Africans permanently residing abroad run at 300,000, 10 % of which is at PhD level (Ainalem 2005).

The other side of the migration phenomenon is shaped by international migration agreements which usually lock poor countries' labour in the country of origin—Mexicans walking through the Arizona desert or northern Africans embarking on boat wrecks to sail across the Mediterranean Sea being the illegal trespassers of these agreements. Those that—either legally or illegally—land a job in the developed world, contribute a great lot to the well-being of their families and native countries: the World Bank estimates that remittances sent back home in 2008 accounted for 2 % of GDP for all developing countries and 6 % of GDP for low-income countries. In fact, these numbers correspond to more than the double of yearly world ODA: roughly 340 billion USD have been remitted to developing countries in 2011 alone. It remains nonetheless impossible calculating missed remittances from those that do not migrate illegally; it remains equally impracticable quantifying the extra-profits that accrue to companies headquartered in OECD countries and that manufacture in or provide services from low and mid-income countries.

ODA, OOF, trade, FDI, capital flight, migration and remittances do not represent the totality of interactions between two countries or regions. Overall relations typically include political and diplomatic agreements on foreign policy issues; vote behaviour in multilateral fora; military and defence cooperation; scientific cooperation; know-how transfer; and way more. The Cotonou Agreement, broadly setting the cooperation framework between the EU and a 79-strong group of countries from the African, Caribbean and Pacific (ACP) region, includes, for example, provisions on a vast array of policy fields arranged over roughly 70 articles.[37] It is simply not possible bringing the totality of a geopolitical relationship into figures or even drawing a fully comprehensive qualitative description—just as it is not possible doing that between two physical persons.

Still, what I had in front of me seemed to be a consistent body of information hinting towards a bizarre phenomenon: while Western ODA rhetoric focused on the face value of development activities, the core of the overall relationship between Africa and Western countries seemed to be concentrated in other sectors and organized in such a way to allow substantial transfers of financial resources and value-adding opportunities from the former towards the latter. China, whose African foreign policy worked under a completely different set of assumptions and showcased its activities through a competing institutional discourse, seemed to maintain with Africa a remarkably similar exchange structure, with the difference of dedicating smaller amounts to ODA. The structure of the relation between Africa and the West and between Africa and China seemed to be of such a nature to advantage Africa's commercial partners. ODA—and OOF for that matter—represented only a small, consensual dent in an otherwise consistent and smoothly running machine that regularly transferred financial resources from Africa towards Western countries and China.

Did that hint had any validity?

Notes

1. This chapter relies on observations and analyses gathered during the author's experience as a United Nations (UN) Fellow in Angola (2005) and as a European Union (EU) political and trade analyst in South Africa (2006–2008). References to specific events are the result of personal experiences.
2. This idea appears in a number of EU institutional documents, and has lately been reiterated in the *Agenda for Change*: "[...] supporting developing countries' efforts to eradicate poverty is the primary objective of development policy and a priority for EU external action in support of EU's interests for a stable and prosperous world" (EU 2011, p. 3).
3. The EU's understanding of "sustainable development" further includes good governance, human rights, and political, economic, social and environmental aspects (European Parliament 2005).
4. Official Development Assistance is typically divided between humanitarian aid and assistance in crisis prevention, on the one side, and development aid, on the other; while the former may include unsustainable activities (such as distributing imported food or providing temporary shelters), the latter aims at creating the conditions for endogenous development.

5. "The primary and overarching objective of EU development cooperation is the eradication of poverty in the context of *sustainable* development" (European Parliament 2005, p. 4); "We reaffirm our support for the principles of *sustainable* development" (UNGA 2000, 4§22); "[…] promote an open, non-discriminatory and equitable multilateral trading system that *will enable all countries—in particular, the developing countries—to improve their economic structures and improve the standard of living of their populations through sustained economic development*" (UNCED 1992, 2.9.A); "We resolve to ensure *centrality of sustainable poverty reduction in development co-operation*, particularly at country level" (OECD 2001a, p. 10).
6. These include *sustainability*, *national ownership*, *policy coherence*, *aid harmonization* and *coordination*. "National ownership" reflects the idea that development programmes are "aligned on government policies and build on government systems and processes to manage and coordinate aid rather than creating parallel systems to meet donor requirements" (OECD 2006, p. 18). "Aid harmonization and coordination" relates to the setting up of framework and objectives that allow development cooperation partners to enhance aid effectiveness. "Policy coherence" is aimed at ensuring that government policies are mutually supportive of a country's development goals—it translates in ensuring that national policies in developed countries do not counteract or hinder the action of development policies.
7. These are often as disparate as the agenda of a national government. Some donors, or donor's subagencies, specialize on specific sectors—as in the case of the Food and Agriculture Organization (FAO) and the many other UN specialized agencies—while others intervene in multiple sectors. The bigger players typically operate across a broad policy spectrum: governance, human rights and democracy, civil society, migration, environment, health, education, culture and employment are some of the fields of EU's activity in the developing world.
8. The spectrum of development aid tools include *project aid*—implemented either directly or indirectly, *sector programme support*, *sector* or *general direct budget support*, and *technical cooperation* agreements. Project aid includes all type of interventions where the donor is "fully in control of all the inputs required in the production of the developmental good" (Cordella 2003, p. 12). "Sector or general direct budget support" refer to transfer of money either "in support of a narrow range of development or reform policies"

or transfer in support of "a broad range of development or reform policies as set out in a national strategy". "Technical cooperation" refers to the "payments to consultants, advisers and similar personnel as well as teachers and administrators serving in recipient countries (including the cost of associated equipment)" (OECD 2001b).

9. To be sure, aid agencies regularly issue papers on their development vision; these strategies refer, however, to rather general concepts which build from pre-set assumptions and avoid establishing a clear route map. Examples include the EU Agenda for Change (EU 2011) and the 2013 World Bank Group Strategy (Bank 2013).
10. As a matter of example, the EU indicates the necessity to enable "[...] vectors for inclusive and sustainable growth, notably a stronger business environment and deeper regional integration" (EU 2011, p. 7), without venturing into the question of what businesses and what typology of common markets are mostly conducive to growth.
11. A number of implementing agencies (non-governmental organizations, national development agencies or international organizations) receive large budgets against ODA project proposals; at their own turn, these organizations may decide to subcontract some parts of their projects. Most of these projects are in specific areas and are measured against specific objectives rather than the general objective of economic growth.
12. Capital goods are understood as any physical asset used in production rather than for consumption.
13. Statistical indexes from these organizations include their online databases, the World Economic Outlook and Africa Economic Outlook (OECD), the Human Development Report (UNDP) and the World Development Report (WB).
14. These concepts have long been fostered by the IMF across the development spectrum: lower-, lower-middle, upper-middle and high-income countries. For a sample, see IMF (2010).
15. Some of them focus on the donor's side, while others scrutinize the beneficiary side. Most of them share the idea that aid is not working because of corruption, incapacity and lack of leadership, including Robert Calderisi (2007), Steve Berkman (2008), and Michael Maren (1997).
16. ODA from all donors to all recipients. Source: OECD Statistics, retrieved June 2014.

17. This "sweeping" exercise grossly fails from time to time: the European Court of Auditors found that 1 billion euros in ODA to the Republic of Congo was grossly misappropriated between 2003 and 2011 (ECA 2013).
18. Entire international conferences are dedicated to aid coordination and effectiveness, the most notable having been the 2002 International Conference on Financing for Development, resulting in the Monterrey Consensus; the 2003 Rome High Level Forum on Harmonization, resulting in the Declaration on Harmonization; the 2005 OECD Paris conference, giving rise to the Declaration on Aid Effectiveness; the 2008 Accra High Level Forum, agreeing on the Accra Agenda for Action; and the 2011 Busan High Level Forum adopting the Partnership for Effective Development Cooperation.
19. As it will be discussed in Chap. 2, most of the literature on development aid could be defined as technically driven, to the extent that it deals with aid as an existing policy field that needs being administered by looking at its polity, policy-making, financial and bureaucratic aspects. Within this group, part of the existing literature serves as a guide for aid administrators, while other texts focus on aid analysis by striking a balance of the phenomenon, usually distinguishing between aid that has provided tangible results and aid that has gone wasted. For a limited selection of texts pertaining to the first group, see David Lewis (2001) and Cusworth and Frank (1993). For a limited selection of inputs pertaining to the second group, see Roger Riddell (2007).
20. Cybernetics is the interdisciplinary study of systems, including problems of *control*, *recursiveness* and *information*. On the concept of cybernetics and second-order cybernetics analysis, see Heinz Von Foerster (1973).
21. As a matter of example, Article 17a of the *Staff Regulations of Officials of the European Communities* establishes that "[…] an official who intends to publish or cause to be published, whether alone or with others, any matter dealing with the work of the Communities shall inform the Appointing Authority in advance. Where the Appointing Authority is able to demonstrate that the matter is liable seriously to prejudice the legitimate interests of the Communities, the Appointing Authority shall inform the official of its decision in writing within 30 working days of receipt of the information. If no

such decision is notified within the specified period, the Appointing Authority shall be deemed to have had no objections". Other international organizations have similar clauses in their staff regulations. While justifiable from the institutional perspective, these clauses effectively limit the freedom of speech of officers working for governmental bodies, including on ODA programmes.

22. "[...] for it would, of course, be a condition of imperial assistance that any plant or material required should be ordered in this country", as Winston Churchill put it. In fact, Churchill, who was speaking in his capacity of Secretary of State for the Colonies, did not think of the colonies' economic benefit as a positive by-product for itself, but rather as a *mean* to enhance "[...] the purchasing power of individuals in the colonies, with future benefits to British trade" (Havinden and Meredith 1993, p. 140).
23. The EU does this through "Framework Contracts", which are sample contracts pre-negotiated with a limited number of service providers used in some ODA implementation activities, including M&E and M&R.
24. As a matter of example, the international community has hailed the 2002–2014 GDP growth in Afghanistan as an indication of economic success due to regime change and ODA strategies, when such growth was simply reflecting the enormous amounts of financial injections poured by the international community, rather than a genuine development in the national economy. In 2014, the Afghan economy continues adding extraordinarily little value to the goods and services it produces and its GDP growth perspectives have drastically changed (from 11.2 % between 2004 and 2014 to an estimated 4.8 % a year till 2025) as a direct consequence of international disengagement, thus leaving the question of what will be left behind after 12 years of international presence and massive ODA injections. Source: World Bank (Joya and Khan 2014).
25. ODA saves lives and saving lives—it could be said—enables human development by creating the very minimum conditions for development to happen. This argument is sound from an ethical ground but does not, however, hold water from an economic perspective: larger numbers of people do not automatically translate into greater chances for an improved quality of life—quite the contrary.
26. Most of the reports used throughout the book—issued by organizations such as the IMF, WB, OECD, UNDP and UNCTAD—are generally considered as objectives by both academics and practitio-

ners. However, their statistics and interpretations are often inconsistent. Also, it is not uncommon to find data and analyses organized in such a way as to under-represent or over-represent certain trends, while the wording of their different analyses is carefully spelt to best reflect and defend the organization's vision, mandate and interests.

27. OECD Statistics (http://stats.oecd.org/qwids/ retrieved November 15th, 2011): All donors' ODA to all recipients: 2537.815 billion USD; All donors' ODA to Africa: 711.077 billion USD; All donors' total flows (ODA + OOF + Private flows) to all recipients: 5589.367 billion USD; All donors total flows (ODA + OOF + Private flows) to Africa 1000.285 billion USD.
28. 2008 prices inflation adjusted.
29. Statistics from commodity-driven economies, including those of Gabon, Nigeria, Mauritania, Algeria, Libya, Equatorial Guinea, Zambia, Democratic Republic of Congo, Republic of Congo, Sudan and Angola have, at times, give an indication of being on a path of steady and self-sustainable growth: on deeper scrutiny, they were, in fact, hostage of boom and bust cycles in commodity prices.
30. Economic and Monetary Community of Central Africa (CEMAC), Economic Community of the Great Lakes Countries (CEPGL), Common Market for Eastern and Southern Africa (COMESA), Economic Community of Central African States (ECCAS), Economic Community of West African States (ECOWAS), Southern African Development Community (SADC) and West Africa Economic and Monetary Union).
31. Statistics from UNCTAD, retrieved 30 November 2011.
32. This also reflects in the cacophony of results shown by quantitative studies reviewed in Chap. 2.
33. William Easterly estimates that the total figure of people working for official development agencies is as high as 90,000 (W. Easterly and Pfutze 2008, p. 20). No figure could be found concerning the estimated amount of workers in the private international aid industry (NGOs; charity organizations; think tanks specializing on analyzing / monitoring development aid; etc.)
34. ODA data from OECD DAC (http://stats.oecd.org/qwids/) retrieved on 15 November 2011. EU trade data from EU DG Trade (ACP African countries + South Africa + Morocco + Algeria + Tunisia + Libya + Egypt); USA trade data from USA Census Bureau AGOA; PRC trade data from Global Trade Information Services.

FDI data from UN Conference on Trade and Development (UNCTAD), retrieved on 15 November 2011.

35. The PRC was the only partner to have a positive trade balance in 2009 (+ USD 6.56 Billion).
36. In 2010, this group of countries accounted for over 74 % of the value of African exports to China, 58 % to the EU and 60.8 % to the USA.
37. Policy fields and subfields are enumerated in articles going from Article 7 to Article 79. They include as many provisions as: political dialogue; human rights, democratic principles and the rule of law, good governance; other elements of the political environment; peace building, conflict prevention and resolution, response to situations of fragility; fight against terrorism; cooperation in countering the proliferation of weapons of mass destruction; migration; investment and private sector development; macroeconomic and structural reforms and policies; economic sector development; fisheries; tourism; social sector development; youth issues; culture and development; support of regional cooperation and integration; gender issues; HIV-AIDS; environment and natural resources; climate change; institutional development and capacity building; economic and trading arrangements; cooperation in international fora; trade in services; competition policy; protection of intellectual property rights; standardization and certification; sanitary and phytosanitary measures; trade and environment; trade and labour standards; consumer policy and protection of consumer health; fishery agreement; food security; financial cooperation; support for debt relief; structural adjustment support; micro-projects and decentralized cooperation; humanitarian, emergency and post-emergency assistance; technical cooperation.

References

Ainalem, T. (2005). *Brain drain and capacity building in Africa*. Ottawa: International Development Research Centre.

Berkman, S. (2008). *The World Bank and the gods of lending*. Sterling, VA: Kumarian Press.

Boyce, J. K., & Ndikumana, L. (2008). New estimates of capital flight from Sub-Saharan African countries: Linkages with external borrowing and policy options. In *PERI Working Papers, 144*. Amherst, MA: Political Economy Research Institute.

Calderisi, R. (2007). *The trouble with Africa: Why foreign aid isn't working*. New York: St. Martin's Press.

Cordella, T., & Dell' Ariccia, G. (2003). Budget support versus project aid. *IMF Working Paper, 03*(88). Washington, DC: International Monetary Fund.
Cusworth, J. W., & Franks, T. R. (1993). *Managing projects in developing countries*. Burnt Mill, Harlow: Longman Scientific & Technical.
Easterly, W., & Pfutze, T. (2008). Where does the money go? Best and worst practices in foreign aid. *Journal of Economic Perspectives, 22*(2), 29–52.
ECA. (2013). Special Report N. 9. Addis Ababa: United Nations Economic Commission for Africa.
EU. (2011). *Increasing the impact of EU development policy: An agenda for change*. Brussels: European Union.
European Parliament, Council and Commission. (2005). The European consensus on development. *Official Journal of the European Union, 46*(1), 1–19.
Goodrich, L. (2011). *Cultural studies*. Sudbury, MA: Jones & Bartlett Learning.
Havinden, M. A., & Meredith, D. (1993). *Colonialism and development: Britain and its tropical colonies, 1850–1960*. London: Routledge.
IMF. (2010). Lifting Euro area growth: Priorities for structural reforms and governance. *IMF Staff Position Note, 10*(19). Washington: International Monetary Fund.
Joya, O., & Khan, F. (2014). *Afghanistan Economic Update*, April 2014. Kabul: World Bank.
Lewis, W. A. (1984). The state of development theory. *American Economic Review, 74*(1), 1–10.
Lewis, D. (2001). *The management of non-governmental development organizations: An introduction*. London, New York: Routledge.
Maren, M. (1997). *The road to hell: The ravaging effects of foreign aid and international charity*. New York: Free Press.
OECD. (2001a). *The DAC guidelines. Poverty Reduction*. OECD Publishing.
OECD. (2001b). Development cooperation report. *The DAC Journal, 3*(1). OECD Publishing.
OECD. (2006). Survey on harmonization and alignment of donor practices. *OECD DAC Journal, 6* (Supplement 1). OECD Publishing.
Riddell, R. (2007). *Does foreign aid really work?* Oxford, New York: Oxford University Press.
UNCED. (1992). *Agenda 21*. Rio de Janeiro: United Nations Conference on Environment & Development.
UNCTAD. (2005). *Economic development in Africa – Rethinking the role of Foreign Direct Investment*. New York and Geneva: UNCTAD.
UNEP. (2005). *UNEP project manual: Formulation, approval, monitoring and evaluation*. Nairobi: UNEP, Programme Coordination and Management Unit.
UNGA. (2000). *United Nations Millennium Declaration*. 8th Plenary Meeting.
Usher, E. (2005). *The millennium development goals and migration*. Geneva: International Organization for Migration.
WB. (2013). *World Bank Group Strategy*. Washington, DC: World Bank.

CHAPTER 2

The Theory of Economic Development

My very first port of call for answering that question was the academic literature in development economics. It was hardly an original question: in 1977, the Indian-American economist J.N. Bhagwati noted, in somehow bare terms, that "developing countries are linked to the developed countries through trade, aid, investment and migration. The central issue for them is whether these links work to their detriment or advantage" (Bhagwati 1977). As simplistic as it may sound, this question has elicited a surprising number of controversial answers, suggesting that reading the developed-underdeveloped nexus as a fundamentally positive or negative variable in the development of poor countries is not necessarily too simplistic or reductionist an endeavour.

A multitude of disciplines take issue with the question, including economics, political science, international relations and law. These disciplines are home to different schools of thought, holding at their own turn widely disparate views. Most of these views explore relations among developed and developing countries within the broader question on the origin and mechanisms of economic growth,[1] albeit with remarkable exceptions. Their most striking feature is their radically different accounts on how economic growth happens: such a multifaceted theoretical portrait already hints at the difficulty of using economic theory alone as a basis for policy prescriptions.

S. Raudino, *Development Aid and Sustainable Economic Growth in Africa*, DOI 10.1007/978-3-319-38936-3_2

1 Assessing Economic Relations Between Developing and Developed Countries

1.1 Malign Links

Does the international system work against the interests of its weakest members? A host of political economists have replied to this question with a resounding “yes”. The intuition that relations between countries is what causes, and explains, the unequal distribution of wealth among them underlies a body of literature spanning from Lenin’s *Imperialism, the Highest Stage of Capitalism* (Lenin 1965) down to the latest edition of Ha-Joo Chang’s *Bad Samaritans* (H.-J. Chang 2009).

The underpinning idea—states entertain international relations with the aim of getting as much as possible from each other, with the stronger being in a position to take advantage of the weaker—can be traced back to the forefathers of the realist tradition in political science, at a time when war was considered a legitimate means of state interaction. In the sixth century BC, Chinese strategist Sun Tzu already suggested that restrain and moral reasoning are not useful to government rulers (Tzu 1963); writing roughly around the same time about the history of the Peloponnesian Wars, Thucydides plainly noted that the “[...] strong do what they have the power to do and the weak accept what they have to accept” (Thucydides 1972, p. 402).

Having written about the rowdy state of Italian politics during the Renaissance, Niccoló Machiavelli became later known for having justified political ends through any means (Machiavelli 1998); although an over-simplification of his political thought, some of his quotes have long conveyed the idea that international relations is not a business for the faint-hearted.[2] American realism, after World War II, introduced the idea that international politics is governed by universal laws based on standard national interests (Morgenthau 1973). Structural realism refined these stances by arguing that international relations are shaped by the self-help nature of the international system: states not organizing themselves for survival in a self-help system (e.g. states renouncing war capability) will be at a structural disadvantage (e.g. risk of political and military subjection) (Waltz 1979). Whether pushed by human nature or structural conditions, a strong scholarly tradition in political science has long maintained that states act egoistically and predatorily, a world vision very much compatible with the idea that strong nations take advantage of their economic relations with weak nations.

This general perspective translated into economics to form what J.N. Bhagwati has called the doctrine of "malign neglect" (Bhagwati 1977): the idea that economic links between poor nations and rich nations are exploited by the latter and imposed upon the former. The argument has a long tradition; before Marx and Engels (1974), this line of reasoning already appeared in the work of the early nineteenth-century German economist Friedrich List (1916). These authors draw inspiration from the unbalanced economic relations Europe established during 500 years of transcontinental relations through colonialism, unequal treaties and imperialism.[3] With the beginning of the decolonization process in the 1950s, a flourishing literature on developed-underdeveloped relations began scrutinizing economic relations between former colonizers and newly independent states, with structuralist, dependentist and neo-Marxist schools portraying wealth differences across countries as determined by the different international economic specializations entailed by laissez-faire policies, including free trade, free investments and restrained labour migration.

Argentinean economist Raúl Prebisch posited the economies of peripheral and underdeveloped countries as relying upon the export of raw products, consequently losing value-adding opportunities and profit margins to countries purchasing, processing and reselling those commodities (Prebisch 1950).[4] According to Prebisch, manufacturing countries also benefit from higher productivity growth rates, organized labour structures and high wages, all these elements contributing to assigning the bulk of manufacturing and trade profits to developed countries. Raúl Prebisch and Hans Singer (Singer 1950) further argued that the terms of trade of primary products exported by developing countries have constantly declined against the value of manufactured goods exported by developed countries, thus feeding a structurally unjust trading system, in which the producers of primary goods (and simple manufactures) transfer value to the producers of (complex) manufactures.

The work of Prebisch, and particularly his 1950 *The Economic Development of Latin America and its Principal Problems*, set the ground for a critical debate around the liberal international economic system that had recently been established in Bretton Woods. Shortly after him, Swedish economist Gunnar Myrdal (1957) suggested that open trade would have become instrumental in increasing wealth differences between rich and poor nations. Myrdal also found that large western multinational corporations (MNCs) investing in developing countries can bring havoc by disrupting salary structures and creating growing disequilibria

(Myrdal 1956, 1957). Similar arguments found vocal proponents across American scholars: Chilean economist Osvaldo Sunkel (1972) argued that the integration of developed countries in the international economy leads towards their domestic disintegration; American neo-Marxist economist Paul A. Baran (Baran and Sweezy 1969) argued that the bourgeoisie in developing countries often allies with landed interests and international capital to barren economic reforms that would not only be conducive towards sustained economic development but also cause labour radicalism and populist upheaval; Brazilian economist Celso Furtado (1970) and German-American economist Andre Gunder Frank (1971)—both widely identified with the more radical dependentist school—argued that the economic development of the centre (e.g. rich countries) actively contributes to the underdevelopment of the world periphery (e.g. poor countries).

These positions vary greatly; all of them share however the idea that there would not be a rich North (or centre) as we know it without a poor South (or periphery). In the *malign link* view, such a relationship goes beyond structural linguistics (the idea of "development" would not exist without the idea of "underdevelopment", just as the idea of "black" would not exist without the idea of "white") to reach the very empirical world of trade and financial flows. As Brazilian economist Theotonio dos Santos has put it, these authors see "[…] a certain structure of the world economy such that it favours some countries to the detriment of others, and limits the development possibilities of the subordinate economies" (Sanchez 2003, p. 32). Whereas liberal mainstream economists saw underdevelopment as a temporary and necessary condition in which countries find themselves on their path towards the developed status, the *malign link* view understands underdevelopment as a permanent stage in which certain countries remain trapped, exactly because of their relationship with the developed world.

Under these conditions, the neoclassic assumption that developing countries were undergoing a childhood period before reaching maturity was flawed: instead, low-income countries were living as stunted adults in an international society unwilling to address the structural imbalances that caused their pathologies. Development and underdevelopment are seen as two sides of the same coin, feeding off each other's mechanisms and being embedded in a zero-sum game structure that cannot cater to the interests of all involved parties. Since the very same economic system that creates wealth for some nations generates poverty for others, it is unreasonable to expect solutions to come from within the system itself.

The *malign link* view devised a number of solutions for generating economic growth in low-income economies, including by substituting foreign imports and financial services through locally manufactured products and locally raised capital via a policy formula known as Import Substitution Industrialization (ISI).[5] These solutions were implemented in Latin America and received some positive results in the 1960s, when industry became the dominant sector in Argentina, Brazil, Mexico and Chile. By and large, these national markets proved, however too small, undercapitalized or short of know-how to set up credible and lasting industrial alternatives to foreign production. Several governments implementing ISI policies failed to grasp the complexities attached to market intervention, allowing free domestic competition in industries with high fixed costs and in desperate need of large-scale output in order to bring costs down: for example, in the late 1960s, the annual output of cars and trucks in eight Latin American countries was only 600,000 units shared by 90 firms, giving an average of 6700 units per firm (Baer 1972).

Up to these days, dependentist and world system scholars argue however that there is consistent evidence showing that countries which managed to successfully create a national industrial basis in the second half of the twentieth century have mainly done so by protecting their markets and infant industries. These include countries with the most successful development track record since the 1980s: China, India, Taiwan and South Korea. Similarly, several Latin American economies experienced the greatest economic expansion when they were the least dependent upon international capital and trade: Argentina, Brazil, Mexico and Chile grew most rapidly during the two World Wars, the Great Depression and the 1960s.

1.2 Benign Links

Do, conversely, economic links between poor and rich nations contribute to the trade expansion and economic growth that allowed some western countries to develop in the nineteenth century to recover from the misfortunes of World War II and, pushed China, India, parts of Latin America and South-East Asia towards the developmental path they have undertaken since the 1970s? Is this process comparable to the expansion of trade and investment flows that brought wealth to parts of Europe, since the Renaissance, and progressively expanded into the temperate colonies (the USA, Canada, Australia, New Zealand, South Africa) and Japan? A large part of the mainstream liberal and neoliberal scholarship—whether in political science, international relations or economics—sees little reason to doubt it. Economic liberalism maintains, in more or less direct terms, that international economic dynamics play a role of "benevolent neglect" upon the economies of underdeveloped (or less developed) countries: poor nations gain from their links with rich nations. Liberalism under its different declinations sees economic specializations and different trade patterns (nature of goods/services exported and imported) as reflecting the neutral principle of comparative advantages, while foreign direct investment (FDI) is understood to be a permanent catalyst for transfers of capital, expertise and good practices.

In political science, benign visions can be found in the liberal tradition going from the Glorious Revolution's forefathers to John Stuart Mill's *On Liberty*: the idea that societies are best organized by leaving as much liberty as possible to individuals is grounded in the belief that social and economic interactions are a positive-sum game. Believing that "[...] the sole end for which mankind are warranted, individually or collectively, in interfering with the liberty of action of any of their number, is self-protection" (Mill 1913, p. 13), necessarily requires a strong faith in human inclinations, or interests, or both: such a reading is incompatible with the idea of inherent conflicting interests among societies, an intuition that naturally leads towards cautiousness in international economic relations. It is, on the contrary, complementary with the idea that open relations stand to benefit all involved parties. In international relations (IR), the liberal tradition goes very much along these lines: Immanuel Kant's *Perpetual Peace* sets out the idea that war could be avoided *if only* states could be turned into representative republics and could create adept institutions, such as federations of states (Kant 1948). The underlying idea is that republics representing their people's interests would be peaceful because their citizens would naturally avoid war and its consequences: fight, pay the cost of military mobilization, reconstruct the devastation, shoulder the ensuing public debt and more. Kant generally perceived the human character as egoistic, but also understood human beings as driven by enlightened self-interest, an element leading towards successful compromises and mediations. Such a view implies that war occurs as a sort of system failure or communication breakdown and not because of intrinsic incompatibilities in people's interests, desires or aspirations.

Similarly, scholarly traditions alternatively identified with *Rationalism* and the *English School* in international relations argue that because there are no supranational institutions guaranteeing security and welfare, it is in the best interest of national governments to spontaneously find a way towards international mediation and accommodation. Hedley Bull (1977) believed that states inhabit an *anarchical society*; since anarchy is the given setting and welfare is the goal, states develop and abide by norms that allow successful cohabitation. The capacity of turning an international *system* (group of states interacting among them) into an international *society* (an international system sharing a set of rules and institutions) is by itself proof of the nation states' ultimate capacity to compromise on each other's interests.

In economics, the idea that open international exchanges work in the interest of everyone draws legitimacy from the belief that checks and balances are inherently built into market economies. The work of classical economists, beginning with Adam Smith (1966) and David Ricardo (1911), did uphold the idea that everyone has to gain from free trade (at least in the long run) while reassuring the public as to the fact that the market economy is self-regulating. By introducing the idea of an "invisible hand" acting in everyone's interest—a concept to be later scorned by heterodox economics as a Panglossian *Weltanschauung*, an irrational belief depicting the current economic state as the best that it is possible to achieve—Adam Smith introduced a revolutionary principle which later became posited by classic economics as self-evident. Similarly, David Ricardo publicized the law of comparative advantages as the logical proof that trade advantages two countries, even if they produce exactly the same commodities and even if one of the two always does so at lower prices. In Ricardo's understanding, international trade is always beneficial: as long as each country has a relative advantage of production—a better ratio of labour enshrined in the exchanged commodity—every party has to gain from it.[6] Both the self-regulating and comparative advantage principles went on to become foundational beliefs of the liberal tradition in economics, surviving two centuries of alternate vicissitudes in the history of economic thought.

With the rise of the neoclassic theory of economics, which is symbolically placed at the end of the nineteenth century, mainstream economics confirms the key role played by open economies in spurring growth. Other schools of economics concurrently contribute in cementing this belief: open trade and international investments also feature in the arguments of the imperialist historical school, which claims the eminently positive impact of imperialism upon colonies. According to these views, the economic misfortunes of certain countries are either to be ascribed to market failures or to poor institutions: because these countries are incapable of creating the necessary normative framework allowing national and international market forces to behave freely, they fail. Thus, in the neoclassic narrative, international market forces constitute an eminently positive universe, sitting and waiting for the right institutional conditions to appear before they can unleash their potential for promoting growth via trade and investments. Between the nineteenth century and the Great Depression, this model went substantially unchallenged, and understandably so: why would western economists question the obvious benefits that foreign market access was granting to western industrial economies?

Mainstream economic confidence towards open trade policies was, however, abated by the Great Depression of 1929, the subsequent adoption of beggar-thy-neighbour policies and Keynesianism gaining traction in questioning some of the key neoclassic tenets. The international economic system established in Bretton Woods managed nonetheless to re-establish confidence in the liberal belief that economic openness, positively and unconditionally, correlates to economic growth. Some economic ideas developed in those years contributed to the revival of liberal and neoliberal tenets: the Heckscher-Ohlin (H-O) model developed in the 1930s confirmed the leitmotiv that markets are self-regulating and that free movement of goods, services and capitals contributes towards growth, in both capital- and labour-intensive economies.[7] Paul Samuelson's elaboration of the H-O model introduced the concept of factor price equalization, which added to this belief an almost messianic message: since an open international economy pays the factors of production—capital and labour—with similar remunerations independently from the place where they sit (Samuelson 1948), labour in developing countries needs not to go abroad to benefit from the win-win advantages of economic liberalism. According to Samuelson, salaries and return on capital in developing countries with open economies are destined to catch up with levels in developed countries, at least in the long run.

The western political changes of the 1980s—traditionally identified with the neoliberal policies of Margaret Thatcher, Ronald Regan and Helmut Kohl—contributed in popularizing a radical declination of the international neoclassic paradigm, known as the *Washington Consensus*. Within this declination, academics such as Milton Friedman and Ludwig von Hayek and practitioners such as World Bank presidents Lewis Thompson Preston and James Wolfensohn promoted the integration of low-income countries within the international economic system as a means to induce trickle-down effects and poverty alleviation. In those same years, neoclassic counter-revolutionary economists describe stagnation as resulting from poor resource allocation and policy failure at the national level and prescribe free trade, export expansion and openness to FDI (Friedman and Friedman 1980) as recipes to improve resource allocation.[8] Allowing the market to establish its own rules for trade and investment exchanges and letting countries specialize in what they are good at is the mantra that gets revamped in this new liberal theoretical declination. While the *Washington Consensus* found vocal critics in all theoretical camps and is today seen as largely dismissed,[9] it did inform—and arguably continues to inform—the economic reform agenda of International Financial Institutions (IFIs).

1.3 ODA Literature

Relations between low-income and high-income countries are a privileged topic of discussion in the literature dealing with Official Development Assistance (ODA) and development cooperation policies.[10] In fact, the ODA literature often represents the first source of information for both specialists and non-specialists when thinking about international relations and socio-economic development. This partially comes as a result of a common misperception: the idea that ODA is the main economic link between donor and beneficiary countries—a link operating through the liberal logic of cooperation and mutual benefits. It is a fitting misperception, since it corroborates with the view of mainstream economics that developing countries lack integration with the world economy, while also responding to the institutional communication requirements of the donor community.

A wealth of academic work analyses the role of ODA in beneficiary countries under the assumption that ODA plays, or has the potential to play, a major role in the developmental dynamics of beneficiary countries, subsequently asking whether aid is good or bad for development or investigating what type of aid works best. This assumption seems to be largely unjustified by evidence; consequently, its ensuing questions are often inconsistent. To understand ODA as a standalone component of development, while ignoring the more complex and conspicuous relations between developing and developed countries, amounts to ignoring the influence of balance of payment (BoP) items such as trade, FDI and factor income upon economic development processes in low- and mid-income countries.[11] It also indicates a failure to grasp the much broader understanding of what is needed for socio-economic development to happen[12]: since ODA activities are mainly welfarist in nature, focusing on ODA to explain economic growth means ignoring the dynamics that have brought today's OECD countries and newly industrialized economies (NIEs) to their high-income status.

Interestingly, the marginality of research questions focusing on ODA to explain economic growth is proved by their own answers: econometric studies have investigated for decades whether aid is good or bad for development and what type of aid is working best, with no consistent answers. The plethora of quantitative studies on aid produced since the 1960s has failed to come up with any solid results. Empirical studies on the subject have indirectly proved the irrelevance of ODA upon economic growth at the very moment in which they have attained, in roughly equal quantities, one of the following four conclusions: (1) aid has a positive effect on growth; (2) aid has a positive effect on growth only under given circumstances; (3) aid has no effect on growth; (4) aid has a negative effect on growth.[13] While some of these studies might have caught relevant aspects of the ODA-growth nexus in specific national cases, time periods and contingent circumstances, their widely divergent conclusions show that, globally, the ODA-growth nexus holds extremely weak explanatory power. As discussed in Chaps. 1 and 4, this has also been revealed from simple, long-term correlation analyses between world regions that have received conspicuous ODA quantities and those that have not.

Unsurprisingly, donor agencies promote or directly finance a large part of research on ODA. Some of these works do that from a purely institutional perspective, often representing little more than a public relations exercise for the institutions promoting them: a number of regular publications from the World Bank Group, the United Nations, the European Union, the OECD and the many think tanks financed through these institutions offer good examples of this type of literature.[14]

The ODA industry also supports a large body of technically driven research: these publications deal with ODA as a policy making, bureaucratic, administrative and managerial phenomenon. The underlying assumption of this literature is that ODA exists as a public policy and as an industry; it does not concern itself with ODA's underlying meanings or raison d'être, much in the same way as manuals on investment banking or export management do not concern themselves with the foundation of the international trading system. The management of ODA requires specialist knowledge and executive skills in the same way as other industries do: this literature caters to this need.[15] A similar approach within the ODA literature is represented by analytical inquiries posing "problem-solving" type questions: who are the actors? What do they do? What are the key problems with ODA and how could those be solved? Most of these studies remain largely descriptive; some question however the role of aid in the larger international relations framework: how to establish whether ODA is working? What should be the yardstick for such an assessment? If ODA is not working, why are these institutions continuing in their endeavours?[16]

Finally, there is a growing body of the ODA literature openly taking critical stances against international development policies. These criticisms come from different angles. A number of them take issue with assistentialism and the implementation of abstract plans for Africa, along with their alleged counterproductive results (W. R. Easterly 2007; Moyo 2011). Other authors, often coming from a journalistic background and relying on anecdotal experience, share the idea that poor coordination, corruption, inefficiencies, incapacities and cultural differences are at the basis of ODA's limits and harmful effects (Hancock 1989; Maren 1997). Others focus on the limits and self-interested scope of the donors' agenda, with particular malicious accounts of World Bank and International Monetary Fund activities, as being guilty of pushing projects lacking transparency and decent governance standards (Caufield 1996).

Most of these works put forward relevant points, and yet they seem to be missing a key passage: the main limit of the ODA-growth nexus does not seem to lie with ODA itself but with all the other items of the donor-beneficiary relation. ODA only represents a tiny amount of the overall Africa-west and Africa-China exchanges: most likely below 6 % in the former case and below 2 % in the latter case. Purposefully focusing on this limited amount means ignoring the elephant in the room, eschewing the obvious question of what kind of impact the remaining 94 % (or 98 %) of exchanges entail. Existing ODA quantitative studies confirm this rather natural intuition: the ODA-growth nexus is weak, and even a perfectly functioning ODA would bear no guarantees of stimulating endogenous growth processes rather than simply fuelling externally subsidized welfare systems. These results are miles away from the successful economic reforms that today's developed countries, including OECD countries and newly industrialized economies, have undertaken throughout their histories.

All in all, the ODA literature seems under-equipped to answer questions relating to international wealth disparities and to provide a basis for normative policy prescriptions. This inadequacy begs for further research into the larger field of international political economy, stretching well-beyond the restricted perimeter of ODA.

2 Research Questions in Context

Are there scientific answers to Bhagwati's (1977) question? Can relations between "rich" and "poor" nations be audited to determine whether they are benefiting or harming the latter group? The literature dealing with relations between developing and developed countries showed no clear answers and inevitably referred to a broader universe, for example, the general literature on economic growth. Logically so: an impact assessment of international economic relations upon the socio-economic standing of low-income countries must necessarily tread into the many topics dealt with by general theories of economic growth, including, among others, savings and investments, increasing and diminishing marginal returns, economies of scale, value-adding levels, value chains, terms of trade, returns on investments and more. If we want to assess the impact of these variables, we also need to be able to provide an objective measure. Yet, one can only measure, once a yardstick has been defined.

How should these variables be measured and assessed then? Different economic theories lend different meanings and weights to the same variables. For example, faced with the factual reality that the ratio of African raw exports to African total exports has increased since the 1980s, it is necessary to decide upon the theoretical tools that will interpret such a phenomenon as eminently positive, neutral or negative. Differences among existing theoretical tools are stark: while the neoliberal school will recognize in this higher ratio a manifestation of Africa's comparative advantages and its increased integration in the world economy (and welcome such a development), import-substitution theories will deprecate the recurring pattern of African specialization at the lower-end of the value-adding chain.

Deciding which theoretical tool should be used corresponds to creating a yardstick—a metre of comparison that can subsequently be used to carry out policy analyses. This necessitates a foundational step: establishing what is good and what is bad for a country's development *in general*, something that can only be done by determining first what promotes domestic economic growth *independently* from the international economic relations a given country entertains with its partners. This requires integrating the literature on relations between developing and developed countries within the larger literature on economic growth.

Many disciplines have explored this question from different angles. As it happened for the more circumscribed question of "What is the impact of economic relations between developing and developed countries", a multitude of schools of thought within those disciplines have elaborated alternative approaches through their theoretical and empirical declinations. Looking at these approaches provides an overview of the different research venues that have already been explored to explain the causes of the wealth and poverty of nations. More interestingly, it allows observing a plain fact: the conclusions reached by academic disciplines dealing with economic growth often reach too widely diverging and far-fetched views to provide stable guidance for political praxis. This observation stands in stark contrast to the exceptional similarities that can be observed in the economic policy praxes followed by countries that have developed successfully, an exercise that is carried out in Chap. 3.

3 The Broader Picture: Theories on the Wealth and Poverty of Nations

What explains the wealth and poverty of nations? Philosophers, economists, political scientists and jurists have provided different classes of answers to this question.

The broadest possible answers leave out as few social and natural dynamics as possible: these approaches, which could be defined as "omni-comprehensive", have drawn attention from disciplines as different as anthropology, medicine and geography. Other authors have been less comprehensive, but not necessarily less ambitious, in their explanations, focusing upon human agency as the foremost cause of disparities in international wealth. Most of these theories pertain to the discipline of economics: theories explaining growth and development through correlation patterns among economic variables. Other theories pertain to the disciplines of political science, international relations and law, having mainly dealt with the question of how political and legal institutions favour or hinder socio-economic development.

3.1 *Omni-Comprehensive Approaches*

Have all nations—developing, rising and developed—faced different, but overarching, structural conditions that had already stacked the cards in favour of some and against others, and ultimately contributed in determining their socio-economic development? Is human agency just a flimsy and short-lived act performed on the rock of historical determinism? Solid accounts coming from geographers, biologists and virologists suggest that historical determinism and social Darwinism may have played a strong role in distributing wealth across the globe. Exhaustive compilations of the long-term determinants of comparative development have been provided, inter alia, by Jared Diamond (1998), William McNeill (1976) and Alfred Crosby (1986). Some economists have also taken issue with the relevance of variables such as diseases, religions and cultures in explaining income differences across former European colonies (Acemoglu et al. 2001).

Most of these approaches throw into the cocktail as many ingredients as possible: climate, germs, latitudes, religions, technology, inheritance traditions, public institutions, natural endowments and ethnic origins, to name a few. The results are passionate and deeply revealing accounts of the many directions one could look at when pondering the question of why some nations became rich and other stayed poor.

Yet, these works leave a number of unanswered analytical questions and an unfulfilled normative vacuum. Unanswered questions relate to the relative weight, causal direction and temporal order linking the variables that have contributed in shaping the history of the world economy. Theories failing to prioritize and systematize their many answers to a given research question have not only limited analytical value but also limited social utility. Accounts of *all* the potential elements that *may* have had an influence upon socio-economic development processes are also destined to leave a normative vacuum, relating to the impossibility of deriving a road map for action: what are we to do with all these potential answers? If temperature, rainfall, ocean currents, bacteria, ethnic compositions, natural inclinations, historical determinism, religions, Darwinian selection, social institutions, political structures, economic organizations are all, *equally*, inextricably and non-chronologically responsible in determining a new-born's chances to grow up in a society allowing a decent existence, do we not incur the risk of surrendering to fatalism?

3.2 *Economic Approaches*

When looking at wealth differences across countries, economic theories have traditionally focused upon domestic variables. Although few economists would openly claim that growth is unaffected by the international system, many works discuss domestic policies without considering the international structure they are embedded in. Historically, this might be due to the fact that classic and neoclassic theories have largely been formulated by western authors for western audiences, at a time when the impact of Second and Third World market dynamics was seen as either predictable or irrelevant. Other economic schools have also downplayed the impact of the international environment upon domestic growth: the institutional political school, for example, developed largely independently from considerations on international dynamics.[17]

Globalization is also a relatively recent phenomenon when compared to the cultures, traditions and inventions that allowed a number of civilizations to grow rich.[18] Relatively wealthy, knowledgeable and well-administered civilizations inhabited the ancient world at times of limited international exchanges: societies in Egypt, Greece, Arabia, Persia, pre-Columbian Central America, China and Japan bear testimony to the numerous and independent routes undertaken in the past to achieve economic growth and social development. How does economic theory account for these successes throughout history and how does it explain income differences between these societies and other contemporary civilizations?

Somehow, artificially, mainstream economics individuates the first answers to these questions in the work of Adam Smith (1966). Needless to say, Smith did not "invent" the theory of economic growth: his work built upon a long European tradition that had been looking at financial affairs since, at least, Aristotle's *Politics* (Reeve 1997) and Xenophon's *Oeconomicus* (Pomeroy 1995) in the fourth century BC, while benefiting from several economic treaties written during the European renaissance and dealing with the issue of the spectacular economic development managed by some regions in those centuries.[19] Adam Smith's *Wealth of Nations* had however the extraordinary merit of systematizing a large body of knowledge that, if already existent at his time,[20] was nonetheless dispersed and poorly interrelated. In particular, Smith compellingly individuated three factors leading towards economic growth: (1) division and specialization of labour; (2) accumulation of capital and; (3) self-adjusting market mechanisms, which naturally allowed free markets to function in the general interest. Some 40 years later, David Ricardo further stressed the importance of capital accumulation when he predicted that any economic activity runs the risk of experiencing diminishing marginal returns—successively lower extra outputs from adding equal extra inputs (labour, land and/or equipment). Because all economic activities are subject to this limit, Ricardo saw capital accumulation and increasing investments as the only strategy to offset diminishing returns and achieve indefinite growth. No investments, no growth: this leitmotiv quickly became the basis of the love story between the classic/neoclassic school of economics and the emergent European industrialist class, which used this refrain to claim that tax breaks allow to fruitfully invest credits that would otherwise go wasted into sterile redistribution.

Savings and investments have continued representing the classic school's key to economic growth till our days. Such a view has been lambasted for failing to take into account, inter alia, the role of technology, change, political preferences and national security in choosing and implementing policies that affect economic growth across the different layers of society. Ricardo has, for example, been poignantly criticized on the ground that technology has allowed agriculture to avoid diminishing marginal returns in many countries and for many centuries, thus, avoiding the grim scenario he portrayed in his 1817 *Principles of Political Economy and Taxation*, which was likely inspired by another no-technology scenario bias, in which his friend Thomas Malthus predicted future famines for an ever-enlarging population (Malthus 1958). Further criticism of Ricardo has focused on the centrality of public investments in sensitive industries, a practice that might hinder economic growth in absolute terms, but that has widely come to be seen as a preliminary condition for developing stable and independent societies in first instance.

Interestingly, the major counter-theory to economic classicism in the nineteenth century, Marxism, was also biased towards the role of capital. Contrary to classic economics, the Marxist analysis accounted for the possibility of social change, but was equally marred by an underestimation of capitalism's capacity to adapt to new environments. Marxism explains socio-economic changes, including growth, through historical materialism, a model borrowed from the Hegelian idea of evolution through the thesis-antithesis-synthesis stages: changes in social relations and political organizations stem from (r)evolutions in production modes. In the passage from feudalism to capitalism to socialism, Marxism individuates the main drive towards evolution in the changing relations between production factors. Marxism has however been criticized on account of failing to take into consideration the all-important role of reforms. By underestimating variables such as political processes and social psychology, it overlooked elements that allowed capitalism to successfully co-opt nineteenth-century labour classes into the bourgeois system, allowing them to share the benefits of economic growth and convincing them to renounce revolutionary options. By sticking to a static view of economic dynamics, Marx gathered the belief that capitalism would have been unable to evolve and was consequently vowed to self-destruction. That belief proved historically wrong: not only did Marxist revolutions not happen in Western Europe, more compellingly, where they did happen, they led to systems that redistributed wealth, but failed to keep up with the pace of wealth creation achieved by capitalist economies.

At the end of the nineteenth century, a major change took place in economic circles: positive epistemology became common currency in the economic discipline—a metamorphosis that ferried "political economy" into "economics", transforming an "art" into a "science". The (1) adoption of the positive method came hand-in-hand with (2) a newly found analytical (rather than normative) ethos and (3) a shift of attention towards microeconomic dynamics: these three features marked a major development in mainstream economics, sometimes defined as the passage from "classic" to "neoclassic" economics. The idea that economic processes can faithfully be represented through algebra—an intuition going back to David Ricardo and further refined through the works of Léon Walras (1977), William Stanley Jevons (Jevons and Jevons 2001) and Francis Ysidro Edgeworth (2003)—contributed a great deal towards cementing the belief that economists should relate to societies in the same way biologists relate to cells: detached objects of analysis.[21] Neoclassic economics became more concerned with procedural and operational questions than with normative ratios: how the economy works rather than how the economy should work; what are its functioning mechanisms rather than how it should develop. One of the possibilities for this switch of interest towards micro-management could be found in the belief that the west had already found the "right formula" of macroeconomic growth: in the second half of the nineteenth century, laissez-faire economics was benefiting Europe with impressive growth trends, leaving little reason to doubt the validity of liberal policies. Particularly in the UK, the pragmatic results and optimism that sprung from the Victorian age became a poor fit for alternative economic theories questioning liberal fundamentals. Substantial economic results for large chunks of the population were under everybody's eyes and it made little sense questioning whether the bases were sound: liberal economics and free trade were working very well for Britain and Europe. Instead, general wealth made people interested in micro-economic visions that explained how to maximize daily economic achievements.

Within this new paradigm, macro-level readings of economics as a social phenomenon with its own laws gave way to micro-level understanding depicting economics as the sum of individual rational behaviours. The two readings (macroeconomic and microeconomic) were not mutually exclusive; rather, there was a shift of attention from the former towards the latter, from society towards households and firms. Because the economic discipline becomes more related to the rational behaviour of single individuals rather than to social dynamics, it also loses its political character. People are seen—and increasingly see themselves—as behaving in an economic world that is naturally given; within this framework, the only thing people can do is try their best to improve their situation as players, not as rule-setters. At the same time, economists grew increasingly interested in studying the behaviours of economic players from a purely analytical perspective, claiming to renounce normative prescriptions: the economic discipline becomes less interested in indicating a direction, if not in describing what it perceives as scientific rules.

It is against this background that math and abstract modelling take centre stage in mainstream economics. This has a double effect: on the one hand, it creates expectations as to the capacity of the economic "science" to solve real-life economic scenarios through unrealistic assumptions (people are, as a matter of example, assumed to be rational actors exclusively interested in maximizing pleasure); on the other hand, it drifts attention away from the determinants of long-term growth in the real economy, including industrial strategies. Economic circles instead lend increasing attention to structural macroeconomic conditions such as interest, inflation and exchange rates. Critics of the neoclassic theory suggest that math becomes a weapon of mainstream economics to uphold unsound theories favouring international macroeconomic conditions that are compatible with western corporate interests keen to expand their markets overseas, but not necessarily with pre-industrial economies.

Economic Theories of Late Industrialization Growth

In the 1950s, a number of authors became specifically interested in the issue of late industrialization and growth in low-income countries. These authors, mostly trained in neoclassic economics, recognized the specificity of problems faced by developing countries battling against widespread poverty in an increasingly financially polarized, and yet interdependent, world. Stimulated by the decolonization process, theories of economic growth started propping up, both from "developed" and "developing" countries. While the former typically asked how rich countries could build on experiences such as the Marshall Plan to stimulate growth, the latter looked at the possibility of emulating public policies adopted by developed countries. Because of their innovative approach, ethos and the specific historical phase they developed in, these theories have been largely identified with the shaping of "development economics", as a separate subdiscipline within economics. Perhaps naively, some of these approaches posited the possibility of a quick catch-up between developing and developed countries.

Nobel laureate Arthur Lewis is often indicated as the forefather of the academic discipline of development economics. His structural-change theory (W. A. Lewis 1955) focuses on the positive effects of surplus reinvestment in economies characterized by an over-supply of labour, allowing for low wages and high returns on investments (ROI). According to Lewis, when the unlimited supply of labour dries up, salaries go up, profits shrink and investments wane. At that point, economic growth slows down, having reached a point of relative maturity. Lewis believed that the key dynamic allowing economic growth was in the passage of labourers from low-value-adding activities (normally agriculture) towards high-value-adding activities (normally manufacture) created by industrial investments. National economies grow because of this process of labour transfer, which creates new jobs and allows output growth. The Lewis model has been criticized on the basis of doing little more than taking microeconomic tools to exemplify historic processes without adding much to the understanding of why this happens; for example, why and how some countries successfully manage to shift workers from low- to high-value-adding activities, while others do not. Lewis's theory heavily relies on classic assumptions—saving and investments are the key towards growth—while keeping a strong focus on domestic economic determinants.

Similar assumptions underlie the controversial work of American economist Walter Rostow (1971) considered the forefather of the linear-stage theory. Rostow argued that transitions towards development require all nations to pass through fixed developmental stages,[22] and that low-income countries needed standardized rules to get through these stages. Among these, the single most important factor is high saving rates, which is seen as translating into high investment rates. If countries could not grow at the desired rate, this was due to the incapacity or impossibility to save and therefore invest. Rostow's theory translated into normative policies promoting foreign investments, either in the form of FDI or ODA. However, Rostow did not provide a differentiation between different typologies of investments, nor did he provide an endogenous explanation for the passage from one stage to another. Africa has been the main world recipient of ODA; yet, this financial plug has largely been used to foster the consumption of imported goods and services, thus, being of little assistance in promoting investments and job creation, two necessary steps in the passage towards the take-off stage. Rostow's approach has also been criticized for being a-historical as it freezes (or ignores) the environmental conditions in which economic development happens: as a matter of example, his theory does not account for the fact that today's developing countries interact in a different financial and trading environment than nineteenth century Europe.

Other domestic-focused approaches in development economics set off from the so-called vicious-circle theory, which carries the intuitional assumption that poverty is self-nurturing: poverty alone is a sufficient condition for its reproduction. The vicious-circle theory displays immediate evidence: a society that is poorly fed and in poor health conditions is obviously incapable of engaging in productive activities. Similarly, poverty-stricken societies spend a relatively high proportion of their energy and time in survival activities, thus being unable to engage in higher-value-adding activities. The theory holds some empirical validity: once states graduate from a given level of GDP per capita, they seem to benefit from international market forces taking their growth rates on a convergent path with developed economies (Barro and Sala-i-Martin 2004).[23]

These observations have invited a number of policy prescriptions. In his theory of balanced growth, Ragnar Nurkse (1953) argued the necessity of simultaneously developing all sectors of the economy rather than specializing only on a few, as it typically happens for the primary sector in developing countries. Nurkse understood that the expansion of exports in primary products is not in itself a guarantee of growth: dozens of countries have known impressive economic expansions under commodity boom periods to subsequently drag into heavy recession and debt unsustainability once faced with falling commodity prices. Engaging in a round of heavy investments across different sectors—a strategy also known as the "big push" theory—has also been proposed as an effective policy to create the very market demand that ensures a market for the products of these industries. Complementarily to this vision, Rosenstein-Rodan (1943) suggested that variables positively affecting economic growth do not accrue incrementally but discretionally, e.g. via developmental jumps. Investing in infrastructures, for example, is useless unless the whole project can be completed—a process which necessarily requires sizeable investments: railways, bridges and roads cannot be used until they are fully financed and completed. The critique to this position is that governments do not usually have the capacities and resources to invest in different sectors at the same time. African countries like Angola, Equatorial Guinea and Gabon found themselves, at different points in time, with strongly positive current accounts due to the oil bonanza; yet, they represent more an exception than normality. Most African governments work with a severely limited budget and suffer from chronic shortages of expertise and capital goods, a situation that is hardly compatible with a "big push" policy option. Similarly, it would be a counter-intuitive decision for relatively well-off economies based on the export of primary products to start neglecting agriculture or mining in an effort to promote manufacturing investments from scratch. Abandoning commodity exports producing consistent, albeit unstable, sources of hard currency would also be an unpopular policy option among the elites of developing countries.

An alternative path is signalled by proponents of the strategy of unbalanced growth (Hirschman 1973), suggesting investments in selected industries allowing technology, expertise and investment capacity in leading sectors to progressively spill-over into other sectors. In this view, the most technologically advanced sectors hold a strong potential for creating high-value-adding jobs (forward linkages), while stimulating the provision of goods and services from providers specializing in low-value-adding sectors (backward linkages). The unbalanced growth theory, perhaps even more than the balanced growth theory, requires advanced planning and managing skills: governments need channelling investments towards selected industries holding the potential for kick-starting other economic sectors. To this extent, Hirschman's theory is incompatible with empiric observations suggesting that private actors are better placed than governments in individuating the most profitable economic sectors and business ventures.

3.3 *Political and Institutional Approaches*

A large body of literature in political science, comparative politics and international politics has long dealt with the influence of political and legal institutions upon economic and social development. Reflections along these lines also come from the discipline of economics itself, at least since John Maynard Keynes publicized the idea that markets need "[...] rules of the road and governmental actions" (Samuelson 1946, p. 43) to function, a contention that unsettled the neoclassic credo that markets are self-regulating and self-sustainable. More recently, Douglass C. North and Robert Paul Thomas (1973) inaugurated an institutional tradition in economics exposing how efficient economic organizations in Europe relied upon key institutional arrangements, including property rights and rule of law. North (1981) also argued that good institutions need to provide the legal framework that enables economic transactions, in particular, by supporting private contracts and avoiding government expropriation. The argument is further developed in the work of institutional economist Daron Acemoglu who suggested that "[...] the social, economic, legal and political organization of a society, that is, 'its institutions' is a primary determinant of economic performance" (Acemoglu et al. 2001).[24] Dani Rodrik (2000), also writing from an economic perspective, suggested that market economy mechanisms work only in the presence of institutions.[25] Rodrik further suggests that participatory democracies allow higher-quality growth, defining quality in terms of stability, resilience and distributional outcomes.

A number of political and law scholars have also tried establishing positive correlations between political regimes and socio-economic development. Writing for the World Bank, Daniel Kaufmann (Kaufmann et al. 2005) suggests that the rule of law is a key factor in determining the growth of developing countries. This position underpins the governance agenda adopted by most western international institutions, including International Financial Institutions, from the 1980s onwards: according to this view, legal, political and economic norms are *conditio sine qua non* of economic growth. Despite being widely publicized in institutional environments, this argument does not go unchallenged. Law scholar, Frank Upham, suggests that liberal institutions are a culturally biased way of reading development, as "[…] they leave no sense that there may be other path to development other than through an effective, efficient and fair legal system, and they imply that nothing can happen until these institutions are perfected" (Upham 2002, p. 10). Criticisms of the centrality of liberal institutions also come from the fields of development economics, philosophy and cultural studies. Heterodox economist Ha-Joo Chang (2002) compellingly argues that the lack of what the liberal world conceives today as pro-growth institutions—including intellectual copyrights, patents, bankruptcy laws and a liberalized trade and investment regime—has neither hindered development processes in eighteenth- and nineteenth-century Europe nor represented a problem in recently developed Asian NIEs. Harvard-based Chinese philosopher, Tu Wei-Ming, notices that modernization in East Asia has not necessarily meant assimilation with western models, adding that eastern modernization standards are as much "universalizable" as western standards (Ming 2000).

The debate on the role of institutions in economic growth also includes works on the democracy–development nexus. International liberal scholarship largely assumes that democracy and political liberalism are conducive, or are even prerequisites, for economic growth and social development. In *Capitalism and Freedom*, Milton Friedman (Friedman and Friedman 2000) argues that political and economic freedom are mutually reinforcing. A long-standing academic tradition suggests direct proportionality between governance, openness and democracy levels, on the one hand, and economic growth, on the other. This is also the official position of a number of international institutional players.[26] Yet, several empirical studies have not found clear positive correlations between GDP growth and democracy indexes.[27] Using data from 134 countries over a time span of 34 years, Robert Barro concludes that "[…] the net effect of more political freedom on growth is theoretically ambiguous. The quantitative analysis indicates that the overall effect is weakly negative but not statistically different from zero" (Barro 1996, p. 6).[28] This is not difficult to imagine: one only needs to think of cases like the middle-eastern resource-based countries (Saudi Arabia, Qatar, Kuwait, the United Arab Emirates, Bahrain and Oman) plus Russia and China, which all together accounted for some 15 % of the world's GDP in 2012, to realize that it is not easy to establish a positive and statistically relevant correlation between open political institutions and economic performances.[29] Natural resources in many of these countries are paying for strong welfare systems that have allowed dramatic socio-economic improvements, as has also happened in some of the most notoriously illiberal but pro-poor regimes of the 1990s and 2000s: Libya under Muammar Gaddafi and Venezuela under Hugo Chavez. A number of hybrid cases, countries considered as partially free, such as Ethiopia, Thailand and Indonesia, have coupled poor governance, democratic shortcomings and human right violations with good, albeit unequal, economic performances over the last 20 years. Some of Asia's star performers, like Hong Kong, Macau and Singapore, are not democracies. History has also shown that developmental dictatorships have often achieved spectacular economic growth in spite of—and, according to some scholarship, thanks to—lack of participatory democracy: Fascist Italy until World War II (1922–1939), Brazil during the military regime (1964–1985) and South Korea under the dictatorship of Park Chung-hee (1961–1979) are all relevant examples (Gregor 1979). Similarly, if the Democratic Peace Theory (DPT) has long been hailed as firm proof that democracies rarely fight one another and are more peaceful in general, thus establishing a direct correlation between democracy and peaceful, predictable, pro-growth political environments, its validity has long been questioned. Scholarly work suggests that the theory is untenable, because it is statistically weak or because it circumvents rigorous definitions of "democracy" and "war" (Henderson 2002; Spiro 1994). It has also been noted that countries with powerful intelligence services and abundant soft-power resources, including the USA, the UK and Israel, could afford the luxury of violent interventions in the international scene while avoiding been caught in open warfare, a technique sometime defined as *covert intervention* (Downes 2010).[30] Others, looking from an economic perspective, suggest encompassing economic coercion in the definition of "conflict", to subsequently show that democracies resort to violence with each other at least as often as authoritarian regimes do, thus implying equal risks of exogenous economic disruption (Heather 2009). All in all, if the link between modern liberal institutions and positive economic growth has proved a useful lead in understanding wealth distribution around the world, it remains complex, controversial, not exclusive and difficult to pin down.

4 No Common Ground

What are we to make of this large body of interdisciplinary academic literature proposing radically different readings of socio-economic development among nations? No single approach, theory or explanatory framework seems to be able to cater to all the variables influencing the dynamics of socio-economic growth. What is worse, different academic traditions across different subjects are unable to find a minimum common ground on what low-income countries need to do in order to promote growth and socio-economic development.

Even within the discipline of economics, there is no such a thing as a general agreement on basic policy prescriptions. Neoclassicism/Monetarism (suggesting that opening the market and stabilizing inflation are key pre-conditions of development); neo-Keynesianism (underlining the importance of public governance and direct state intervention in the real economy) and, Structuralism (favouring industrialization and the development of a sound national manufacturing basis in a biased system privileging the interests of the centre against those of the periphery), to name only three approaches, propose diametrically opposed policy prescriptions. They all have mixed track records. All of them ostensibly claim a privileged understanding of the dynamics regulating the wealth and poverty of nations and can call to witness countless empirical studies validating specific elements of their theoretical framework. Yet, history also shows how they have, at times, inspired disastrous policy recipes. More generally, the world of academic theories is inhabited by cultural lineages iterating, and reiterating, mutually incompatible positions on economic growth, thus suggesting that the academic discipline of economics as a whole is neither in a position to provide conclusive answers to the question of how to achieve economic growth, nor is it capable of endorsing a consistent set of measures for public policy praxes in low-income countries.

Being faced with a wealth of economic theories pointing in mutually exclusive directions, one might think that the economic praxes of countries that have already graduated, including selected OECD countries and the Asian newly industrialized economies (NIEs), could be of much better normative guidance. Development praxis, rather than development theory, could then be used as the "yardstick" of measurement against which western and Chinese policies in Africa could be assessed.[31]

Notes

1. Economic growth is standardly defined as the "increase in the market value of the goods and services produced by an economy over time". Economic growth is often, and generally, indicated by increasing real Gross Domestic Product. As it will be discussed in Chap. 3, GDP growth alone does not automatically translate into

better social conditions for people and this is why more comprehensive socio-economic indexes, such as the Human Development Index, have been created by national statistic agencies and Official Development Assistance organizations. However, the only possibility of achieving social improvements without economic growth is by re-distributing existing wealth in a more equitable way – a measure that, by itself, is not sustainable over time. This means that over the mid- to long-term horizon there is no escape to the development-economic growth nexus: hence, if a purely economic perspective of social development does not provide the full picture, it still remains an essential and enabling condition for development to happen.

2. "In the actions of all men, and especially of princes, where there is no court to appeal to, one looks to the end. So let prince win and maintain his state: the means will always be judged honourable, and will be praised by everyone" (Machiavelli 1998, p. 71).
3. Mainstream western historiography identifies the European colonial period as stretching from the early fifteenth century (Portuguese conquest of Ceuta in 1415) until 1870, when a sudden increase in the degree of competition and in the pace of foreign territorial acquisition justified the identification of a new phase known as "Imperialism", which lasted until World War I. The outright acquisition and direct administration of foreign territories co-existed with other forms of asymmetric relations with formally independent countries, including via unequal treaties.
4. Prebisch is recognized as the most authoritative figure in the structuralist school, having inspired the work of Celso Furtado, Fernando Henrique Cardoso and Osvaldo Sunkel. Prebisch's intellectual venture also led to the setting up of institutional houses of heterodox thinking in economics, as he headed the United Nations Economic Commission for Latin America and the Caribbean (ECLAC) and the United Nations Conference on Trade and Development (UNCTAD).
5. ISI measures included "[…] protective tariffs and/or exchange controls; special preferences for domestic and foreign firms importing capital goods for new industries; preferential import exchange rates for industrial raw materials, fuels and intermediate goods; cheap loans by government development banks for favored industries; the construction by governments of infrastructure espe-

cially designed to complement industries; and the direct participation of government in certain industries, especially the heavier industries, such as steel, where neither domestic nor foreign private capital was willing or able to invest" (Baer 1972, p. 98).

6. The logic being the following: if China produces one ton of rice every 10 working hours and one car every 100 working hours while Germany does the same every, let's say, 8 and 70 working hours respectively, then the two countries would still have an interest in trading among them. For Germany could renounce producing one ton of rice and with the 8 working hours saved it could produce instead 8/70 = 11.42 % of a car, which would sell for 11.42 Chinese working hours, allowing Germany to buy 1.142 tons of Chinese rice. On its side, China would gain 100/10 = 10 tons of rice for every car it renounces to make, and with that amount it would be able to purchase 80 German working hours, corresponding to 80/70 = 1.142 German cars.
7. The Heckscher–Ohlin model (H–O) posits that a nation's comparative advantage is determined by its relative abundance of production factors (labour or capital). Nations abounding in a production factor will have a comparative advantage in activities that are intensive in that particular factor. The neoclassic growth model of Robert Solow exemplifies the new view: growth of saving rates, population and technological progress are mathematically compounded to produce a model explaining production and economic growth in a given time period. The model is mathematically strong and yet unable, and uninterested, to explain growth over the long term, or to suggest normative action.
8. The 1980s neo-classical counter-revolution theory is counter-revolutionary to dependentist theory that largely dominated development studies in the 1960s and 1970s. Its most well-known proponents include Lord Peter Bauer, Deepak Lai, Ian Little, Harry Johnson, Bela Blassa, Julian Simon, Jagdish Bhagwati and Anne Krueger.
9. Interestingly, also from within the neoclassic camp: Jagdish Bhagwati and Dani Rodrik have both expressed strong doubts that short-term capital liberalization may contribute towards stability and economic growth.
10. By "Official Development Assistance" (ODA) is here understood the sum of the loans, grants and projects that are financed by the

international community, as per the OECD definition. By "development cooperation policies" is understood the broader cooperation framework that, aside from ODA, includes all the conditionality policies coming with ODA, as well as the international agreements between OECD and G90 countries in fields as different as finance, trade and migration. These policies, under suggestion of the same donor community, are increasingly treated as part of the "development policies" proposed to G90 countries.

11. Frustration with mainstream ODA debates is aptly expressed by Andrew M. Fischer in noticing that there is "[...] no sense in discussing whether aid is good or bad for development, or whether more or less aid is required for development, outside of a much broader understanding of what is required for development to happen" (Fischer 2009, p. 863). This point seems indeed lost in most of the ODA mainstream literature.
12. As it will be argued in the following chapters, these include, but are not limited to: specialization on activities characterized by increasing marginal returns, shift of resources towards industries characterized by higher-value added activities, strong entrepreneurial role played by the government, market imperfections that can favourably play in its national interest, strong normative framework regulating FDI, industrial, trade and financial policies aimed at retaining and wisely investing hard currency, and sunk public investments.
13. A similar argument is made by David Roodman, who suggests that such diversity of results in ODA-growth correlation studies is, by itself, an indication of their fragility. He subsequently shows that seven important aid-growth papers suffer from large arbitrary specification choices, but minimal arbitrariness in testing choices. Talking about these papers, Roodman notes that "[...] Aid is measured a certain way. A certain epoch is studied. Periods have a certain length. And so on. Some of these choices imply assumptions about the world, such as, say, that aid is exogenous to growth. All limit the scope of a strict interpretation of the results. A question of great importance for the literature is, how many of such implied assumptions can be dropped without harming the conclusions?" (Roodman 2007, p. 17). For a good meta-bibliography of ODA quantitative studies, aside from Roodman, see Gymah-Brempong et al. (2012) and William Easterly (2003).

14. For a limited selection of institutional publications with a discernible institutional communication agenda and limited scientific content, see the annual reports on the European Union's development and external assistance policies and their implementation; the UNDP national human development reports and the World Bank Africa's human development series.
15. For a limited selection of texts pertaining to this group, see David Lewis (2001), Cusworth and Franks (1993), and James Manor (2007).
16. Roger C. Riddell (2007), Arjan de Haan (2009), Karin Arts and Anna Dickson (2004), and Degnbol-Martinussen and Engberg-Pedersen (2003) provide some examples of this type of research on ODA.
17. John Adams notes that "American institutional economists have devoted very little attention to the international economy" (Adams 1987, pp. 289–290). The widely-acclaimed work of economists, Acemoglu and Robinson, is a good example of this lack of attention within the American institutional school of economics, since it suggests that colonialism had a role in determining today's low-income and mid-income countries' fate, only insofar as it influenced the institutions that were later to be adopted by these countries and not because it shaped the nature of their economic relations with western countries (Acemoglu et al. 2001).
18. Mainstream historiography individuates the phenomenon of globalization anywhere between the "proto-globalization" that followed European colonial ventures in the seventeenth century AD up to the first modern globalization wave resulting from the nineteenth century British revolution.
19. Including Antonio Serra (Serra 2011) and Giovanni Botero (Botero 1589; Botero et al. 1588).
20. Several economic historians concluded that Adam Smith contributed little to eighteenth century analytical understanding of market mechanisms. Among them, the Canadian economist Jacob Viner noticed that "On every detail [...] Smith appears to have predecessors in plenty. On few details was Smith as penetrating as his predecessors" (J. Viner 1927, p. 199) while the Austrian-American Joseph Schumpeter trenchantly remarked that "The wealth of Nations does not contain a single analytical idea, principle or method that was entirely new in 1776" (Schumpeter 1955, p. 184).

21. Aside from Ricardo, other authors had laid the bases for the "positivization" of economics, early in the nineteenth century. The German, Johann Heinrich Von Thünen, used calculus by extensively applying Ricardo's marginal principle to the spatial differentiation of economies. In 1838, the Frenchman Augustine Cournot discussed profit maximization and price targeting in mathematic terms, while a few years later, his fellow countryman, Jules Dupuit, was among the firsts to define utility maximization as a key concept in economics. An engineer by background, Dupuit insisted that utility, just as supply, demand and any other key concept in economics, should be given a mathematical form through empirical estimates. The Prussian civil servant Hermann Heinrich Gossen dealt with the concept of marginal utility, publishing in 1854, a book that already contained the bases of the law of diminishing marginal utility. The works of a second generation of neoclassic authors, including Alfred Marshall, Eugen Von Böhm-Bawerk, John Bates Clark, Vilfredo Pareto; and Irving Fisher, contributed in further specifying assumptions set out by early marginalists.
22. Rostow individuated five passages: (1) traditional society; (2) preconditions for takeoff; (3) takeoff; (4) drive to maturity; (5) and age of high mass consumption.
23. Over the period 1960–1985, the authors confirmed that growth rates of OECD countries had a tendency to converge, whereas the growth rates of poor countries and those of rich countries tended to diverge.
24. Using the number of formal legal procedures required to resolve a case of collecting an unpaid check as a proxy for "contracting institutions" and the Heritage Foundation's assessment of private property protection as a proxy for "property right institutions", Acemoglu shows a positive statistical correlation between institutional development and GDP levels across former European colonies (Acemoglu et al. 2001).
25. Rodrik defines institutions as "[...] a clearly delineated system of property rights; a regulatory apparatus curbing the worst forms of fraud, anti-competitive behaviour, and moral hazard; a moderately cohesive society exhibiting trust and social cooperation; social and political institutions that mitigate risk and manage social conflicts, the rule of law and clean government" (Rodrik 2000, p. 4).

26. "[…] the objectives of development, democracy, human rights, good governance and security are intertwined" (EU 2011, p. 3).
27. For a selection of studies on this topic, see Schiffbauer (Schiffbauer and Ling 2010).
28. Robert Barro refines considerations on the democracy-growth nexus by noticing that "[…] there is some indication of a nonlinear relation in which more democracy raises growth when political freedoms are weak but depresses growth when a moderate amount of freedom has already been attained" (Barro 1996, p. 6).
29. All these countries were classified as "authoritarian regimes" by the Economist's 2012 Democracy Index.
30. Among some of the examples raised in this paper: the USA–UK engineered downfall of Iranian prime minister Mohammad Mossadeq in 1953; the USA toppling of Guatemalan president Jacobo Arbenz in 1954; USA assistance to overthrow Sukarno in Indonesia in 1957–58; the USA/Belgian removal of Patrice Lumumba in Congo in 1960; the USA removal of Cheddi Jagan in British Guyana and João Goulart in Brazil in the 1960s; Richard Nixon's attempt to prevent Chilean socialist Salvador Allende from taking office in 1970 and support to the 1973 military uprising.
31. The term "praxis" is often defined in philosophy as thoughtful practice or practice that is informed, purposeful and deliberate, thus representing, in simplified terms, the sum of theory and practice. Karl Marx suggested that the difference between bees and architects is that bees build marvellous structures based on practice, while architects build marvellous structures based on praxis, the difference lying in the fact that architects are involved in reflective practices, while bees behave following natural instincts: "[…] But what distinguishes the worst architect from the best of bees is this, that the architect raises his structure in imagination before he erects it in reality". Following Marx's reasoning, architects "think" about what they are doing and constantly re-evaluate their values, skills, theories and knowledge as they apply to the structure they are building. Contrary to "practice", "praxis" also draws from the repertoire of past experiences in order to understand situations and develop new possibilities for action. Because of their highly reflective and thoughtful nature, political and economic actions will be referred in this dissertation as "praxes" rather than "practices".

References

Acemoglu, D., Johnson, S., & Robinson, J. A. (2001). The colonial origins of comparative development: An empirical investigation. *American Economic Review, 91*(5), 1369–1401.

Adams, J. (1987). Trade and payments as instituted process. *Journal of Economic Issues, 21*(December), 1839–1860.

Aristotle. (1998). *Politics* (C.D.C. Reeve, Trans.). Indianapolis/Cambridge: Hackett Publishing Company.

Arts, K., & Dickson, A. K. (2004). *EU development cooperation: From model to symbol.* Manchester: Manchester University Press.

Baer, W. (1972). Import substitution and industrialization in Latin America: Experiences and interpretations. *Latin American Research Review, 7*, 95–122.

Baran, P. A., & Sweezy, P. M. (1969). *Monopoly capital: An essay on the American economic and social order* (1st Modern reader paperback ed.). New York: Monthly Review Press.

Barro, R. J. (1996). *Getting it right: Markets and choices in a free society.* Cambridge, MA: MIT Press.

Barro, R. J., & Sala-i-Martin, X. (2004). *Economic growth.* Boston, MA: McGraw-Hill.

Bhagwati, J. N. (1977). *The new international economic order: The North-South debate.* Cambridge, MA: MIT Press.

Botero, G. (1589). *Della Ragion di Stato: Libri dieci.* Venice: Giolito.

Botero, G., Martinelli, G., Aracoeli, C. d. S. M. i., & Romano, G. C. (1588). *Delle cause della grandezza delle citta libri 3. Di Giouanni Botero benese.* appresso Giouanni Martinelli.

Bull, H. (1977). *The anarchical society: A study of order in world politics.* New York: Columbia University Press.

Caufield, C. (1996). *The World Bank and the poverty of nations.* New York: Henry Holt.

Chang, H.-J. (2002). *Kicking away the ladder: Development strategy in historical perspective.* London: Anthem Press.

Chang, H.-J. (2009). *Bad Samaritans: The myth of free trade and the secret history of capitalism.* New York: Bloomsbury Press.

Crosby, A. W. (1986). *Ecological imperialism: The biological expansion of Europe, 900–1900.* Cambridge: Cambridge University Press.

Cusworth, J. W., & Franks, T. R. (1993). *Managing projects in developing countries.* Burnt Mill, Harlow, Essex, England: Longman Scientific & Technical.

de Haan, A. (2009). *How the aid industry works: An introduction to international development.* Sterling, VA: Kumarian Press.

Degnbol-Martinussen, J., & Engberg-Pedersen, P. (2003). *Aid: Understanding international development cooperation.* London: Zed Books.

Diamond, J. M. (1998). *Guns, germs, and steel: A short history of everybody for the last 13,000 years.* London: Vintage.

Downes, A. (2010). Overt peace, covert war? Covert intervention and the democratic peace. *Security Studies, 19*(2), 266–306.

Easterly, W. R. (2003). Can aid buy growth? *Journal of Economic Perspectives, 17*(3), 23–48.

Easterly, W. R. (2007). *The white man's burden: Why the West's efforts to aid the rest have done so much ill and so little good.* Oxford: Oxford University Press.

Edgeworth, F. Y. (2003). *Mathematical psychics and further papers on political economy.* Oxford: Oxford University Press.

EU. (2011). Increasing the impact of EU development policy: An agenda for change.

Fischer, A. M. (2009). Putting aid in its place: Insights from early structuralists on aid and balance of payments and lessons for contemporary aid debates. *Journal of International Development, 21*, 856–867.

Frank, A. G. (1971). *Capitalism and underdevelopment in Latin America: Historical studies of Chile and Brazil.* Harmonsworth: Penguin.

Friedman, M. (2000). *Capitalism and freedom.* Chicago: University of Chicago Press.

Friedman, M., & Friedman, R. D. (1980). *Free to choose: A personal statement.* Harmondsworth, Middlesex: Penguin Books.

Furtado, C. (1970). *Economic development of Latin America: A survey from colonial times to the Cuban revolution.* Cambridge: Cambridge University Press.

Gregor, A. J. (1979). *Italian fascism and developmental dictatorship.* Princeton, NJ: Princeton University Press.

Gymah-Brempong, K., Racine, J., & Giapong, A. (2012). Aid and economic growth: Sensitive analysis. *Journal of International Development, 24*, 17–33.

Hancock, G. (1989). *Lords of poverty: The power, prestige, and corruption of the international aid business.* New York: Atlantic Monthly Press.

Heather, C. (2009). The nexus between the democratic peace theory and economic coercion: Why democracies fight each-other?. *Winter, 8*(4).

Henderson, E. A. (2002). *Democracy and war: The end of an illusion?* Boulder, CO: Lynne Rienner Publishers.

Hirschman, A. O. (1973). *The strategy of economic development.* New Haven: Yale University Press.

Jevons, W. S. (2001). *The theory of political economy* (4th ed.). Basingstoke: Palgrave MacMillan.

Kant, I. (1948). *Perpetual peace.* New York: The Liberal Arts Press.

Kaufmann, D., Kraay, A., & Mastruzzi, M. (2005). Governance matters IV: Governance indicators for 1996–2004. *World bank policy research working paper* (3630).

Lenin, V. I. (1965). *Imperialism: The highest stage of capitalism: A popular outline*. Peking: Foreign Languages Press.
Lewis, W. A. (1955). *The theory of economic growth*. London: Allen & Unwin.
Lewis, D. (2001). *The management of non-governmental development organizations: An introduction*. London, New York: Routledge.
List, F. (1916). *The national system of political economy Reprints of economic classics* (pp. xxxi, 454 p.).
Machiavelli, N. (1998). *The Prince* (H. C. Mansfield, Trans.). Chicago: The University of Chicago Press.
Malthus, T. R. (1958). *An essay on the principle of population*. London: Dent.
Manor, J. (2007). *Aid that works: Successful development in fragile states*. Washington, DC: World Bank.
Maren, M. (1997). *The road to hell: The ravaging effects of foreign aid and international charity*. New York: Free Press.
Marx, K., & Engels, F. (1974). *On colonialism*. Moscow: Progress.
McNeill, W. H. (1976). *Plagues and peoples* (1st ed.). Oxford: Blackwell.
Mill, J. S. (1913). *On liberty* (People's edition). London: Longmans, Green.
Ming, T. W. (2000). Multiple modernities: A preliminary inquiry into the implications of East Asia modernity. In L. E. Harrison & S. P. Huntington (Eds.), *Culture matters: How values shape human progress* (pp. 256–266). New York: Basic Books.
Morgenthau, H. J. (1973). *Politics among nations: The struggle for power and peace* (5th ed.). New York: Knopf.
Moyo, D. (2011). *How the West was lost: Fifty years of economic folly and the stark choices ahead* (1st American edition). New York: Farrar, Straus and Giroux.
Myrdal, G. (1956). *Development and under-development: A note on the mechanism of national and international economic inequality*. Cairo: National Bank of Egypt.
Myrdal, G. (1957). *Economic theory and under-developed regions*. London: Duckworth.
North, D. C. (1981). *Structure and change in economic history*. New York: Norton.
North, D. C., & Thomas, R. P. (1973). *The rise of the Western world: A new economic history*. Cambridge: Cambridge University Press.
Nurkse, R. (1953). *Problems of capital formation in underdeveloped countries*. Oxford: Blackwell.
Pomeroy, S. B. (1995). *Oeconomicus*. Oxford: Clarendon Press.
Prebisch, R. (1950). *The economic development of Latin America and its principal problems*. New York: United Nations Department of Economic Affairs.
Ricardo, D. (1911). *The principles of political economy and taxation*. London: Dent.
Riddell, R. (2007). *Does foreign aid really work?* Oxford, New York: Oxford University Press.

Rodrik, D. (2000). Institutions for high-quality growth: What they are and how to acquire them. *Studies in Comparative International Development, 35*(3), 3–31.

Roodman, D. (2007). The anarchy of numbers: Aid, development, and cross-country empirics. *The World Bank Economic Review, 21*(2), 255–277.

Rosenstein-Rodan, P. N. (1943). Problems of industrialization of Eastern and South-Eastern Europe. *The Economic Journal, 53*(210/211), 202–211.

Rostow, W. W. (1971). *The stages of economic growth: A non-communist manifesto* (2nd ed.). Cambridge: Cambridge University Press.

Samuelson, P. A. (1946). Lord Keynes and the general theory. *Econometrica, Journal of the Econometric Society, 14*, 187–200.

Samuelson, P. A. (1948). International trade and the equalisation of factor prices. *Economic Journal, 58*(June), 163–184.

Sanchez, O. (2003). The rise and fall of the dependency movement: Does it inform underdevelopment today? *Estudios Interdisciplinarios de America Latina y el Caribe, 14*(2), 32.

Schiffbauer, M., & Ling, S. (2010). Democracy vs. dictatorship: Comparing the evolution of economic growth under two political regimes. *Economics of Transition, 18*(1), 59–90.

Schumpeter, J. A. (1955). *History of economic analysis*. London: George Allen & Unwin.

Serra, A., edited by Reinert, S. A. (2011). *A short treatise on the wealth and poverty of nations (1613)*. London: Anthem Press.

Singer, H. (1950). The distribution of gains between investing and borrowing countries. *American Economic Review, 40*, 473–485.

Smith, A. (1966). *An inquiry into the nature and causes of the wealth of nations*. New York: Kelley.

Spiro, D. E. (1994). The insignificance of the liberal peace. *International Security, 19*(2), 50.

Sunkel, O. (1972). Big business and "dependencia": A latin American view. *Foreign Affairs, 50*(3), 517–531.

Thucydides. (1972). *History of the Peloponnesian war* (R. Warner, Trans.). Harmonsworth: Penguin.

Tzu, S. (1963). *The art of war* (S. B. Griffith, Trans.). New York and Oxford: Oxford University Press.

Upham, F. (2002). *Mythmaking in the rule of law orthodoxy*. Washington, DC: Carnegie Endowment for International Peace.

Viner, J. (1927). Adam Smith and Laissez Faire. *Journal of Political Economy, 35*(2), 198.

Walras, L. (1977). *Elements of pure economics, or, The theory of social wealth*. Fairfield, NJ: Kelley.

Waltz, K. N. (1979). *Theory of international politics* (1st ed.). New York: Addison-Wesley.

CHAPTER 3

The Praxis of Economic Growth: Lessons from History

The theoretical review of development economic literature neither proved nor disproved first-hand impressions and preliminary information collected from the field. Development economic literature abounds with studies establishing positive, irrelevant or negative correlations between ODA levels and economic growth—thus failing to provide any consistent empiric proof as to the correlation between development aid and economic developments. Multidisciplinary theories on relations between developed and developing countries did not prove any more conclusive. The overview of general theories of economic growth also suggested that different traditions in economics, political science and law could either agree or disagree with preliminary field analyses.

Yet, if the history of economic ideas could not provide stable guidance on how to assess Africa's international economic relations, the history of economic praxes could possibly do such a service.[1] There are, today, 31 countries classified as high-income by the World Bank/OECD and it is theoretically possible to review the political measures that, at crucial times in their history, have contributed in advancing their economic status. Since the academic discipline of history of economic praxes does not exist in mainstream academia, this review has to rely on isolated studies on the subject as well as on primary and secondary sources dealing with economic policies in modern and contemporary history.

S. Raudino, *Development Aid and Sustainable Economic Growth in Africa*, DOI 10.1007/978-3-319-38936-3_3

1 On Development

Ever since men came down from trees, their history has been one of development through progressive stages of personal and social betterment. Reports and novels abound with descriptions of endemic misery in those same regions that later became the richest countries on earth: Europe, North America, Japan and Oceania. In 148 AD, the Physician Galen of Pergamum (modern day Turkey) described how, following the end of the winter, the peasantry was "[…] literally compelled for the rest of the year to feed on noxious plants, eating the shoots and tendrils of trees and shrubs, the bulbs and roots of unwholesome plants" (Chao 2006, p. 81). Between 1315 and 1322, the whole of northern Europe—present-day Germany, Belgium, the Netherlands, Luxemburg, northern France, the British islands with the exception of northern Scotland, the Baltic states and the southern portions of Scandinavia—suffered from a major famine that claimed the lives of millions (Jordan 1997). Famines were a regular occurrence in Europe all throughout the Middle Ages, and continued to plague some Western European countries until the nineteenth century: between 1845 and 1852, the Great Famine claimed the lives of an estimated 20 % of the Irish population. Scarce agricultural yields were cyclical occurrences comparable to natural disasters: highly unpredictable, because they were dependent upon a number of unforeseeable factors, including inclement weather and crop diseases. However, the fact that these cycles regularly resulted in devastating famines indicates that Europeans lived at a level of such precarious subsistence that they could not accumulate surpluses to shoulder hard times. Food scarcity was not the only factor keeping life on a brink: poor sanitary conditions resulted in regular pandemic outbreaks. From the eleventh until the nineteenth century, Europe suffered from recurrent pandemics of bubonic plague: in 1348–1350 alone, after having annihilated 60 % of the Chinese population, the "Black Death" travelled West and likely halved the overall European population.

Widespread poverty in the Western world continued throughout contemporary history and well into the industrial revolution. The *Commission on the Employment of Children and Young Persons* described the work of minors in English mines in1842: "Chained, belted, harnessed like dogs in a go-cart, black, saturated with wet, and more than half-naked—crawling upon their hands and feet, and dragging heavy loads behind them […]" (Routh 1989, p. 126). Witnesses testified to the Commission as to the standard working hours: from 2 am to 8 or 9 pm—one day off a week.

Child labour and 16 hours-long working days were not the exception, but the statutory norm. Exceptional, according to the American economist, Heilbroner (1980, p. 105), was the brutality used by English employers, as described by a 1828 article in the magazine *The Lion:* children were "[...] whipped day and night to stimulate their flagging industry; kicked, punched and sexually abused; left almost naked in the cold of the winter and brought in a trough, scrambling with the pigs, for their daily slops".

Today, virtually no one suffers from hunger in these regions. "Food insecurity", a milder concept than plain hunger, still affects roughly 4 % of the population in the USA.[2] Child labour has virtually disappeared since the 1980s. Absolute poverty has been almost eradicated, while the percentage of relative poverty in OECD countries varies between 17 % in the USA and 5.4 % in Finland.[3] More importantly, these regions are characterized by a strong middle and upper-middle class, estimated by different studies as encompassing anything between the absolute majority and the totality of their population.[4] Most of these countries have enforced sound legislation providing a great deal of welfare assistance, while consistent portions of their population are wealthy enough to make private donations or engage in charity work. Among these countries, education and health are considered almost everywhere as basic rights and are either partially subsidized or plainly provided by the government. Seen through the statistical development tools of the United Nations, these results translate in the status of countries with a "Very High Human Development Index": high GDP per capita, long life expectancy and high literacy rate.

How did they do it?

2 The Role of Economics in the History of Development

Much has been done since the 1990s to decouple the concept of development from the simple idea of income: concepts such as "human security" and "human development" have fostered the idea that people need to access services that cannot easily be translated in monetary terms. Econometrics can estimate the cost of primary education, universal vaccination or access to internet and mobile communication, but not the value that these services add to societies. Even more difficult is putting into numbers the psychological gratification deriving from self and social esteem—elements that are strictly dependent upon the chances of positively contributing in the management of our own lives and those of the communities we live in. Social development goes beyond the mere accumulation of capital and the adoption of successful economic policies; it also crucially depends on variables that are not always related to economics, including safety and public health, cultural and professional development and, moral gratification.

Socio-economic development is by no means a linear or irreversible process simply linking economic growth to people's well-being: pandemics, wars and incapable political regimes are examples of natural and man-made disasters that have turned around the sorts of otherwise wealthy and healthy populations. Over the last few decades, the HIV pandemics brought a number of African societies on their knees, despite the encouraging economic signs they had displayed in the previous decades. This has been the case for Botswana and South Africa, two countries that in the early 2000s showed unsustainable rates of HIV prevalence,—running well above 20 % in the adult age group—despite having managed impressive economic and social progress in the previous decades. History has also shown how wars can quickly shatter well-developed societies: the destruction of Germany between 1942 and 1945 brought the second largest economy of the world to its knees in a matter of a few years. American reports of 1947 Germany referred to vast chunks of the population living on rations that provided hardly more calories than those that condemned thousands of people to starve to death in Nazi concentration camps.[5] Ideologically misled or simply incapable, corrupted, botched-up regimes provide another set of examples of how promising socio-economic trends can quickly undergo U-turns, or how prosperous regions can be brought to ruins. Uganda under the ferocious and odd administration of Idi Amin, China during the Great Leap Forward and the Cultural Revolution of Mao Zedong, Argentina with the hyper-liberalist reforms of Carlos Menem and Zimbabwe under the iron grip of Robert Mugabe are all cases in point.

How economic growth happens and how the fruits of such growth are distributed in the society also bears consequences on the well-being of the overall population and on the capacity to induce further growth. Between 2000 and 2010, Angola has been growing at an average rate of 11.1 % annually; yet, since this growth relies entirely on oil and mining operations and because Angola had little welfare support, it had a limited impact on the well-being of the general population: more than 40 % of Angolans, today, remain below the absolute poverty line. Similar, albeit more nuanced, patterns are clearly discernible in fast-growing economies across the developing world: Nigeria, which between 2000 and 2010 grew at an average of 8.9 %, in 2009 had a Gini coefficient of 43 %[6], Colombia (with a Gini coefficient of 53.5 % in 2012), Guatemala (52.4 % in 2011), Rwanda (51.3 % in 2010) and the Democratic Republic of Congo (42.1 % in 2012) are all economies that have seen fast, but unequal, growth in the 2000s. Deeply seated economic injustices have characterized other countries for a longer time, making social mobility difficult to improve, despite the political measures taken to specifically tackle social justice problems; they include South Africa (with a Gini coefficient of 63.4 % in 2011), Namibia (61 % in 2009), Botswana (60.5 % in 2009), Brazil (52.7 % in 2012) and Argentina (42.5 % in 2012).

The history of economic development reveals a number of other long-term trends. The first concerns the role of macroeconomics in human development: if GDP growth alone does not necessarily translate into better social conditions for people, it is also true that there is virtually no possibility of achieving long-term social improvements without economic growth. Some temporary results can be achieved by redistributing existing wealth in a more equitable way—as socialist revolutions have done in many countries—however, over the mid to long run, there is no escape to the development–economic growth nexus. Economic growth is a *conditio sine qua non* of human development: a purely economic perspective does not provide the full picture, but any other perspective is incomplete unless it keeps economics within the picture. Economic growth might not be sufficient, but it remains a necessary condition of social betterment.

Second, there is an historic pattern showing that political units ("states" as they are called in the post-Westphalian system) improved the conditions of their *masses* (life expectancy, health, literacy, working conditions, access to property) through endogenous policies. That is, empirical evidence suggests that economic growth can only be endogenously generated: there is virtually no example in history of a country that managed to attain a high socio-economic status while being administered by foreign governments, running an externally planned economic system, receiving foreign subventions or depending upon international aid.[7] Material and social progress cannot be simply financed from outside, because it needs to be continuously serviced and expanded. To the same extent, successful reforms, public institutions and societal models cannot simply be "given" from outside, because they need to be paid for and be accountable to the communities adopting them. Domestic dynamics are largely accountable for the adoption and implementation of endogenous policies, but international relations often bear an enormous weight in influencing their outcome.

Third, at any time in history, certain political units have obtained much better socio-economic results than others. Whether because of their domestic or international policies, it is an historical fact that certain governments have been way more successful than others in promoting their citizens' socio-economic well-being—from the rise of sedimentary civilizations in 3000 BC onwards. Whether the two phenomena—the relative development of certain political units and the relative under-development of other political units—are interlinked is open to debate; what should not be open to debate, instead, is the idea that the world should have accumulated by now enough hands-on-experience to discern what policies promote socio-economic development from those that hinder it.

The review proposed in this chapter accounts for these three key patterns in the history of economic development of some OECD countries and NIEs,[8] namely: (1) development cannot happen without economic growth, (2) economic growth has always been achieved through "virtuous cycle" endogenous economic policies and (3) "virtuous cycle" endogeneous economic policies are constituted by the reiteration of specific economic praxes that have proven successful throughout history.

3 How OECD Economies Have Grown Rich: An Historical Perspective

Relatively wealthy, knowledgeable and well-administered civilizations inhabited, at different times and different places, the ancient world. Societies in Egypt, Greek city-states, African kingdoms, parts of the Roman republic and empire, Arabia, Persia, Central America, China and Japan bear witness to the different routes that can be taken—and have been taken—to improve socio-economic standards. Their experiences would be invaluable in the study of how societies undergo social and economic development. Yet, such accounts would carry little relation to the processes and policies that brought the world to where it is today: a strong concentration of socio-economic development in the OECD and newly industrialized economies, vast poverty in G90 countries and a mixed picture in a number of mid-income countries.

Arguably, the earliest developments that can be linked to today's socio-economic maps can instead be found in the economic, industrial and trade policies that allowed several northern Italian and Flemish city-states to start accumulating capital in the twelfth century AD. Henry VII (1457–1509) arguably took England along the same path in the 1480s, thus emulating what France under Louis XI (1423–1483) had started only a couple of decades earlier. Large areas of Germany remained untouched by these reforms until Frederick the Great (1712–1786) introduced state capitalism in the second half of the eighteenth century. In 1776, the USA achieved independence and started pressing forward on a number of similar reforms, mainly geared at establishing economic independence from and industrial alternatives to Europe, a process that intensified following the end of the American Civil War in the 1860s. Japan set on a route of emulation of Western industrial and trade policies in the 1880s and never departed from them. Several other Eastern Asian countries, including Hong Kong, Singapore, Korea, Taiwan and Malaysia underwent in the 1960s what Japan had started 80 years earlier. In the 1970s, taking advantage of surges in oil prices, some Middle-Eastern resource-rich countries, such as the United Arab Emirates and Qatar, used their income from natural resources to diversify their economies and promote a number of reforms that bear striking similarities with other successful developmental cases in Eastern Asia. China, somehow represents the child prodigy of twenty-first century development; if its 1.4 billion-strong population makes it a bit of a special case, most of the reforms it promoted since 1979 can, however, be seen as lessons learnt from other Asian development experiences.

Conversely, the economic policies—or lack thereof—of Spain, southern Italy and Sweden in the late Middle Ages and early modern era, when continental Western Europe was undergoing a period of major economic expansion, provide interesting insights as to the impact of these measures on a country's capacity in creating endogenous growth. Similarly, the ups and downs that several Latin American economies have experienced in the twentieth century—including Mexico, Argentina and Chile—reflect not only the instability of a region marred by political infighting and strong foreign interests, but also of discontinuous and alternating economic policies. The timid growth displayed by some African countries in the first post-colonial period—including Ghana, Tanzania and Ivory Coast—is equally far telling as to the existence of a positive relationship between incipient industrialization, economic diversification and growth trends. The economic slump in which most Sub-Saharan, non-commodity exporter states are today mirrors the reciprocal side of this very same story: the structural limits in creating endogenous growth without nurturing manufacturing activities through competent state intervention.

A number of remarks should be noted at the outset. First, the historical accounts that follow deal with the *praxis* of economic development rather than with the *theory* of economic development. Facts—including laws, edicts, ministerial strategies, publicly commissioned reports and official statistical data—occupy central stage; theories, ideas and opinions—resulting from academic works, civil society campaigns, institutional communication, debates and opinion polls—will only be used where they contain references to facts or where there is proof that they have successfully influenced public policies. It is a necessary distinction if reality has to be kept separated from fiction in a field where strong national and class interests have traditionally generated substantial amounts of propaganda and ideologically driven literature, either directly (through institutional communication) or indirectly (by financing researches, journals, think-tanks and professional institutions).

Second, we shall also deal with the role of economic development in the Middle Age and the early modern era (twelfth to eighteenth century) rather than exclusively focusing on the modern and contemporary industrial revolutions (mid-eighteenth century to date). Technological developments in eighteenth- and nineteenth-century Europe likely allowed Western countries to undergo the most radical economic acceleration in their history and to strengthen their supremacy over other regions of the world. However, most of the mechanisms that created the conditions for this jump to happen were already there: statecraft skills, well-tested industrial and international trade policies, incorporation and stock exchange norms, banking and financial instruments had all been created and perfected before the eighteenth-century European industrial revolution; in all likelihood, they massively contributed towards the present-day situation of the world economy. This explains the interest in stretching the historical review back to the twelfth century, while paying particular attention to fifteenth and sixteenth century economic dynamics.

A third remark concerns the nature of the public policies here discussed, which have been categorized into "positive", "negative" and "soft" policies. "Positive" economic policies are aimed at fostering a country's own potential for economic growth. They include a selective promotion of manufacturing activities characterized by increasing marginal returns;

a purposeful and timely creation of "market imperfections", including monopolies, state subsidies and patents; opening of large markets for the export of goods and services; public investments in human resources and technology; the setting up of areas specifically dedicated to manufacturing activities and benefiting from labour specialization and economies of scale; and the promotion of an assertive foreign policy through diplomatic and military means. "Negative" economic policies encompass all activities aimed at reducing the competitiveness of potential rivals: they aim at hindering other nations' activities in order to advance the relative economic standing of those promoting them. Historically, these policies have included the limitation of export of raw materials to other countries through quota, taxation or outright prohibition; the promotion and protection of domestic industries and markets against the influx of manufactured goods and services; the imposition of foreign market access through coercive means; the imposition to subdued countries of severe limitations on the number and quality of economic activities they were authorized to engage in; and the limitations in the mobility of key productive factors, including labour and capital. A third group of activities—serving the purposes of both "positive" and "negative" economic policies—relates to what Joseph Nye famously described as "soft-power" activities (Nye 2004). They include public diplomacy and institutional communication, export of culture, belief systems and traditions, management of religious affairs, control over the distribution of information, production of social science theories—anything, in other words, that can contribute in attracting and co-opting others towards intended and pre-established behaviours, without resorting to force.[9]

There is no clear-cut distinction between these three categories, as they often refer to different aspects of the same policies. Mercantilist policies in one country are usually aimed at expanding domestic production also by hampering other countries' access to their domestic market; in so doing, the same policy eventually generated both "positive" and "negative" byproducts. "Positive" economic policies—policies that promoted certain activities at home—often had exactly the same, albeit inverse, content of "negative" economic policies—policies that forbade or tried to hamper these same activities abroad. However, the distinction remains significant for several reasons. In first instance, it helps clarifying that—contrary to liberal beliefs—vast areas of international economics have always been under the rules of a zero-sum-game: gains on the one side are to be directly coupled with losses on the other. Large chunks of interests on one side of the world are intrinsically incompatible with those in other parts of the world; had this not been the case, we would have serious problems in understanding why the Doha Round failed after 14 years of negotiations or why Europe and the USA are increasingly and consistently resorting to trade defence measures in the face of expanding competition from the east. Since today's highly polished international relations environment is left with little room for public straight-talk among allies, the distinction also serves as a reminder that economic antagonism among allied states has always existed and will always exist. Similarly, it helps in understanding that Western policies towards the Global South—those same policies that are today sweetened in the normative language and belief system of development aid—have forefathers deeply grounded in nineteenth century *realpolitik*.

3.1 Northern Italian and Flemish City-States

Although there is scholarly agreement about the fact that technological advancements contributed in improving the living conditions of twelfth- and thirteenth-century Europeans, so-called "improvements" must be put into the early Middle Ages perspective.[10] Throughout these two centuries—and for much longer afterwards—Europe remained an overwhelmingly rural society, with an estimated 90 % to 95 % of the population living in rural areas. Life in the countryside was characterized by epidemics, famines and an endemic scarcity of food. A 1267 AD survey in the region of Namur, France, shows how 81 % of 255 farm tenures were insufficiently large to allow their tenants to support themselves by farming alone. Small landowners had no surplus whatsoever; having barely enough to survive, their precarious destiny was in the hand of fortune. If disease or death struck the father of the family and the new head of the family could not find work, the family would quickly fall into pauperism. Help for these people could only come on a voluntary basis from charitable institutions. This help was not enough to prevent widespread social problems and popular disturbances, as testified by the movement of the Pastoureaux in 1251, when thousands of hungry and dispossessed people invaded cities in France and the Low Countries. Life in most European urban centres was relatively better, but nonetheless plagued by illness, poverty, crime, scant sanitary conditions and ignorance.

However, at the turn of the twelfth and thirteenth century, the economies of three Italian maritime republics—Genoa, Venice and Pisa—were flourishing, along with those of Milan, Florence and a number of Flemish cities. Commerce was the main source of profits for the Italian maritime republics, both for home manufactured and for re-exported goods. The constant expansion of trade routes, aimed at simultaneously creating sourcing and destination markets, was the key element in maintaining a flourishing trade business, an element that justified the efforts the maritime republics put in establishing new international agreements. By the end of the twelfth century, historical sources report of 291 ships in the port of Genoa, probably only a fraction of the whole merchant marine the city could count on. Venice and Pisa likely had fleets of a similar size (Pryor 1999, p. 426). These ships were used to carry commerce with virtually every kingdom, sultanate or republic in the Mediterranean and in the Middle East: by the thirteenth century, Genoa was trading with Malaga, Sicily, Safi, Tangier, Oran, Tunis, Tripoli, Alessandria, Constantinople, Thessaloniki, and Crimea; Venice was mostly dealing with the Balkans, Crete, Greece and the Aegean Islands, the Middle East, Cyprus, the Black Sea, Constantinople and Romania.

Income derived from commerce was partially invested in public works, including road pavements, bridges, churches and communal buildings, as well as in the refurbishing of already existing infrastructures. All three republics had, in point of fact, extensive public building programmes, financed by public authorities, private wealthy citizens and the church. Works paid by public authorities allowed keeping high employment rates and salaries even among those working classes that were not directly related to the trading or manufacturing industry. In all the three cities, the Government played a major role in the public economy; Venetian authorities, more than anyone else, interfered heavily in the city's development by building galleys—either directly or by auctioning them to private bidders—, managing factories, establishing prices within the freight industry and militarily protecting their merchant marine.

The other group of cities that thrived throughout this period were the manufacturing cities of Italy and the Flanders: Milan, Florence, Bruges, Ypres and Ghent were the European—and world—centres of woollen cloth, the main industrial product of the time. England and the Spanish kingdoms, at this time, were only exporting raw wool to the Low Countries and Italy, thus allowing foreign manufacturers to weave and re-export these products. These cities kept consolidated supplies of food, raw material and working tools within their borders, allowing a number of master artisans to efficiently work around the clock. Arguably, these were among the first early examples of economies of scale and increasing marginal returns, whereby an increase in output corresponded to lower production costs, a phenomenon that had not characterized agriculture until then.

The advantages brought by systematic production processes and foreign trade proved long-lasting: in 1500, the world's richest areas with the most impressive concentration of trade, industry and wealth were still northern Italy and the strip of the Low Lands that went from Ypres up north-west towards Antwerp. Wealth coming from industry and foreign markets spilled over to banking, accounting and trading techniques, with crucial inventions such as the double-entry book, the stock exchange and the letter of credit originating exactly from these same regions. Since the beginning of the fifteenth century and well into the seventeenth century, the wealth of these regions could also afford the luxury of nurturing culture and attracting foreign artists, thus turning industrial capitals into cultural capitals of the world, expressing scientific and artistic talents of the calibre of Galileo Galilei, Leonardo da Vinci and Jan van Eyck. Remarkably, both northern Italy and the Atlantic coast from Flemish Belgium to Holland have remained comparatively rich European regions throughout modern and contemporary history.

3.2 England

In 1485, Henry VII acceded to the English throne and decided that England should have established its own textile industry rather than relying on the export of raw wool to the continental Low Lands and Italy. The logic was straightforward and the mission simple: keeping inside the country those activities—manufacturing rather than cattle farming—that guaranteed higher profit margins, while creating a viable market for these newly produced national goods. England started having a system of industrial protection that was later to be praised by mercantilist thinkers (Lamond 1893) and damned by the classic school lineage—from Adam Smith down to the latest edition of Samuelson's *Economics*. Contrary to much of today's mainstream economic theory, such a system relied on simple empirical observations: reserving supplies of English raw wool for the English cloth industry, while prohibiting the import of manufactured woollens was the easiest way to create a national industry and move up the ladder of economic profitability.

Plain, hands-on-business logic had long worked in royal courts: before Henry VII, Edward IV (1442–1483) had already promoted a royal edict that turned into a felony the export of bullions to other countries—a prohibition that remained valid till 1663. What was later to be defined as faulty mercantilist logic was an act of law justified by two plain reasons: (1) preserve the country from being drained of its currency and (2) avoid the political dangers associated with a government that did not have any treasures to face emergencies. In a system in which precious metals represented the ultimate reserve of value and war was a legitimate means to solve divergences of interests, having a positive inflow of bullions simply meant to be engaged in activities that ensured profits rather than losses and to stand ready to face a fresh bout of war.[11] Other mechanisms were devised in those same years to avoid unprofitable trade. A string of legislative provisions regulated private contracts between English and foreign companies in such a way as to maximize exports and the entry of liquidity: the *Statutes of Employment* and the institutions charged with supervising trade and custom matters—including the Customers and the Royal Exchanger—, requested English merchants to bring back to England a portion of their proceedings from overseas sales, while foreign traders were obliged to spend a portion of their proceedings on English goods.[12]

The attention towards the balance of trade was a matter of "practical statecraft"—as remarked by John Maynard Keynes—well before it became a subject of discussion among economic schools. Allowing a positive balance of trade not only signified an inflow of bullions, if not an increase in the tax basis and a larger degree of national self-sufficiency. It was clear to most thinkers of the time that increases in export could most easily be promoted via public interventions aimed at raising the quantity and quality of national products, a policy that also created jobs. Far from being seen as a myopic accumulation of bullions for their supposed intrinsic value, mercantilist measures were understood as the most realistic, pragmatic and viable policy tools to enhance economic growth—at least by royal courts governing in Europe.

Several legislative provisions adopted in England in the sixteenth and the seventeenth century (particularly between 1620 and 1720) testifies to the double effort at improving the trade balance by increasing national production and creating the necessary market conditions—domestically and internationally—to absorb it. Following poor harvesting in Western Europe in 1556, most countries found themselves obliged to import grain from the Baltic regions, a move that caused drainage of bullions and a subsequent financial crisis. Among the legislative provisions that ensued from that event, a 1566 English Act encouraged the home production of salt; in the Act's preface it is plainly stated that the imports of salt from abroad had costed "[…] great soomes of money to The empoverishment of this Realme by wasting and conveying of the Treasure and Coyne of thys Realme into Forreiyn Parteis […]" (C. H. Wilson 1967, p. 507).

The first English colonial ventures were themselves justified—or at least understood—as part of the efforts to maintain a viable trade balance: accessing the source of goods, such as spices and minerals, that had been long purchased abroad. In the sixteenth century, hefty prices were paid for Portuguese sugar imported from Brazil via refineries in Antwerp as well as for Spanish tobacco imported from New World colonies via Iberian ports, which paid large profits to Spanish merchants and duties to the Spanish Crown. The reign of Queen Elizabeth I (1558–1603) decided that time had come to stop this vicious circle and emulate Spain and France by expanding overseas trade. This was done by setting up joint-stock companies to establish an English commercial presence overseas: the English East India Company and the London Company of Virginia were set up in 1600 and 1606, respectively, to cater to English trade interests. Specific edicts also referred to the necessity of reducing English reliance upon foreign sources, with all the vulnerability and costs that such reliance entailed.

In the 1660s, and in line with national legislation in France as well as in Italian, Flemish and Hanseatic cities, the Stuarts devised a comprehensive navigation policy (1651 *Navigation Act*; 1660 *Navigation Act*; 1663 *Act for the Encouragement of Trade*) that made it difficult for foreign shipping companies to transport goods in and out of England and its colonies: only English ships were allowed to carry national goods.[13] The logic was crystal clear: why allow foreigners to strip England of profit margins accruing from the manufacturing and sale of English goods? The 1663 Act requested more than leaving English trade to English ships: it obliged all European goods bound for America and all American raw materials bound for anywhere else to pass through England first, where they could be inspected and taxed. In practice, the Act implemented most of the provisions that a governmental *Commission of Enquiry* had already put forward in 1623 as a comprehensive package of measures to deal with the economic crisis that hit most European states in the early 1620s.[14] These measures plainly reflected the credo of most European governments of the day: building up the value and volume of exports, while satisfying as much as possible of the national aggregate demand.

English economic policies gradually evolved not only as a consequence of national economic developments but—more significantly—as a consequence of a changing relationship between the English Kingdom and the international environment. The 1663 *Act for Encouragement of Trade* not only extended the English crown's control upon trade flows, but also abolished the outright prohibition on the export of bullions. What happened is that England had become aware that Dutch merchants, being allowed to freely trade with bullions, were profiting from the possibility of paying cash for goods that could subsequently be re-exported against cash to third countries. English merchants were losing out on foreign business opportunities because public regulations were limiting their liquidity by restricting payment modalities. The international environment had also dramatically changed from the years in which export of bullions was prohibited: the expansion of acreage of cultivated land and the improvement of agricultural techniques had lessened England's reliance on foreign imports of food, which had previously contributed towards a negative balance of trade.[15] The interplay between commercial interests and changing international conditions spurred change in English economic policies.

Exporting manufactured goods and importing bullions were policies that could only go hand in hand with economic and industrial policies aimed at incentivizing production. While a number of Acts within medieval statute books already promoted wool-growing, cloth-making and shipbuilding, these often relied on specific definitions of products in order to limit the amount of producers allowed into the market and create reasonable profits for those entrepreneurs that decided to invest in new industries or new areas of the Kingdom. In later edicts, there is a weakening of the attention towards these aspects and a strengthened concern towards market access abroad. More generally, it is interesting to notice the government's activism to expand sales markets (both domestically and overseas), promote a positive inflow of bullions and strengthen manufacturing industries. In the first half of the eighteenth century, an economically growing UK was still full-swing into this vision: Prime minister and Chancellor of the Exchequer Robert Walpole (1676–1745) announced in 1721 his intention to simplify the growing and confusing body of existing trade legislation, taxes, duties and excises on the basis of the clear and simple conviction that "Nothing would more conduce to [the riches and grandeur of this nation] than to make the exportation of our own manufactures, and the importation of the commodities used in the manufacturing of them, as practicable and easy as may be; by this means the balance of trade may be preserved in our favour, our navigation increased and greater numbers of our poor employed." (Brisco 2013, p. 130)

For some, the publication of Adam Smith's *Wealth of Nation*, David Ricardo's *Principles* (1817), the defeat of Napoleon (1814) and the repeal of the *Navigation Acts* (1849) are all events contributing to the British renouncement of long-used principles of mercantilist trade in favour of *laissez-faire* as a radical policy alternative. This might have been the case, considering the necessity for British industries to penetrate increasingly larger markets in order to sustain its growing industrial basis, but it is a fact that Britain never renounced mercantilist opportunities whenever and wherever these could still be seized. In 1806, London requested the independent USA to drop all trade with foreign powers, engaging in a war when the latter refused to abide. In the early 1840s, Britain militarily engaged China in order to continue exporting massive quantities of opium, thus maintaining a trade balance that would have otherwise disproportionally favoured the Chinese. Following successful military campaigns against the Qing Dynasty, London imposed exclusive commercial concessions, including low and unilaterally established duties, a most favoured nation clause and extraterritoriality rights for its merchants residing in China. Almost 30 years later, following disputes on the implementation of these provisions, the UK engaged China in a second war (Second Opium War, 1856–1860) aiming at reinstating its trade privileges. In fact, most of the British colonial wars of the late nineteenth century and the early twentieth century can, indeed, be seen as an effort to maintain mercantilist economic, trade and property rights in dealing with foreign economies.

3.3 France

Some of the political economic reforms that Henry VIII initiated in 1485 had been already underway in France since Louis XI (1423–1483) took upon a ground-breaking strategy of national identity-building around the idea of *bien commune* (common wealth). Louis XI's founding strategy was to substitute the feudal aristocracy with an industrial bourgeoisie as the leading national class. This was done by creating national industries, protecting their markets and discouraging the landlords' rent-seeking behaviour. Taxes started being levied by inverse proportionality to the taxpayers' productivity: feudal princes were thus asked to pay higher percentages than entrepreneurs and workers. Contrary to other European Kingdoms, France also encouraged the nobility and the clergy to engage in productive activities. Tax income—which increased almost fourfold in the 20 years of Louis XI's reign—was subsequently used to subsidize cities and their nascent industries. The state started financing public works in a number of sectors, including the enhancement of canals' viability and ports' capacity, as well as supporting selected industries, including the armament manufacturers. France also started incentivizing the immigration of skilled workers by protecting their property and temporarily exempting them from income taxes. A number of general regulations were issued in an effort to build an environment conducive towards work industriousness and increased efficiency, including a set of edicts aimed at improving sanitation standards as well as water and food quality. Another edict prescribed the free circulation of grain to allow wheat distribution at affordable prices and avoid malnutrition among the working population. A national currency was introduced to cut down transaction costs; a similar logic further suggested the introduction of a unified investment plan and a national credit policy to foster capital-intensive investments. State investments were also channelled towards human resources, with the creation of new Universities dealing with civil and canon law, medicine and liberal arts.

Louis XI's modernization plan crucially relied on a key development in the national economic basis to pay for its multiple reforms: France was to pass from an agrarian, aristocracy-led country into a manufacturing, capitalist-led nation. Masterly crafted investment policies could have done little without this foundational economic change, which relied on ideas similar to those entertained by the English royal house in those same years: "money is in body politics what blood is in the human body"[16]: allowing a country to prosper meant ensuring that enough blood was circulating by nourishing national production. Attention was to be lent, on the one hand, to necessary activities that injected more blood into the system and, on the other hand, to those risky activities that drained it; manufacturing, export and protection of infant industries pertained to the former group; purchasing of finished foreign goods to the latter group.

Louis XI set the direction; French policies throughout the sixteenth century followed along that path. Sixteenth century historical reports show how the French state incentivized private investments in specific industries by providing limited numbers of manufacturing licences, by exempting entrepreneurs from taxes or by giving outright financial subventions. A *cahier* (register) discussed in the *Estates Generales* in 1576 suggested that money will be gained if France can manufacture the raw materials of which it abounds. By then, a 1572 edict had already banned the import of foreign textile and prohibited the export of raw goods, on the ground that French people "[...] can better devote themselves to the manufacture and working up of wool, flax, hemp and tow [...] and so get the profit that foreigners now make" (C. H. Wilson 1967, p. 524); few years later, in 1583, the Assembly pleaded tax-free entry of these same raw materials. Cardinal Richelieu, who became Secretary of State in 1616, gave the next strong impetus towards industrialization, state investments, subsidies and foreign market access: in 1627, he decreed that all French trade had to be shipped by French merchant vessels; in 1629 he incentivized the nobility to become entrepreneurial by guaranteeing that they would not lose their social status because of their engagement in productive activities; in 1628, he began establishing the Great Trading Companies—including the *Company of New France* and the *French West India Company*—, which aimed at encouraging colonial settlements. In his role of *Controller General of Commerce* and President of the *Conseil de Commerce*, Barthélemy de Laffemas devised a public institution dedicated at encouraging entrepreneurship and regulating industries. Despite being judged by historians as a cumbersome machine generating endless meetings of doubtful utility, Laffemas's *Commission de Commerce* did everything conceivable to encourage industrial investments in France. In an estimated 150 separate sessions over the 1601–1602 period only, the Commission investigated matters relating to trade in goods and services, including textile manufacturing, horse breeding, leather works, glass, tiles, tapestry, rival and canal works, shipbuilding and much more. Proof of the centrality of state dirigisme in the economic development of France is also to be found in the discussions of the *Estates Generales* of 1614 and in the *Assembly of Notables* in 1626.

Louis XIV relentless minister Jean-Baptiste Colbert was the man who, more than anyone else, set out to fully implement the vision firstly delineated by Louis XI: France was to become economically self-sufficient, while gaining markets over its major competitors. In the 20 years of his tenure as Minister of Finance, France managed to "conquer" what Colbert himself defined an "economic warfare" against other European Nation states, surpassing everyone with the sole exception of the Dutch. Under political directions of *Roi Soleil*, Colbert created new trading companies or renewed existing ones, while strengthening the protectionist principles introduced over a century earlier. Commerce with the Spanish kingdom was individuated as particularly favourable, because of the great liquidity that Spain derived from its monopoly over Central American silver mines and the ease with which it used this liquidity in paying for foreign commodities.

At the same time, attention was paid to avoid state trading companies from running trade deficits with the commodity-rich kingdoms of the Levant. A seemingly endless list of industrial regulations was introduced, specifying rules that went from the obligation of pertaining to a guild to the allowed number of threads per cloth. Those *règlements* (regulations) that were later to be mocked as short-sighted bureaucratic mentality by classic economists and that became an unbearable burden to eighteenth- and nineteenth-century capitalists, had very practical scopes, which were arguably achieved: (1) ensuring an environment of profitable and imperfect competition by granting monopoly, subsidies and cartelizing privileges; (2) promoting industrial and technological development aimed at introducing new manufacturing activities in France and (3) advancing the standards and quality of manufactured goods in order to foster the reputation of national industries. Historians suggest that Colbertism slowly produced a bureaucratized society that became increasingly corrupt and inefficient, but there is also some agreement about the suitability of the economic system itself to the time, and there is no doubt that under Colbert, France grew to become the strongest European power (Sargent 2013).

3.4 The USA

The economic development of the USA is strictly entangled with emancipation from what we have defined as "negative economic policies": public policies that purposefully hampered the economic growth of other regions as a mean to enhance one's own economic growth. Being the first colony to undergo the systematic economic and industrial changes that allowed a catch up—and a later overtake—of European economy, the USA represents a leading example of how well-engineered economic, industrial and trade policies can go a long way towards socio-economic emancipation and development.

Traditionally, European colonies had been used as a source of raw material and end markets for manufactured goods. This appears not only from mercantilist pamphlets of the early modern era discussing British, French and Dutch economic policies, but also from official transcripts, such as parliamentary debates and royal edicts. Colonies were further prohibited from establishing any manufacturing activity that could have locally competed with manufactured products coming from the mother country or even managed to compete in the mother country's own domestic market. The USA was no exception: until the 1780s, the only manufacturing activities—usually limited to foodstuffs and textiles—took place within farm households at a very small scale.[17] This situation was certainly favoured by the abundance of land and natural resources in the early days of American colonization, but was also the result of a conscious and long-lasting British policy vis-à-vis the New World. Such policy has been explained by the historian, McCusker, under three headings: (1) England (Great Britain from 1707) was to be the exclusive beneficiary of the trade in the products of its colonies, (2) England was to be the exclusive beneficiary of the trade in the supply of goods to its colonies and (3) England was to be the exclusive beneficiary of the carrying trade of the colonies (McCusker 1996). This translated in London unilaterally deciding what to buy and sell, through whom and at which conditions. Maintaining a monopoly on trade flows with the colonies was the key mechanism to ensure a steady flow of revenues towards the English Crown and ensuring profits to those merchants that represented the strongest political allies of the Crown.

The deal was not totally unfair to European settlers in America, at least at the beginning. Settlers living in the New World were subjects of the British Crown exactly in the same way English citizens were. Their property and businesses were under the tutelage and jurisdiction of the English Kingdom. Despite legal regulations on the subjects allowed to trade with the colonies, between 1600 and 1660, European settlers were, in practice, left free to do business with whomever they preferred, with Dutch trading and shipping companies being often preferred to English. Things, however, changed with the introduction of the 1660 and 1663 Trade Acts, by which London obliged all carriers to and from the New World to pass through England first.[18] These statutes were aimed at strengthening the management of the empire as a machine, where the periphery was tasked with the export of raw material, kept away from industrialization and prohibited from trading with non-British subjects. Within this logic, the USA was a cogwheel in a large imperial machine operated by the English government and the economic classes that sustained that government.

From the eighteenth century onwards, other British laws begun to encroach on the interests of the New World. In the 1720s and early 1730s, the UK parliament passed a law designed to hamper any direct trade between the North Americans and the foreign West Indian colonies. Here again, the British wanted trade to be processed via England, where they could take a cut of every transaction. The Molasses Act of 1733 imposed a sanction on New England on sugar imports coming from non-British colonies, in such a way as to hinder and detour the trade that had been flourishing between the North American colonies and the French, Dutch and Spanish West Indian possessions. More limits were to come in the 1760s and 1770s: the *Sugar Act* of 1764 further taxed and regulated trade centred in the West Indies, while the *Currency Act* of 1764 curtailed the emission of independent currencies that New England believed indispensable to expand trade.

These were about the last straws the colonists would take; one year after, in 1765, the non-importation movement retaliated by asking Americans to refrain from purchasing British manufactured goods, and particularly cloth, as well as agricultural goods coming from other British possessions, particularly tea. The movement was meant to encourage local production of goods previously imported or their substitution with alternative products locally manufactured or grown. This same strategy had been used for 300 years in Europe, was about to be theorized by the German economist Friedrich List and was destined to become popularized almost 200 years later under the name of *Import Substitution Industrialization* (ISI). The *Continental Congress Association* that organized the boycott also linked political liberty with autonomous international commerce—it was clear that the latter presupposed the former. The boycott went on for a few years with a certain degree of success; the Tea Act of 1773 further exacerbated tensions until the situation precipitated the following year, when the British Parliament passed a series of punitive laws known as the *Intolerable Acts*. These were read by the Americans as an act of overt aggression and an impingement upon their constitutional rights rather than as a credible trade request; shortly after, in April 1775, the American War of Independence broke out.

What the American colonists had witnessed over almost 200 years of colonial relationship with Britain was a system of economic dependence that initially benefited anyone who was linked to its levers—independently from his nationality or place of residence—but progressively restricted the opportunities for general economic growth in America. After the USA proclaimed its independence in 1776, the newly established sovereign country did not take long to replicate the mechanisms the UK had followed to ensure its own economic development. A number of legislative provisions aimed at encouraging manufacturing expansion were introduced following Secretary of Treasury Alexander Hamilton's *Report on Manufactures* (Hamilton 1791), which pointed to the benefits accruing from the growth and development of industries. Hamilton—whose advises contained in the report were almost entirely adopted by the Congress—introduced import duties to protect the nascent USA industry while raising fresh revenues for the new administration, used part of these revenues to pay direct subsidies to national industries, opened immigration to allow for increases in the labour force and launched a patent system to encourage inventions and technological innovations.

The new American administration acted swiftly, but production was slow in taking off—15 years after the introduction of these incentives, there were still little signs of progress. Some indirect incentives came from the 1812 war with Britain and the embargo that ensued, which indirectly spurred national production. Patriotic appeals were also used to arouse the public sentiment in favour of economic autarchy. The first major breakthrough arguably came with the development of the cotton textile mills, which were based upon three economic pillars: the principle of economies of scale (large factories), cheap labour (almost entirely consisting of women), and innovative technology (which allowed, among other things, to transmit water power). Shortly after, technological developments (like the use of steam) allowed industrial expansion into new regions and increased efficiency, to which contributed the concentration of manufacturing activities in urban areas. The Civil War (1861–1865) also provided an indirect occasion to support specific industries that were to remain vital in the USA economic ascendancy, including armaments and food processing.

There is a shared consensus about the fact that the most impressive period of American growth happened between the end of the American Civil War and the end of World War I (1865–1919). In that 50 years' time span, the USA managed to grow from an emerging country with a world GDP share comparable with that of the UK or France, into the first-world economy, having a GDP that fell slightly short of the German, French and British GDPs combined. Not only had the USA become a commercial superpower that had overtaken its former colonial masters, its economy was also nurturing and maintaining one of the strongest military apparatus worldwide. There is little doubt that the economic boom was due to the manufacturing sector, which underwent major transformations in those years: the size of industrial units had increased sensitively (number of employees per establishment doubled between 1870 and 1890) along with the share of labour force employed in manufacturing, which rose from 13.8 % in 1860 to 22.1 % in 1910. All in all, the share of manufacturing in the American GNP rose from roughly 24 % in 1869 to 33 % in 1899.

The transformation owed to multiple determinants, yet little could have happened in the absence of a skyrocketing demand for consumable goods, including foodstuff and apparels. This demand grew spontaneously along with the demographic growth and the USA capacity to attract migrants from all over the world, but new market opportunities were consciously sought via import substitution and increased penetration into foreign markets—manufactured exports as a share of total exports rose from 28 % in 1860 to a staggering 60 % in 1910. In this period, the USA became a new world player using old methods: over these 50 years, Washington dusted off the mercantilist policies of its former colonial masters and raised tariff rates for manufactured imports several times over. A huge domestic market and a natural abundance of raw materials (mineral, vegetable, animal, leather and fibres, timber, coal, iron, copper) meant that the USA had a limited need to procure safe supplies of basic commodities or expand market access abroad.[19]

The booming of manufacturing activities was entirely due to the private sector. There is little doubt that the USA had a much less interventionist model than Europe had had before; however, different levels of the USA government—federal, state and local—did pass laws aimed at incentivizing and/or restricting industrial activities according to their contribution to the national economy. Industrial subsidies and import duties on manufactured goods had remained two stable pillars of the American economic policy since Alexander Hamilton's proposal of 1791. Import duties' nominal rates generally increased between the 1790s and 1832, with the full support of the Treasury Department. The *Compromise Tariff* of 1833 lowered custom protection levels, but the need for revenue generated by the American Civil War induced a new sharp increase in tariffs in 1861—that level was generally maintained high until World War I. In fact, with the McKinley Tariff of 1890, the USA had become the country with the highest tariff rates in the industrialized world. On top of these key tools, the USA economy benefited from a number of other governmental systemic interventions, including the promotion of technological progress via measures sustaining innovations—these included patent rights and the institutions designed to support trade in these patents.

3.5 *Japan*

Several reasons contribute in making Japan a case as significant as the USA in understanding the role of economic, industrial and trade policies towards social development. The first is that since the seventeenth century and until the American-imposed *Kanagawa Treaty* of 1854, Japan had been an almost completely isolated country. This means that the Japanese islands were not affected—in the good and the bad—from the consequences of interacting with other developing economies, a phenomenon that crucially characterized the interlinked histories of the European countries and the territories they administered. The second is that, compared to Europe and the USA, nineteenth century Japan had a modest economy and weak military power: well into the 1870s, Japan still maintained a feudal system, a largely agrarian economy and an administration based on hereditary office-holding. The country's relative backwardness was, in fact, the key reason that induced its strongly anti-Western elite to accept, after a frantic resistance of two years, the Unequal Treaties imposed by the USA first and by other European nations later. The third reason is that during the Meiji period (1868–1912), Japan had likely achieved the world's most successful socio-economic growth after the USA. Japan replicated a similar economic miracle in the post-World War II period until the 1980s, working as a catalyst of economic development for several other Eastern Asian nations.

When in 1868 Japan initiated its modernization, it had two defining conditions: economic underdevelopment and a history of seclusion that stretched back to 1635—hence, little consequences from other nations' "positive" and "negative" economic policies.[20] The setting up of modern Japan was a humungous task; it spanned from measures aimed at ensuring the allegiance of the militaries to the liquidation of the existing public debt; from the abolition of the fiefs to the establishment of certificates of title for the land; from the organization of a tax system to the issuance of "rules of conduct" for Japanese nationals travelling abroad. What linked this maze of reforms were a few leading themes, including the abolition of previous societal structures—seen as a hindrance towards growth—and a quest for knowledge abroad, in a conscious and deliberate effort to emulate foreign economic, political and legal institutions. In 1871, the "founding fathers" of modern Japan, including Ito Hirobumi (1841–1909), Iwakura Tomomi (1825–1883), Ōkubo Toshimichi (1830–1878) and Kido Takayoshi (1833–1877) set off for a trip to the USA and Europe in a mission aimed at acquiring knowledge on statecraft and economic growth. After almost two years, the group became convinced that a programme of domestic reforms similar to those undertaken in Western countries could have ensured a safe and prosperous Japan.

The steps taken towards that direction betray a heavy indebtedness to the logic and praxes of nineteenth century Western economic policies. Education, communication facilities and legal institutions were all understood as underpinning elements of economic growth, and, as such, provided by the government. However, in planning its own model of state economic intervention, Japan went one step further than Europe and two steps further than the USA, intervening in far more complex tasks than simply creating a favourable environment to industrialization. The Japanese government became, instead, the leading national entrepreneur when it took over a number of recently established companies, including shipyards, weapon factories and communication companies. After the Unequal Treaties had brought into the country a flood of cheap foreign manufactured goods, inducing strong trade imbalances and a constant drain of species throughout the period 1868–1881, the Japanese government reacted by engaging in competition with foreign industries.

As in Washington 100 years earlier, people in Tokyo acted swiftly, mainly with the conviction that, in the increasing world militarism of the late nineteenth century, late or sluggish performances could have costed Japan its own sovereignty. The government attracted foreign technicians and sent Japanese students abroad for training, set up local technical schools, organized trade exhibitions, imported foreign capital goods to be studied and replicated, engaged directly in international trade and used the proceeding to finance its many investment ventures, including the creation of factories—often commercially and financially unviable—for the purpose of serving as training centres or as pioneering import substitution facilities. Later on, in the 1880s, when the financial burden of these investments started becoming intolerable, some of these industries were sold, government grants and subsidies reduced and new taxes introduced.[21]

The economic results achieved countrywide in a time span of only 20 years were impressive. By the 1890s, Japan had managed to achieve import substitution in the textile sector and was competing with British products in China and India. Japanese shipping companies successfully competed with European vessels, not only in Asia but also on transcontinental routes. Shortly after having managed import substitution in key industries, Japan decided to emulate its Western mentors in other, more controversial ventures: colonial expansion was initiated in Taiwan (1895) and followed in Manchuria (starting from the Liaotang province in 1905) and Korea (1910). Japanese economic policies in these colonies bore a striking resemblance to European imperialist policies in Africa and the

Middle East: colonial territories were developed according to the mother country's needs, typically consisting in having a stable source of cheap raw material and hungry markets for manufactured products. Manchuria was dedicated to the extractive industry. In Taiwan, the motto of the foreign administration in the 1910–1930 period was "industry for Japan, agriculture for Taiwan"—thus making Formosa one of the world's biggest producers of sugar cane, which, along with rice and other agricultural products, was only authorized to be exported to the mother country. An exception to this rule was opium and cocaine sold to China: the Japanese had learned from the British the double benefits accruing from selling highly priced drugs to enemy countries. Both Korea and Taiwan were forbidden from engaging in manufacturing activities that could have competed with industries in the mother country, while their domestic markets were barren of foreign products by way of high import duties. Contrary to most European nations, Japan invested an enormous amount of attention, resources and skills in the management of its colonies, planning their "development" very much along the model it had successfully followed at home. Agricultural production in Taiwan could become successful thanks to large-scale financing and heavy subsidies from Tokyo (often sponsored through deficit financing), the setting up of semi-governmental monopolies and the efforts of a highly skilled and competent administration which managed, in a matter of ten years, to turn Taiwan into a fiscally self-sufficient region.

3.6 Asian Newly Industrialized Economies (NIEs)

In the 1970s, Singapore, Hong Kong, South Korea and Taiwan became known under the term Asian newly industrialized economies (NIEs), Asian newly industrialized countries (NICs) or, more colloquially, as the four Asian tigers—all indirect references to their newly achieved, sustained and prolonged economic growth rates.[22] In 1960, the GDP per capita of Singapore and Hong Kong were below those of Turkey and Venezuela and at par with South Africa and Jamaica; today, they consistently rank better than several Western European countries. South Korea and Taiwan were, in 1960, in the same GDP league as the Ivory Coast and Sierra Leone, outperformed by countries like Liberia and Honduras; in 2013, they were ahead of the most developed among eastern European countries.[23]

Asian NIEs were—and remain—fundamentally different among them. Historically, Hong Kong and Singapore had been part of the British

Empire for 155 years and 135 years, respectively,[24] whereas Taiwan and South Korea had been Japanese colonies for "only" 50 years and 35 years, respectively. They had long maintained different international statuses: Singapore and South Korea became sovereign countries in the 1960s; Hong Kong passed from the status of British colony to the status of Special Administrative Region (SAR) of China in the 1990s; while Taiwan has been battling since 1945 to maintain its status of sovereign country. Politically, these countries have been through widely different systems: Singapore has been an authoritarian regime since its independence in 1965, South Korea and Taiwan are considered fully fledged democracies since the 1980s, while Hong Kong has never achieved independence. Their industrial model varies to such an extent that there is, today, some shared agreement about the absence of a standard "East Asian model" of industrialization: each country pursued different objectives through different intervention mechanisms. If there is a common denominator, this is to be found in the lack of democracy during the crucial phases of these countries' developmental paths and the strong role of the government in the economy.

At independence in 1945, Korea was, quite literally, among the poorest countries in the world: the GDP per capita in the Korean peninsula stood well below the level of most African countries, while the literacy ratio was barely above 20 %. The little industries that were allowed under Japanese occupation were destroyed shortly after independence, when the Soviet Union-backed North and the American-administered South engaged in a fratricidal war that lasted over three years (1950–1953). In the war, the South Korean portion of the peninsula lost 50 % of its manufacturing basis and 75 % of its railways; in 1961, its GDP per capita still stood at half the per capita value of Ghana (82 USD against 179 USD) (H.-J. Chang 2009, p. 3). A military coup in 1961 set the stage for the first set of reforms: the military regime of Park Chung-hee decided to press forward with an ambitious, centralized, state-controlled reform programme. In 1973, the *Heavy and Chemical Industrialization* (HCI) programme created the first industrial complexes in the steel, shipbuilding, automotive, electronic, machinery and chemical sectors, with a view to engage in exports. The country sought exactly the same objectives of European mercantilist policies in the early modern era: obtain hard currency from exports, reinvest this currency in foreign capital goods, use these machineries to improve the quality and quantities of consumption goods, increase foreign sales and the associated inflow of hard currency. The description of this process bears striking similarities with sixteenth-century social organicism in Europe: "[...] valuable foreign currency was the blood and sweat of our industrial soldiers fighting the export war in the countries' factories" (H.-J. Chang 2009). USA dollars had substituted bullions, but the mechanism had remained unaltered for six centuries. The South Korean militaries' obsession for avoiding drainage of hard currency evokes, and even surpasses, the gruesome environment of seventeenth century England: in the latter, the economist John Cary asked to introduce the death penalty for exporters of raw material and species (Reinert 2007, pp. 6–7), but in the former the militaries *did* actually introduce the death penalty for violation of foreign exchange control. Between the 1960s and 1980s, the import of some foreign goods was outright illegal, allowed goods were tariffed at an average rate of 40 % in the 1960s, which subsequently came down to a 21 % average rate by the early 1980s. Foreign travels were banned because they entailed drainage of foreign currency. The government ran campaigns against "traitors" purchasing foreign cigarettes, whiskies or cookies on the black market, asking fellow citizens to report to public authorities any such behaviour.

State interventionism through tariffs, subsidies, seed investments and expansion of overseas sales showed exceptional results: between 1970 and 1980, the GDP per capita had soared 505 %, largely pushed by an export growth of almost 2000 %—in average, in the 1970s South Korean exports kept doubling every two years and three months.[25] Regime change occurred in 1979, but the new government had no reason to steer from such a successful economic path, and continued providing public incentives to national exports. South Korean industrial conglomerates—*chaebol*—continued following the investment patterns of their Japanese counterparts, *kareitsu*, engaging in sectors with progressively higher levels of capital investment, research and development, risk and—most importantly—profit margins: semiconductors, automotive, electronics and high precision machineries. Government control further expanded into credit and investments: all South Korean banks remained under state control until fairly recently to ensure stable and cheap credit lines to local businesses. FDI was accepted only in certain sectors where it was likely to induce technology transfer and against foreign investors' engagement to reinvest part of the profit in the country.

Taiwan followed a similar interventionist strategy, although it renounced the creation of heavy industries and giant private conglomerates along the Korean/Japanese model. It maintained, nonetheless, high tariff protection, direct credit and incentives towards exports, technological support for domestic SMEs, a selective interference on incoming FDI and strong public investments in technical and scientific education.

Soon after the *Kuomintang* took control of the island in 1945, the new government confiscated Japanese monopolies to create large public corporations and implemented a vast land redistribution programme—both measures are credited with creating one of the most equal societies in Asia up to now.[26] In 1955, the Taiwanese economy was still heavily reliant on agriculture: 85 % of Taiwanese exports were still agricultural products, while the only manufactured exports were panama hats. In those same years, the government took the first steps towards industrialization, first nurturing SMEs by supporting and coordinating subcontracting networks. Macroeconomic and market strategies focused first on import substitution and, subsequently, moved into the promotion of manufactured exports. Domestic manufactures were protected both by tariffs and multiple overvalued exchange rates; once the domestic market became saturated, efforts focused on exports in manufactured goods with increasingly higher technology and capital content: textile, clothes, radio and television sets, electronic calculators, sewing machines, car parts, machineries and, finally, information and communication technology. Under the later export promotion regime, Taiwan selectively attracted FDI in sectors in which the national industry was the weakest and unable to do much on its own; even in these sectors, the government imposed a normative environment by which investors were obliged to favour technology transfer towards local industries, while guaranteeing high levels of local content and subcontracting to national suppliers. Also, privileges in export processing zones were extended only to businesses which produced goods not to be sold domestically. In all other sectors—where local firms were strong and had solid prospects of growth without any need for foreign intervention—entrance was actively discouraged. As for Korea, Taiwan was also favoured by the (sometime involuntary) coaching provided by early Japanese investors.[27] As for Korea, results for Taiwan came in less than one generation: in 1979, the relatively small tropical island was already the largest exporter of manufactured goods to the OECD group of countries (17 % share) among all developing country and, by 1984, it had further distanced Korea (21 % vs. 15 %).

Singapore differentiates itself from the Korean and Taiwanese models because it did not promote "national champions" among its private industries. The former British colony sought instead FDI in highly specialized, high-value-adding activities. At independence from Malaysia in

1965, the Singaporean government first went for an import substitution strategy by promoting light industrial activities, including garment and semi-conductor assembly. When it became clear that such strategy would not allow Singapore to climb the higher layers of the development ladder, the government aggressively sought FDI in an effort to specialize in the high-value-adding phases of global production, including research and development (R&D). Singapore created the human skills necessary to attract these investments and regulated the normative environment in which foreign investors operated; in particular, foreign companies were requested to contribute in raising the technological content and expertise of the national industrial and entrepreneurial texture. The government still intervened to set up public enterprises in those sectors where it was not possible or it was undesirable to attract foreign interests. Singapore also maintained, all along its developmental stages, an open-market policy. The strategy proved extremely successful: the GDP per capita of Singapore today is the highest among the Asian NIEs—in fact, in 2011, it fared higher than the USA. It has, however, been noticed that only a city-state of a few million inhabitants (5.1 million in 2012) can specialize in a limited pool of activities, becoming a sort of department of the global production chain; its experience may, in other words, be of little relevance to most developing countries.

Along with Singapore, Hong Kong (HK) has consistently been ranked as the freest economy in the world since the early 2000s. HK has also, unsurprisingly, been chosen by the neoclassic literature as the poster boy of liberal policies. This is because HK implemented a successful development strategy without mingling at all with the market, thus following orthodox neoclassic prescriptions: it maintained free trade, an open-door policy to FDI and did not feel the necessity to promote local industries through export incentives, local content rules or promotion of technological spillover from foreign investments. The relative uniqueness of the HK model has been explained on several levels: on the one hand, in the 1960s, it had already enjoyed a distinctive advantage over other Asian countries because of the large number of British companies having established their headquarters or parent companies there; on the other hand, it enjoyed the benefit of sitting on the doorstep of an awakening giant, which began providing substantial market access and capital assets from the late 1970s forward, while having long been a source of cheap engineers and technical workers.

These factors would have likely assisted economic growth in HK independently from the policies chosen by the British territory. Yet, unlikely other Asian NIEs, HK was slow in moving out of the light-labour intensive manufacturing and temporarily suffered the consequences of this delay. When in the 1980s, the cost of production factors increased and profit margins shrunk, HK entrepreneurs relocated to China or elsewhere in the region, and the economy lost some 50 % of its manufacturing jobs in that decade alone. Not having a strong industrial sector to fall upon, the British territory leaped from light manufacturing directly into services, managing to become the financial (banking, insurance, stock brokering, fund management), trading (freight, wholesale, import/export, logistics) and professional services (legal, auditing, engineering, architectural) capital of Eastern Asia. The stunt worked: today, HK's economy relies 91 % on services and only 9 % on industry.[28] HK's development experience is considered unique and with ambiguous lessons learnt, to the extent that its course may be unrealistic—and thus undesirable—for other developing countries.

4 "Negative" Economic Policies

To a certain extent, most economic policies have always been aimed at gaining an advantage over economic competitors, be it through the rather direct means of the mercantilist system (prohibition on the export of liquid assets, duties on exported raw material and imported finished products, prohibition on national commercial vessels to serve foreign interests, trading monopolies with the colonies, piracy against foreign interests, bilateral war) or the more sophisticated policies pertaining to the classic and neoclassic toolbox (non-tariff barriers, safeguards in multilateral trade agreements, public subsidies, trade defence measures, different levels of legal capacity in negotiating international treaties, etc.).

However, while "positive" economic policies can entail negative side-effects on other economies (as it happened with the European import substitution strategies of the early modern era), their primary aim remains to promote economic growth in the country adopting them. On the contrary, economic policies labelled here as "negative" are specifically and purposefully aimed against other economies: harming foreign interests in order to obtain national benefits. There is no shortage of examples of such policies in the 600 years of economic policies reviewed here, from the heydays of the Italian maritime republics until the American New Deal. These measures can be summarized under two broad categories: (1) prohibition/limitations of manufacturing activities and trade in the colonies and in subdued countries; (2) unilateral measures through domestic policies.

As early as in 1699, Britain banned the export of raw wool from its colonies to other industrial countries.[29] Although the measure was primarily intended to undermine the provision of raw material to international competitors such as the Netherlands and France, it equally resulted in a dramatic curtailment of income for Irish and New England wool producers. While prohibiting the export of raw material to competitors, England also enacted a number of laws to facilitate the import of these same commodities: the American colonies, as a matter of example, were granted export subsidies and no import duties on entering the British market. This move served a double-logic: ensure the provision of cheap commodities and push the colonies into specializing as sources of raw material. As Robert Walpole viewed it, encouragement in the export of commodities would "[...] divert them from carrying on manufactures which interfered with those of England" (H.-J. Chang 2009, p. 52).

From a developmental perspective, limitations on other countries' right to industrialize were particularly hideous: European nations that forbade their colonies from engaging in manufacturing activities were doing so with the deliberate intention of hampering their economic emancipation and avoiding commercial threats coming from within the empire. Already in the 1720s, Robert Walpole had banned advanced manufacturing in the USA, prohibiting the construction of technologically advanced rolling and slitting steel mills, while pushing colonies to specialize on low value-added pig and bar iron (H.-J. Chang 2009, p. 45). Faced with the news that American colonists were considering new plans to engage in manufacturing in the 1760s, the then British Prime Minister Pitt the Elder insisted that the colonies should "[...] not be permitted to manufacture so much as a horseshoe nail" (List 1916, p. 55). Early in the 1930s, when the British government realized the great danger of maintaining trade preferences with tropical colonies that had the potential to become industrialized, a British interdepartmental committee decided that colonial industries should not have been "artificially" encouraged, and that already existing local workshops and factories should be restricted on operating conditions and working hours, in order to bring them more in line (and less in competition) with those in the homeland.[30] In 1934, Neville Chamberlain, British Chancellor of the Exchequer, noted that, if it was improbable that West Africa would have managed to set up factories to compete with those in the homeland, there was nonetheless a "real and serious danger" of factories being established in Malaysia and Singapore, as it had already happened in India. Such an eventuality was to be avoided and political efforts were invested towards that end.

Other legal means were used with countries that formally maintained their sovereignty. In 1810, Britain imposed the first Unequal Treaty on an independent country, Brazil. Unequal Treaties quickly became a standard tool of British foreign policy with formally independent countries: Siam was forced to sign the first of such agreements in 1824, Persia in 1836, the Ottoman Empire in 1838, China in 1842 and Japan in 1853. Unequal Treaties were a formidable tool to spur exports: by stripping subdued countries of their sovereign right to regulate customs and by imposing low flat-rate tariffs on manufactured imports from England, they ensured extended and competitive market access to British goods. Subdued countries took decades before recovering tariff autonomy: Japan managed in 1911, China in 1938 and Korea in 1945.[31]

Where military might and diplomacy were of no use, Europeans resorted to unilateral policies. Economists in seventeenth century England envisaged bulk purchases of international raw material and a subsequent disposal of any surplus that could not be consumed or processed by the national industry; some 400 years later, several aspects of the EU Common Agricultural Policy (CAP) closely resemble these same mechanisms.[32] Unilateral negative policies were to be found in several other sectors: in 1719, faced with an increasing stream of qualified human resources moving towards other European countries, Britain decided to introduce legal measures to contain the emigration of skilled workers—a phenomenon that would today qualify as restrictions on the freedom of movement. Recruiting people for overseas jobs became punishable through fines or imprisonment, while UK government officials could issue official warnings requesting British nationals to return home; failing to do so would have normally entailed loss of the right of abode in Britain and loss of any property stationed there.[33] From 1750 onwards, Britain also started introducing legislation aimed at banning the export of capital goods, utensils and machines in key national industries, particularly in the textile sector.[34] British restrictions/bans of the outflow of expertise and capital goods were dropped in the 1830s because international market conditions became more favourable. Nonetheless, modern-day OECD countries' migration policies continue running on the simple principle of keeping cheap labour locked inside developing countries, while luring highly trained professionals into their job market.

Other Western powers did not behave any more generously than Britain. Most European capitals followed London in forcing Eastern Asian countries to sign treaties against the threat of military intervention: China, Japan and Korea were all subdued into Unequal Treaties with the USA, France, Russia and Germany. Western countries saw China as a particularly promising market: following the Boxer protocol of 1901, the Qing dynasty was forced to grant trading concessions to practically all Western powers (aside from those mentioned above, also to Italy, Austria-Hungary, Belgium, Spain and the Netherland). Outside Europe, countries that had suffered from the imposition of negative policies did not hesitate to enforce similar measures upon weaker countries—the USA and Japan proving among the best pupils of European international economic policies.[35]

5 Soft-Power and *Trompe L'oeil* Activities

Norwegian economist Erik S. Reinert points at the exceptional rude transparency used by early mercantilist writers in describing their policy rationale and finalities.[36] There is indeed no shortage of candid malignancy in mercantilist writings. Among eighteenth-century treaties on economic and trade matters, it is possible to find proposals for diverting the colonies' attention from the key mechanisms of economic exploitation in the colonizer–colonized relationship. Writing in 1744, Joshua Gee suggests, for example, that colonies should be given the right to freely export agricultural products to the whole of Europe in order to keep their hands busy and their minds away from realizing the cost opportunity of investing in manufacturing activities (Reinert 2007, p. 166).

Trompe l'oeil or window-dressing strategies have been used in other aspects of the relationship between colonized and colonizers, including in aid policies. Historical records tell us that the British Colonial Development Act of 1929 was primarily aimed at expanding the colonies' demand for British goods and workforce, "[…] for it would, of course, be a condition of imperial assistance that any plant or material required should be ordered in this country", as Winston Churchill put it (Havinden and Meredith 1993, p. 140). Churchill did not think of the colonies' economic benefit as a positive by-product for itself, but rather as a *means* to enhance "[…] the purchasing power of individuals in the colonies, with future benefits to British trade" (Ibid.). The UK started granting aid to its colonies because they spent it on British products, which in turn contributed in creating the conditions for further British exports in the future.[37] The act was, however, "sold" to the public and the international community in a different wrapping: Britain, in the international institutional discourse, was taking responsibility for the development of its colonies. This gap between discourse and praxis continued characterizing the ambiguous nature of development aid in the following decades. When, in 1939, the Great Depression worsened living conditions in all tropical colonies and discontent provoked violent demonstrations in many British colonies, the British Development Fund was strengthened with the aim not only of quelling riots, but also of soothing criticisms from the League of Nations over London's management of international mandates.[38]

International sensitivity on development subjects further strengthened in the post-colonial period. Public diplomacy progressively took stage: today's governments and international organizations go to great lengths not only to craft the words and concepts describing their measures (the vocabulary of the development aid industry is among the most theoretical and creative in the realm of public policy), but also, more importantly, to influence the perceptions of those that are supposed to judge these same words and concepts: the public opinions of donor countries. Western countries have become particularly adept in this exercise. Public grants towards University departments and think tanks are often allocated because of their institutional allegiance rather than on the basis of their scientific records. University graduates are institutionalized to political messages that often lack substantial empirical evidence: "Democracy favours development", "the West supports sustainable economic development in low-income countries", "a free political system is a pre-requisite of economic growth", are all examples in case.[39] Yet, they are so engrained in Western institutional discourse to constitute the basis of common-sense beliefs about the international community: in many European social environments, it is considered in between the tedious and the intellectually shabby to point out that Europe has regularly sustained gruesome dictators in neighbouring Africa and the Middle East—Muammar Gheddafi, Ben Ali, Hosni Mubarak and Bashar al-Assad being the most recent examples, the list including however dozens, if not hundreds, of other cases—in exchange for their geopolitical alliance and favourable economic policies. Doing the same with Latin American dictators propped by the USA is often considered outright banal.

And yet, today's Western political discourse continues being riddled with the same rhetoric that has shaped Western foreign policy since the end of World War II: democracy, free economy, human rights and the West being a force of universal good. Since 1989, terrorism seems to have substituted communism and globalization seems to have gained centre stage, but the nature of the rhetoric has gone substantially unaltered: the West knows the way to socio-economic development. The private sector, and particularly MNCs, if anything, has been even more skilful in soft-power tactics, supported by strong budgets and the expertise of communication professionals, including public policy, public relations and social psychology firms.

What cannot be achieved by rhetoric is often sought by omission. Joseph Stiglitz refers his puzzlement at the IMF and WB's lack of interest in sponsoring official studies on the East Asian economic growth in the 1965–1990 period: for international development institutions, it meant ignoring the elephant in the room. Stiglitz concluded that the only reasonable explanation was that these institutions were embarrassed to highlight success stories that had been achieved in plain disregard of Washington Consensus policies (Stiglitz 2002, p. 91). According to Stiglitz, since success in several of these countries was achieved exactly because of the refusal to follow neoliberal policies, publicizing these cases threatened the credibility of international development institutions.[40]

This phenomenon is not restrained to the ODA world. The humanitarian sector is also heavily influenced by Western foreign policies: with roughly 8000 deaths between 1987 and 2010, the Palestine–Israeli conflict has attracted way more humanitarian assistance and political attention than civil conflicts that have caused over 1 million deaths over the same two decades, such as those in the Democratic Republic of Congo and Sudan.

6 The Virtuous Cycle of Developmental Public Policies

What are the lessons learnt from the praxis of successful developing countries in modern and contemporary history?

First, economic growth is not enough to reduce poverty, ensure sustainable development or promote social emancipation. However, without economic growth, none of these social processes can happen. In logical terms, it can be said that economic growth is a necessary but insufficient condition for sustainable development to happen. This book deliberately targets the economic growth aspects of development in the belief that they represent the permissive conditions of sustainable development.

Second: although there is no single formula for development, historical records suggest that a limited number of rules can be taken as well-tested empirical evidence to build successful public economic policies. These rules have been individuated in economic theories inspired by historical praxes and lessons learnt, as those adopted by the works of Friedrich List (1916), the Historical School of Economics, Joseph Schumpeter and contemporary heterodox economists. Such rules include the importance of: (1) the gradual shift of resources from agriculture and extractive industries towards more technology and capital-intensive sectors, characterized by higher-value-added activities; (2) specialization in activities characterized by the principles of increasing marginal returns and economy of scale; (3) a strong entrepreneurial role played by the government to favour seed investments in sectors of national interest, protect infant industries and create market imperfections that can favourably play in its national interest; (4) a strong normative framework regulating relations with foreign investors in such a way as to optimize the benefits of inward FDI, also by selecting the investment sectors and their vectors, ensuring a fair division of profits by guaranteeing the presence of local shareholders, imposing local content rules, limiting the allowed repatriation of profits and making it obligatory to reinvest a minimum percentage of earnings in the hosting economy; (5) a set of industrial, trade and financial policies aimed at retaining and wisely investing hard currency; (6) well-integrated human resources and migration policies, promoting subsidized higher and vocal education, while avoiding the risks of international "brain poaching" or long-term specialization in the low-value-adding ends of the global production chain.

Most of these rules have been applied worldwide through a set of heterogeneous policies which have managed to lift OECD countries and NIEs out of poverty, and are currently allowing spectacular results in Mainland China. Some parts of southern Asia, Latin America and the Middle East are also benefiting from these policies. What do they consist of? Developing economies have moved as soon as possible from agriculture and mining towards industrial manufacturing and trade. While agriculture has often ensured decent standards of living in many parts of the developing world, there has been no case in history of a country that has achieved continuous and sustainable economic growth by making agriculture the basis of its economy. The extractive industry typically suffers from the same limits, although Western reliance on oil in the twentieth century has allowed a number of African and Middle Eastern countries to develop strong rent economies based on oil cartels.

In all OECD and NIEs, the switch from an agriculture-led economy towards an industry-led economy has only been possible by active state involvement. Capital has been attentively sought, arduously earned, diligently saved and wisely invested. FDI has generally been welcomed only under stringent conditions. The first of such conditions concerned the sector: successful development countries only allowed foreigners to invest in highly profitable and capital-intensive industries, where profit and technology spill-over was likely the highest. The second concerned the modality: incoming FDI was mainly allowed through joint ventures or equity; both options allowed local partners to maintain a strong stake in the firm, while fully foreign-owned enterprises were only allowed at a later stage of economic development. The third concerned the direct beneficiaries in the hosting countries, with the aim of creating jobs not only at the labour level but also at the managerial and cadre levels: often the agreements included provisions for a minimum quota of national hires at the top levels of the company. The fourth concerned obligations on national procurements, backward and forward linkages to the national economy and restrictions to the repatriation of profits back to the investing country.

New national industries have been protected and nurtured by way of tax exemptions or outright financial support. In certain cases, national governments set up their own State Owned Enterprises (SOEs) to operate investments in sectors with interesting profit margins and prospects of social fallouts over the long term, but too many short-term risks to lure the attention of the private sector. In many of these cases, states have lost public money for years—sometime decades—while building the necessary competitive margins to turn them profitable and take on the competition against well-established foreign companies.

Once infant industries have been established, governments have been actively involved in promoting adequate market opportunities for their newly manufactured goods. Domestic market protection through tariffs on imports as well as export subsidies have been a classic for several hundred years, but less gentle policies have regularly been adopted too: the most economically advanced territories have regularly resorted to plain offensive measures such as foreign trading posts, unequal treaties, colonization and forced market access to increase trade ties and business profits. Unilateral policies such as restrictions on the export of technology and expertise and restrictive migration agreements were used to contrast economic competitors that could not be subdued politically or militarily.

Wherever militarily superior countries managed to subdue a colony, they proceeded to set up similar mechanisms of economic interaction: import cheap raw material; process it; sell it in the home market, in the colonies and in as many profitable foreign markets as possible. A set of malignant policies—including the prohibition on exporting raw material to third countries, the prohibition on mechanizing production and the issuing of legislation hampering the free circulation of productive factors—were aimed at ensuring the sustainability of such a system and preventing potential competitors from accessing domestic and international markets.

While much of the academic debate between the classic–neoclassic school and its theoretical competitors was trailing in the inwards/outwards, ISI/export-led, protectionist/liberal dichotomy-type discussions, the most successful governments were proceeding in a pragmatic fashion. If the domestic market was the most profitable, then governments proceeded towards import substitution, as the benefits to national producers offset the increased costs passed on to consumers; if, on the contrary, the domestic market was not able to pay sufficient returns, then successful governments prioritized foreign markets through export-led growth.[41] Under no circumstance did the one exclude the other: most successful developing economies went through ISI first and manufactured exports later. If the ISI/Export-led dichotomy implied some form of trade-off, this was managerial and chronological, certainly not theoretical or ideological. In all cases, a straightforward logic prevailed: the highest the profits, the better—no matter whether these came from domestic or overseas markets.

The role of the state was by no means limited to financial support, market expansion and regulation. Legal provisions made whatever possible to ensure that businesses carried out by national actors accrued to national profits rather than to foreign companies: *cetera paribus* conditions, all countries had systems in place to keep business among national companies. Sometimes, these legal provisions made it compulsory to purchase national goods and services, as in the case of obligations to ship national goods through national carriers. National workers, goods and services received priority in public procurement and hiring processes.

In the initial phases of industrialization, normative provisions allowed the use of foreign hard currency only for profitable activities rather than for consumption. The banking sector has often remained state-controlled to ensure that sufficient credit was provided to national entrepreneurs. Migration provisions encouraged poaching of expertise from abroad, while limiting the freedom of movement of national human resources to avoid the so-called "brain-drain" phenomenon. Double standards applied to patents and copyrights: while all these countries were enforcing internal patent regulations as a tool to incentivize imperfect competition, entrepreneurial activities and the rule of law in economic matters, at the same time, they were lax in respecting foreign copyrights—if not guiltily proactive in procuring trade and economic intelligence through fraudulent means.[42]

Whether liberalism has really managed to free international economics from its traditional antagonistic character (what is gained by one nation is lost by another) or simply managed to displace the issue towards loftier perceptual shores remains a question open to debate. Although world economy is, today, generally understood as a positive-sum game, there is no consensus as to what the conditions that lead two countries to profit or lose from each other's growth or resizing are. More importantly, debates in economic theory do not invalidate centuries of practice in international affairs: political units compete for scarce resources, often resorting to violent means. Indulging in the illusion that neoliberalism in the Cold War aftermath could have provided everyone with a permanent political and economic solution misled not only Francis Fukuyama (1989), but also the many that indulged in a vision of a united international community committed to solving the structural problems affecting its weakest members.

Notes

1. While mainstream and critical literature dealing with Comparative Capitalisms (CC) has an empiric approach to the existing diversities of contemporary capitalism (Ebenau et al. 2015), thus assisting in bridging the gap between economic theories and specific contemporary national economic praxes, the review carried out in this chapter has a more historical and interpretative approach.
2. Food insecurity occurs when the food intake of one or more members of the family is reduced and eating patterns disrupted because of insufficient money and other resources for food.
3. Measurement of absolute poverty considers whether a family can afford a specified amount of goods and services considered necessary for basic living in the country, city, or village in which it lives.

The measurement of relative poverty compares a family's financial situation with that of the rest of the population group to which it belongs. Percentages of relative poverty mentioned here place the poverty threshold at half of the national median income (Alters 2009).

4. Some statistics use a relative definition of wealth, as the Gini coefficient, which is a measure of inequality: a value of 0 indicates perfect equality, while a value of 1 indicates a situation where one person owns everything and the rest nothing. Other statistics use an absolute index of income; if this is set at 2 USD $< x <$ 20 USD/day for the middle class and at $x >$ 20 USD/day for the high income range (per capita, 2005 USD at purchasing power parity), then OECD countries had the entirety of their population split between these two groups in a 1:4 ratio in 1990 and 1:9 ratio in 2008.
5. That amount was estimated as 1080 kilocalories a day—well below the threshold of malnourishment according to FAO's definition—, causing children and adult death rates to jump ten and four times, respectively, over pre-war levels. See Wiggers (2003).
6. World Bank Gini index. As a term of comparison, the most unequal country within the EU is Portugal, standing at 36 % in 2012, while the best performing, Slovenia, stood at 25.6 % in the same year.
7. Some colonies managed to improve their relative socio-economic standing during foreign occupation, as it was the case for Hong Kong and Singapore under the British or, arguably, for Korea and Taiwan under the Japanese. However, these cases should be read in light of the fact that their development was a by-product of the mother country's interests rather than an intentional policy aimed at developing strong and independent economies. The debate on the effect of European colonialism in Latin America, Africa and the Middle East is way more controversial (and partially addressed in the literary review)—suffice noticing here that these same regions coincide today with the poorest areas of the globe.
8. These study cases were chosen because they represent the earliest cases of capital accumulation and economic growth to last till today (Northern Italian and Flemish city states), because of the size of their economies throughout modern history (UK, France), because of their voluntarism in successfully replicating early European development models (USA, Japan) and/or because of their relevance for Africa today (only one generation ago, most Asian newly

industrialized economies had socio-economic indexes largely comparable to those of today's African Sub-Saharan countries).

9. Ironically, it is exactly because institutional communication was not particularly strong before the twentieth century—or simply because the sensibility of the time was different from our own contemporary sensibility—that we have today reports about "negative" policies unmistakably pointing at the role of religion, ideology, national identities and class aspirations in serving very defined, limited and well-organized interests.
10. Accounts of the most ancient "positive" economic policies to affect today's OECD economic status can either be found in contemporary treaties dealing with economic systems of the Middle Ages and early modernity or in economic studies dating back to the Renaissance. In the latter group, see Giovanni Botero et al., (1588), Antonio Serra (1613), Thomas Mun (1621, 2014), Gerard de Malynes (1623). Among the former group, see A. Friis (1950); *The New Cambridge Medieval History* and *The Cambridge Economic History of Europe*.
11. What invalidated this logic was its procedural, distorted and short-sighted application rather than the logic underpinning it: as a matter of example, English merchants were forbidden from purchasing foreign goods in "cash", despite the fact that these could have later been re-sold to foreign customers against cash and with handsome profits.
12. The Statutes of Employment and the Royal Exchanger—an institutional figure that had a monopolistic control over exchange transactions—went out of existence or became inoperative before the end of the sixteenth century. They are both identified by historians as key institutions characterizing the first part of the Mercantilist era—commonly referred to as "bullionism"—against the second Mercantilist era, focused over the issue of the balance of trade.
13. An English ship was defined as one built in England, owned by Englishmen, captained by an English master and sailed by a crew, three quarters of which were English (McCusker 1996, p. 349).
14. "A special commission not composed of privy councilors to inquire into the decay of the clothing trade and to report to the Privy Council such remedial measures as seemed best adapted to increase the wealth and prosperity of the realm" (Andrews 1908, p. 12). On the 1619 crisis, see Kindleberger (1991).

15. Notwithstanding this, England continued having a strong export of silver all throughout the early modern era until the beginning of the eighteenth century, a pattern that particularly characterized English relationship with India and China.
16. From a 1484 Cahiers of the Estates-General. In Charles Wilson (1976, p. 39).
17. The few exceptions included small blast furnaces producing iron in Pennsylvania and some artisan-type activities in other urban areas. See Engerman and Sokoloff (2000, p. 371).
18. The real impact of the Trade Acts upon development in the USA until independence is widely discussed. Some economists noted that this could not have possibly hurt American interests too much if it is true that 100 years after the entry into force of the Trade Acts, English settlers were far better off than both their ancestors and their fellow countrymen living in England, having attained, on average, higher levels of income and wealth than any other group of people in the world. However, English settlers only represented one-third of the population in the areas that later became the USA.
19. In this period, Washington embarked, nonetheless, on its first colonial ventures by taking Cuba, Puerto Rico and the Philippines away from Spain (1899–1902).
20. Japan's isolation policy was initiated by Tokugawa Iemitsu, shogun from 1623 to 1641. His "closed country edict" of 1635 introduced a number of commercial protectionist measures—including prohibiting Japanese ships from leaving for foreign countries, prohibiting Samurai from purchasing any goods originating from foreign ships or directly from Chinese merchants—and a heavily regulated trading system, which authorized only five trading cities (Kyoto, Edo, Osaka, Sakai and Nagasaki) to deal with limited amounts of foreign merchandise. The edict was also aimed at isolating Japan, ethnically and culturally, prohibiting Japanese nationals from travelling abroad, ordering execution for those that returned home after having resided abroad and persecuting Catholic priests and their Japanese followers (Laver 2011).
21. Although many of these industries were sold at below-market price to entrepreneurs with government connections, it seems that the privatization process could be, nonetheless, ascribed to the successes of this period, as it nurtured the government–industrial and financial conglomerate (*zaibatsu*) relationship that contributed

much to Japanese economic development (Myers and Peattie 1984).

22. Most analysis in this section is based on Wade (1990), Lall (1996), and Chang (2009).
23. Nominal GDP per capita in current dollars, data extracted from WB and IMF databases.
24. Both enclaves became subject to Japanese occupation and rule during World War II.
25. Exports went from 836 million USD in 1970 to 17.5 billion USD in 1980. Data from UNCTAD Stats; author's calculation.
26. In 2011, the Taiwanese Gini coefficient stood at par with France (32 %).
27. Gary G. Hamilton and Cheng-Shu Kao notice that "Two former Japanese colonies, Taiwan and South Korea, were the two places Japanese firms placed sizeable investments, first in Taiwan in the late 1960s and then in South Korea in the early 1970" (Yin-wah Chu 2010, p. 131). In the same volume, Yin-wah Chu concludes that "[…] it has been through the couching of Japanese trading companies that Taiwanese industrialists have learnt a brand new way of 'making money' by producing for remote marketplaces" (Yin-wah Chu 2010, p. 229).
28. By comparison, industry in the EU and USA accounts for 25.4 % and 19.2 % of the GDP, respectively.
29. The Wool Act of 1699 plainly states its logic in the preamble of the edict: "Forasmuch as Wool and the Woollen Manufactures of Cloth […] made or mixed with Wool are the greatest and most profitable Commodities of this Kingdom on which the Value of Lands and The trade of the Nation do chiefly depend And whereas great Quantities of the like Manufactures have of late been made and are daily increasing in the Kingdom of Ireland and in the English Plantations in America and are exported from thence to Forreigne Marketts heretofore supplyed from England which will inevitably sink the Value of Lands and tend to the ruine of the Trade and the Woollen Manufactures of this Realme For the Prevention whereof and for the Encouragement of the Woollen Manufactures within this Kingdom Be it enacted[…]" (Fleming 1741, p. 273).
30. *Report of the interdepartmental committee on the industrial development of the empire* of March 1934, quoted in Havinden and Meredith (1993, p. 170). Interestingly, according to a former

Head of Cooperation at the EU delegation in Beijing, this is also the ultimate goal of the European Union's development cooperation efforts to improve labour rights in China: raise the cost of Chinese industrial production and reduce its competitive margins in international markets (Personal discussion, Kabul, October 2013).

31. For a review of the different Unequal Treaties Eastern Asian countries were subdued into, see Craven (2005).
32. Under the CAP established in 1957, the European Commission was authorized to perform a number of market management measures, including the purchase, stock and disposal of excessive agricultural production.
33. The Netherlands introduced similar measures against brain drain and technology transfer in 1751. See Ha-Joon Chang (2002, pp. 54–56).
34. It is worth noticing that these measures certainly entailed short-term negative effects on British citizens and, perhaps, on the British economy as a whole: skilled workers living abroad are often offered better salary than in their home countries (hence the decision to live abroad), and usually spend/invest a relevant part of their income in their country of origin (through remittances, consumption or investments). Equally, exporting machineries is a highly profitable business: capital goods largely accounted for the jump of European and American exports during the industrialization phases of Latin America and Eastern Asia. However, the British government preferred promoting long-term interests: feeling that transferring technology would have allowed other countries to compete in high-value-added industries, it enacted policies deliberately aimed at hampering technology acquisition in third countries.
35. Japan—which had to stand Unequal Treaties with Europe and the USA from 1854 until 1911—imposed its own set of Unequal Treaties on Korea in 1876 and on China in 1895. The USA imposed Unequal Treaties on China (1844), Japan (1854) and Korea (1882).
36. As a matter of example, he reports Joshua Gee to plead that "[…] all negroes shall be prohibited from weaving either Linnen or Woollen, or spinning or combing of Wooll, or working at any Manufacture of Iron, further than making it into Pig or Bar Iron: That they be also prohibited from manufacturing of Hats, Stockings

or Leather of any Kind [...] Indeed, if they set up manufacturers, and the government afterwards shall be under a Necessity of stopping their Progress, we must not expect that it will be done with the same Ease that now it may" (Reinert 2007, p. 165).

37. For a deeper analysis, see George Abbott (1971).
38. The League of Nations instituted several investigations on conditions in the colonies, including on international access to colonial raw material (League of Nations 1937) and on nutrition and public health. The first investigated exploitation of colonial economies by industrial countries and raised doubts on the effectiveness of colonial trusteeship, while the second found widespread malnutrition in tropical colonies. Both contributed in an international drop of confidence in the mandates system (Havinden and Meredith 1993).
39. In quick support of the limits of institutional readings of economic growth, it could be noticed that the economic take-off of OECD countries and NIEs happened when they did not have a democratic system. For a more detailed criticism of the institutional literature in economics, see Chap. 2. As evidenced throughout Chap. 3, these economies were not free either during their booming years, at least when measured against today's IFIs standards.
40. The study was finally pursued following insistence and financial backing from Japan, and published in 1993 as a World Bank Policy Research Report: *The East Asian miracle: economic growth and public policy*.
41. This point is also stressed in comparative capitalism research: talking about different forms of international economic integration, Jan Drahokoupil and Martin Myant notice that, while "[...] there are enormous variations in the relative importance of different forms of integration" it also remains true that "in practice, every country combined more than one form of international integration" (Ebenau et al. 2015, p. 161).
42. While the above sequence of causally inter-related economic policies may appear as a loose minimum common denominator among profoundly different historical experiences of economic development, it is surprising how more focused studies have reached similar conclusions on specific historical national experiences. Talking about the Japanese development model, for example, Bai Gao individuates six key features, many of which overlap with measures

outlined here, including: "[...] use [of] industrial policy to protect infant industries and restrict foreign capital's access to the domestic market, while actively cultivating strategic industries for export to foreign markets; [...] establish endogenous innovation mechanisms to carry out independent research and development [and] promote rapid industrial upgrading in order to produce high value-added products; [...] continue to maintain extremely inefficient sectors that could provide large numbers of jobs" (Huang 2013, p. 69).

References

Abbott, G. C. (1971). A re-examination of the 1929 colonial development act. *The Economic History Review, 24*(1), 68–81.

Andrews, C. M. L. (1908). *British committees, commissions, and councils of trade and plantations, 1622–1675*. Baltimore: The John Hopkins Press.

Botero, G. (1588). *Delle cause della grandezza delle citta. Libri III. Di Giouanni Botero benese*. Roma: Giouanni Martinelli.

Brisco, N. A. (2013). *The economic policy of Robert Walpole*. New York: The Columbia University Press.

Chang, H.-J. (2002). *Kicking away the ladder: Development strategy in historical perspective*. London: Anthem Press.

Chang, H.-J. (2009). *Bad Samaritans: The myth of free trade and the secret history of capitalism*. New York: Bloomsbury Press.

Chao, D., & Vanderzwaag, D. L. (2006). *Poverty in world history: Towards principled access and operations*. Hoboken: Taylor & Francis.

Chu, Y.-w. (2010). *Chinese capitalisms*. Houndmills: Palgrave MacMillan.

Craven, M. (2005). What happened to unequal treaties? The continuities of informal empire. *Nordic Journal of International Law, 74*(3/4), 335–382.

de Malynes, G. (1623). *The Center of the Circle of Commerce. Or, A Refutation of a Treatise, Intituled The Circle of Commerce, Or The Ballance of Trade: Lately Published by E. M.* London: Nicholas Bourne.

Ebenau, M., Bruff, I., & May, C. (2015). *New directions in comparative capitalisms research*. Houndmills: Palgrave MacMillan.

Engerman, S. L., & Sokoloff, K. L. (2000). Technology and industrialization, 1790–1914. *The Cambridge Economic History of the United States, 2*, 367–401.

Fleming, J. (1741). *A collection of all the Irish and English statutes now in force and use*. Dublin: Philip Crampton.

Friis, A. (1953). An inquiry into the relations between economic and financial factors in the 16th and 17th centuries. *Scandinavian Economic History Review, 1*(2), 193–241.

Fukuyama, F. (1989). The end of history. *The National Interest, Summer*, 3–18.

Hamilton, A. (1791). Report on manufactures. Philadelphia: Childs and Swaine.
Havinden, M. A., & Meredith, D. (1993). *Colonialism and development: Britain and its tropical colonies, 1850–1960.* London: Routledge.
Heilbroner, R. L. (1980). *The worldly philosophers: The lives, times, and ideas of the great economic thinkers* (5th ed.). New York: Simon and Schuster.
Huang, X. (2013) (Ed.). *Modern economic development in Japan and China.* Houndmills: Palgrave MacMillan.
Jordan, W. C. (1997). *The great famine: Northern Europe in the early fourteenth century.* Princeton: Princeton University Press.
Kindleberger, C. P. (1991). The economic crisis of 1619 to 1623. *The Journal of Economic History, 51*(01), 149–175.
Lall, S. (1996). *Learning from the Asian tigers: Studies in technology and industrial policy.* New York: St. Martin's Press.
Lamond, E. (1893). *A discourse of the common weal of this realm of England, 1581.* Cambridge: Cambridge University Press.
Laver, M. S. (2011). *The Sakoku edicts and the politics of Tokugawa hegemony.* Amherst, NY: Cambria Press.
List, F. (1916). *The national system of political economy* (Current edition published by Cosimo Classics in 2011). New York: Cosimo Classics.
League of Nations. (1937). Committee for the study of the problem of raw materials. New York: League of Nations.
McCusker, J. J. (1996). British mercantilist policies and the American colonies. In S. L. Engerman & R. E. Gallman (Eds.), *The Cambridge economic history of the United States – The colonial era* (Vol. 1). Cambridge: Cambridge University Press.
Mun, T. (1621). *A discourse of trade from England Unto the East-Indies, 1621: Reproduced from the First Edition.* Facsimile Text Society.
Mun, T. (2014). *England's treasure by foreign trade.* London: Elibron Classics.
Myers, R. H., & Peattie, M. R. (1984). *The Japanese colonial empire, 1895–1945.* Princeton: Princeton University Press.
Nye, J. S. (2004). *Soft Power. The means to success in world politics.* New York: Public Affairs.
Pryor, J. H. (1999). Northern Italy: The maritime republics. In D. Abulafia & R. McKitterick (Eds.), *The new Cambridge medieval history* (Vol. 5, pp. c.1198–c.1300). Cambridge: Cambridge University Press.
Reinert, E. S. (2007). *How rich countries got rich – and why poor countries stay poor.* New York: Carroll & Graf.
Routh, G. (1989). *The origin of economic ideas* (2nd ed.). Basingstoke: Macmillan Press.
Sargent, A. J. (2013). *The economic policy of Colbert.* Hard Press.
Serra, A. (1613). *Breve trattato delle cause che possono far abbondare l'oro e l'argento dove non sono miniere.* Napoli: Lazzaro Scorriggio.

Stiglitz, J. E. (2002). *Globalization and its discontents* (1st ed.). New York: W. W. Norton.

Wade, R. (1990). *Governing the market: Economic theory and the role of government in East Asian industrialization*. Princeton, NJ: Princeton University Press.

Wiggers, R. D. (2003). The United States and the refusal to feed German civilians after World War II. In S. B. Várdy, T. H. Tooley & A. H. Vardy (Eds.), *Ethnic cleansing in twentieth-century Europe*. Boulder: Social Science Monographs.

Wilson, C. H. (1967). Trade, society and the state. In E. E. Rich, & C. H. Wilson (Ed.), *The Cambridge economic history of Europe Volume 4: The economy of expanding Europe in the sixteenth and seventeenth centuries*. Cambridge: Cambridge University Press.

Wilson, C. (1976). *The transformation of Europe, 1558–1648*. Berkeley: University of California Press.

CHAPTER 4

A Quantitative Assessment of Africa's International Economic Relations

What do we know about Africa's current economic position in the international arena? Balance of Payment (BoP) variables provide an objective picture of African relations with its major partners (the European Union, the USA and China), as do other statistics on flows such as capital flight and migration. These data can be used to establish a factual basis to assess whether Western and Chinese policies in Africa are compatible with the historical economic praxes pertaining to the "virtuous cycle" of growth and assess whether they are contributing towards the situation portrayed by available Balance of Payment (BoP) metrics.

1 Econometrics and International Relations

The history of statecraft praxes in today's OECD countries and NIEs provided an overview of apt economic policies that contributed in fostering socio-economic development in the countries that adopted them. To answer Bhagwati's question, it is necessary to understand the impact of West–Africa and China–Africa relations over the development of the latter's economies. More specifically, it is necessary to understand whether these relations are helping developing countries to undergo the same path that has proved successful for OECD countries and NIEs. To do so, the role and weight of ODA and OOF must be contextualized within the broader West–Africa and China–Africa relational context: only by considering the bigger picture will it be possible to understand, on the one

S. Raudino, *Development Aid and Sustainable Economic Growth in Africa*, DOI 10.1007/978-3-319-38936-3_4

hand, whether "rich" countries are helping "poor" countries in undertaking "virtuous cycle" policies for their socio-economic growth, and on the other hand, whether China has initiated anything truly revolutionary in Africa.

These research questions carry a number of implications. The first stems from a methodological doubt: is it possible to "audit" general relations between two countries or two sets of countries? Econometric tools allow a fairly complete review of the quantitative aspects of such a relationship: the BoP—accounting for the balance of trade, investments and returns on investments, cash transfers, and reserve exchanges between two regions—keeps track of important aspects of such relations.[1] Official statistics or estimates about capital flight, migration and relevant political or trade agreements help complement the picture.

However, these data hardly reflect all the variables at stake: many an economist has, for example, noted how mainstream international economics does not account for variables, such as missed remittances from forbidden migration or resource depletion resulting from the extractive industry (Toussaint 2005). What is more, international economics does not tell much about the nature and impact of international agreements underpinning and shaping BoP dynamics. Similarly, quantitative analyses do not tell us about the broader implications of phenomena such as migration (aside from statistics on labour movements and remittances), vote coordination in multilateral fora (aside from the economic implications of punctual decisions resulting from such coordination) or cultural and social exchanges (aside from the value of scholarships and cultural programmes). Political economy provides little description of the winners and losers within each of the national camps that reached an international agreement (capital, labour and state bureaucracies, all have different sets of interests), while shedding even poorer light upon the actors, interests and lobby groups involved in negotiations on trade and financial agreements.

And yet, econometric tools are an invaluable instrument to substantiate analyses in international relations: claims to reality with little empirical evidence are destined to remain philosophical considerations. On the other hand, numbers alone are no substitute for qualitative analysis: statistical evidence needs being interpreted in the light of history and praxis, or risks falling prey to interested or faulty readings that can sometimes graze the absurd. Economic data must go through reality checks or risk getting lost in the maze of useless statistics, on the one hand, and missing, underreported or off-the-radar data, on the other. In an industry where the players are also the referees—ODA/OOF donors or implementers such as the ministries of foreign affairs and national development agencies of OECD countries, the World Bank, the International Monetary Fund and the UN are also the source of most analyses on ODA, OOF and development trends—, the informed observer needs to be aware of smoke and mirror tactics and biased interpretations, or else end up in an Orwellian world.[2]

2 Key Quantitative Data: The Balance of Payments

Trying to find statistically relevant long-term relations between ODA and GDP growth has proved a hollow endeavour. One of the reasons for this statistically poor correlation is the limited weight carried by ODA flows when compared to overall exchanges between beneficiary and donor countries. Measuring such relations is like measuring the impact of climate upon intelligence: there might be some correlations, but these are loose and contingent upon variables having a stronger predictive value.

The role of more relevant variables affecting GDP growth can be weighted by analysing different items in the BoPs of African countries, which account for most of the quantifiable exchanges between Africa and its key economic partners.[3] The scope of this econometric exercise is to provide an "order of magnitude" for all the relevant voices of Africa–OECD and Africa–China relations rather than exact measures; figures will be, however, as precise as available statistics allow.[4]

2.1 *Current Account*

According to the IMF, the Current Account (CA) measures (1) international transactions of goods and services; (2) primary income, and; (3) secondary income or current transfers (IMF 2010).

Transactions in goods and services are by far the major categories of current accounts. *Primary income* (or *factor income*) comprises compensation of employees and investments (*direct investment*, *portfolio investment*, *other investment*): these are profits accruing from national workers and national investments abroad. As such, this voice includes compensation of non-national employees, dividends from non-national equity (dividends accruing from owning equity abroad) and interests from non-national debt securities (interests accruing from owning foreign debt); the latter point is particularly important, taking into consideration the role of external debt upon the economies of Africa and other developing countries.

Secondary income (or current transfer or cash transfers) accounts for transactions provided by one party, without anything of economic value being supplied as a direct return to that party, such as *ODA* and *remittances*.

When a country runs a CA deficit, it means that its purchases of goods and services from abroad exceed its sales of goods and services to foreign buyers. At the same time, in order to finance such deficit, the country is necessarily selling assets to foreigners, net of its purchases of assets abroad, in an amount equal to the current account deficit, or is alternatively eroding its foreign reserves. The net balance on the current account is therefore an indicator of an economy's saving and investment/spending behaviour. Since the CA net balance is the difference between a country's savings and its investment/consumption, a positive account measures the portion of a country's saving invested abroad; conversely, a negative account measures the portion of domestic investment/consumption financed by foreign savings.

When looking at African Current Accounts, the first remarkable data is the overwhelming majority of African countries having a negative balance. Exceptions include oil and mineral exporters plus a limited number of diversified economies in the Maghreb and southern African region.[5] The sum of non-oil, non-mineral exporting Sub-Saharan African countries' Current Accounts has been constantly negative since 1980; the picture for the whole of Sub-Saharan Africa except South Africa is mitigated by mineral exporting countries that have benefited from recurring surges in commodity prices, particularly between 2004 and 2008 (Figs. 4.1 and 4.2).[6]

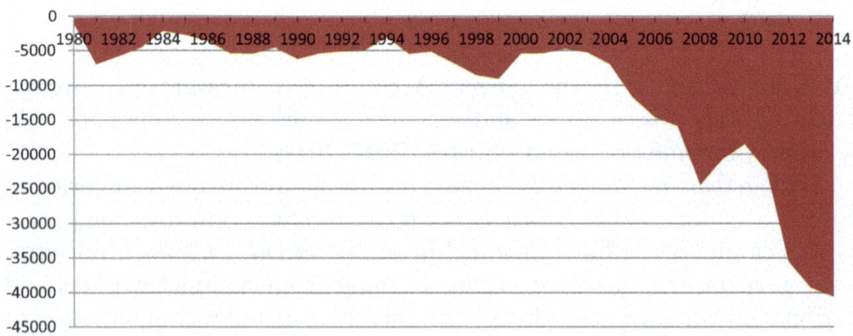

Fig. 4.1 Sum of current accounts of non-oil exporting, non-mineral exporting Sub-Saharan African countries except South Africa, 1980–2014, million USD at current prices and current exchange rate (*Source*: UNCTAD)

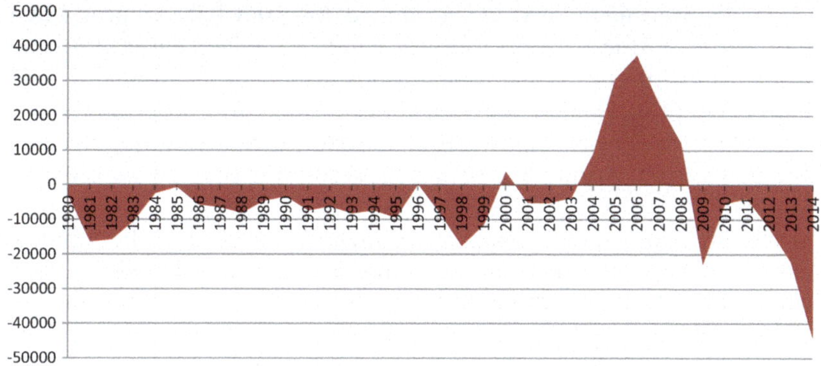

Fig. 4.2 Sum of current accounts of all Sub-Saharan African countries except South Africa, 1980–2014, million USD at current prices and current exchange rate (*Source*: UNCTAD)

This means that, as a whole, the whole continent south of the Sahara, with the exception of short and intermittent periods in which world markets were ready to pay more for natural commodities, has been in a constant state of indebtedness. Sub-Saharan Africa consumes more than it produces, at least in nominal terms: what the world pays for African goods and services is less than what Africa pays for imported goods and services. It would, therefore, be interesting to determine who is selling these goods and services to Africa and who is buying Africa's exports. It would equally be interesting to understand who is granting credits to Africa via the secondary income entry of the current account and the financial account part of the Balance of Payment, thus allowing Africa to both live beyond its nominal means and accumulate debt for protracted periods of times. Answering these questions requires a closer look at the single voices composing the African BoPs.

Trade in Goods and Services

The most important item affecting the economic relations between Africa and Europe, Africa and the USA, Africa and China, and, for that matter, between any two countries or regions of the world, is trade. Most of the Africa–Europe trade is in goods. In 2011, it accounted for 281.7 billion euros (146.7 billion euros of African export to Europe and 135 billion euros of African imports from Europe); trade in commercial services, excluding government services, accounted for 70.3 billion euros (33.4 billion euros of African export to Europe and 36.9 billion euros of African imports from Europe). Total trade (goods + services) amounted to 352 billion euros (180.1 billion euros of African export to Europe and 171.9 billion euros of African imports from Europe), thus accounting for anything between 75 % and 85 % of current account exchanges between the two regions.[7]

Data on Africa–China trade are somehow sketchier.[8] The Chinese Ministry of Foreign Affairs suggests that average annual trade in merchandise over the period 2006–2010 was 88.6 billion USD. Independent estimates relying on Chinese custom data place the 2011 value at 101.96 billion USD (48.52 billion USD of African exports to China and 53.44 billion USD of African import from China).[9]

With such a weight in Africa's international exchanges, trade represents one of the key determinants of the health status of African Current Accounts—and of African overall economies.[10] History has shown that international trade positively contributes towards national economic growth *under* specific conditions, necessary to enter the "virtuous cycle" of growth described in Chap. 3. Historically, Africa has seldom met these conditions: both during the colonial period and the post-colonial years, Africa has specialized in "vicious cycle" trade. This is the result of a trade structure based on mineral extraction, agricultural products, fisheries, minerals and timber: primary commodities. At the same time, African countries import the vast majority of their needs in manufactured goods and services from OECD countries and, increasingly, from China. This is particularly the case for Sub-Saharan African countries, which, with the exception of South Africa, Namibia and Mauritius, have far-less diversified economies than the Maghreb region.

The breakdown of EU–African ACP countries trade in goods (Figs. 4.3 and 4.4) shows that over half (50.7 %) of Africa's exports to the EU in 2011 value were mineral fuels, lubricant and related material, categorized by the UN Standard International Trade Classification with code 3 (SITC3).[11] Other unprocessed African exports included food and live animals (SITC 0), accounting for 13.78 % of total exports; and crude materials, inedible, except fuel (SITC 2), accounting for 8.6 %—the sum of these three categories accounting for 73.08 % of African ACP countries exports to the EU.[12] Conversely, the EU complemented this picture with an export structure largely based on manufactured goods: machinery and transport equipment (SITC 7: 40.1 %), chemicals and related products

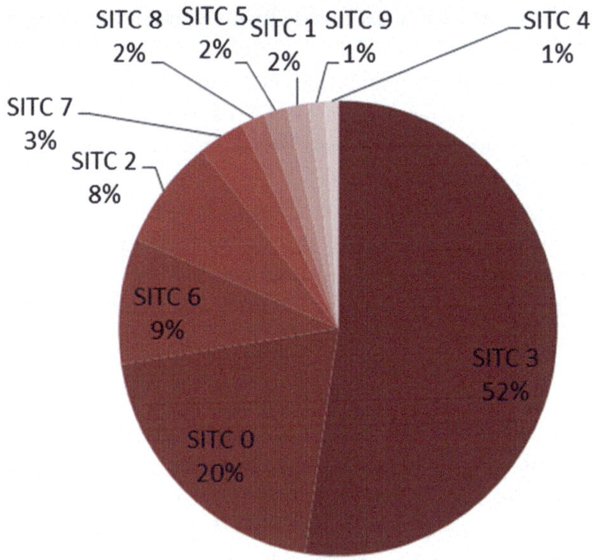

Fig. 4.3 EU–African ACP countries trade structure: EU imports (*red*), 2011 (*Source*: European Commission).

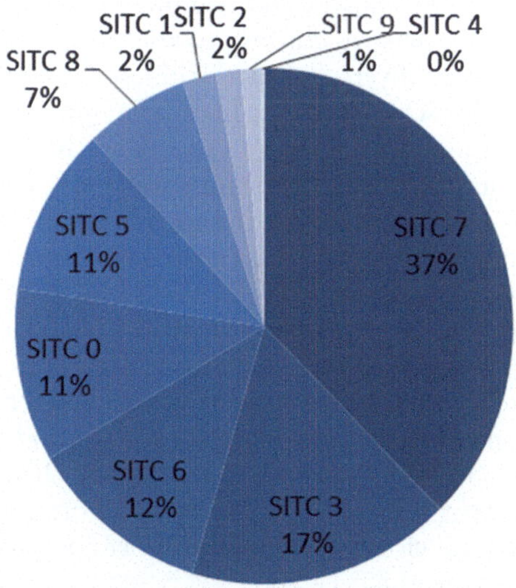

Fig. 4.4 EU–African ACP countries trade structure: EU exports (*blue*), 2011 (*Source*: European Commission).

(SITC 5: 11.3 %) and manufactured goods classified chiefly by material (SITC 6: 11.3 %).

As a result, most European imports of goods from Africa were primary products (79.4 %), with only 17.9 % of manufactures, whereas most African imports from Europe were manufactures (68.7 %), with only 28.4 % of primary products (Fig. 4.5).[13]

Europe is also a net exporter of services to Africa, and particularly to Sub-Saharan Africa (SSA): aside from freight and touristic services—where a number of northern African countries are managing to compete effectively with European operators—EU companies keep a strong lead in most service industries.

Data available on the Africa–China trade structure reflects a similar situation. The Chinese Ministry of Foreign Affairs estimates that between 2004 and 2011, China's import of primary products accounted for over 90 % of total African imports. Among them, fuel accounts for the lion's share (64 % of the total China–Africa trade in 2009), followed by iron ore and metals (24 %) and other bulk commodities, food and other agricultural products (5 %). The same source indicates that in 2009, China mainly exported machinery and transportation equipment (41 % of total exports to Africa) (Lu 2011). A World Bank publication suggests that in 2004 as much as 87 % of all African imports from China were composed of machinery and equipment, textile, apparel and other manufactured products. According to this study, African imports from China are also more diversified than Chinese imports from Africa: using the Herfindahl-Hirschman index, Broadman (Broadman and Isik 2007) unsurprisingly found that Africa's exports are highly concentrated in a few oil- and mineral-producing states, while the same index suggested a considerably greater diversity among the main African importers of Chinese manufactured goods. This is further confirmed by data showing that eight African countries account for up to 92 % of exports towards China (Edoho 2011). Similarly, the World Trade Atlas, indicates that the top 20 products China imports from Africa represent 95 % of total imports; these include mineral products (82 %), precious stones and metals (3 %), parts for motor vehicles (3 %), wood products (2 %) and base metals (1 %). On the other side, the top 20 exports from China to Africa represent only 35 % of the total exports, including machinery (10 %), textiles and clothing (4 %), transport equipment (4 %), footwear (2 %) and plastic products (2 %).

Such trading structure reflects a deeply unbalanced relation: exporting primary commodities—and particularly less dynamic primary commodi-

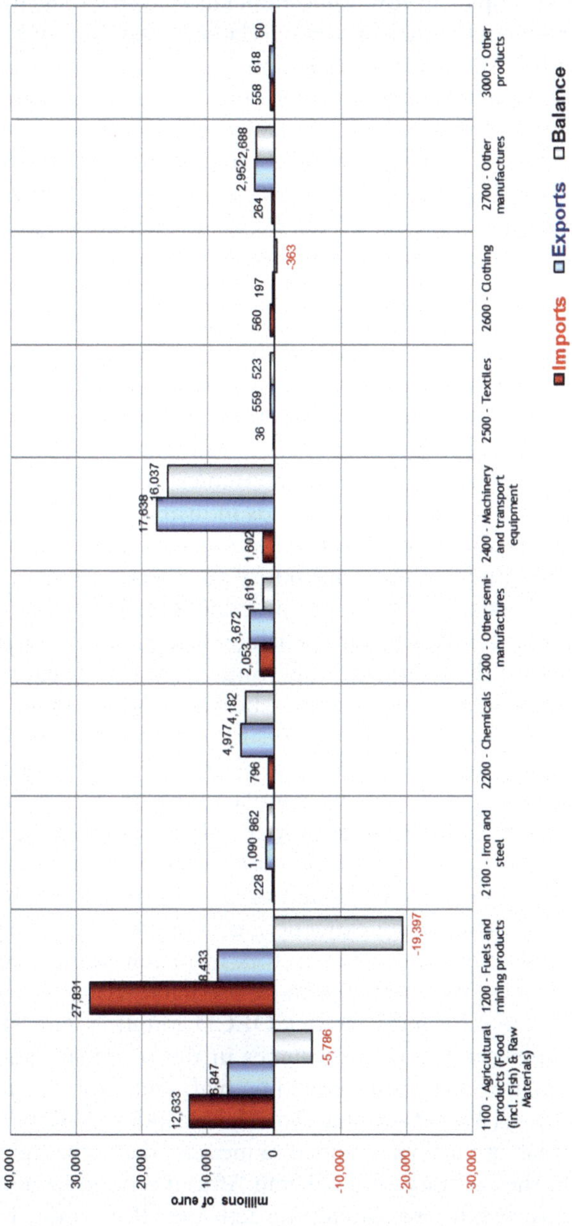

Fig. 4.5 EU–African ACP countries trade balance by industry, 2011 (*Source:* European Commission)

ties such as food crops and low-value minerals—contributes little to job creation and productivity growth. Being relatively easy and inexpensive to produce, they often suffer from oversupply, diminishing marginal returns (the more labour/capital factors invested, the smaller the marginal return on the input), uncertain and highly volatile export and government revenues, unstable and often deteriorating trading terms, and limited links to other sectors of the economy (food crops can only be used for alimentary products, whereas mechanics or IT can be used for limitless applications). Other intrinsic problems relate to resource depletion and environmental degradation.[14]

Conversely, producing services and manufactured goods is instrumental to "virtuous cycle" policies, eventually contributing towards higher-wage and higher-productivity economies.[15] History has shown how such a cycle is powered by increasing marginal returns, economies of scale, higher integration between agriculture, extraction and manufacturing industries (and hence between rural and urban economies) and synergies between consumers, intermediate and capital goods industries. Sub-Saharan Africa does not do that: as noted by UNIDO, this is instead how Africa's trading partners are reaping maximum profit out of the black continent.[16] Africa, on the contrary, is stuck in a cycle of low value-added activities, low productivity and low incentives towards change; integration in international trade has not helped the continent in getting out of this "vicious cycle".

Several indexes confirm this analysis. The Value Added index expresses the amount of added value in any sector, for example, the net output of a sector after adding up all outputs and subtracting intermediate inputs. Because it is "easier" to add value in manufacturing or trading than it is in agriculture, the value added to total output ratio is higher in the manufacturing and trading sectors than in the primary sector. As a matter of example, oil refining, clothing manufacturing and agro-processing typically produce higher value added than mining extraction, cotton growing or staple farming. Because employing production factors in manufacturing (secondary sector) and services (tertiary sector) is more profitable than putting them in agriculture and mining (primary sector), OECD countries and NIEs invest most of their capital and human resources in the secondary and tertiary sectors. This translates in economies yielding high value added in the manufacturing sector (high Manufacturing Value Added index [MVA])[17] as a proportion of the total national value added (a measure that only slightly differs from GDP). On the contrary, Sub-Saharan African economies add most of their value in scarcely efficient agricultural activities (ISIC codes 1 to 5).

Primary Income

The principal entries computed under the primary income (or factor income) voice of the BoP are the returns on foreign investments as well as interests paid to service the foreign debt. Factor income is an important voice for African BoPs considering the predominant role played by foreign firms in the most lucrative sectors of African economies—including mineral extraction and logistic services—as well as the weight of debt instalments in a number of national economies. The latter point, as it will be shown in the next chapter, also covers a key political aspect, as debt servicing has been instrumental in shaping the balance of power between Africa and the developing world, on the one hand, and OECD countries, on the other hand—the latter's position being represented by the WB, the IMF, the Paris Club and the London Club.

FDI to Africa is scarce and there is solid evidence that returns on these investments are generally healthy. In a 2010 poll, UNIDO asked foreign firms to provide information about their major investments in Africa during the last five years. Across the 486 firms reviewed, which reported investing some 1.7 billion USD of new capital, the declared average annual rate of return was nearly 26 %. Scholarly sources (Sautman and Hairong 2007) relying on official data place returns on African FDI in the range of 29 % in the 1990s and up to 40 % by 2005. These figures compare favourably with the rate of return conventionally used in project appraisals in Europe (UNIDO 2012, p. 64). Similarly, using data from 35 Chinese firms operating in Africa, a recent study on Chinese firms concludes that "most CEOs agreed that they were doing 'well' or 'very well' in terms of profitability' (Shen 2013, p. 30).

These data must be taken with a pinch of salt: should the rate of returns always be so favourable, we would expect consistent flows of capital towards Africa rather than the other way round, as it is shown by inward FDI and capital flight indexes (the latter to be discussed in Sect. 4.2.3). This does not happen because Africa is riddled with structural constraints and high business risk levels. However, it remains a fact that a number of economic reports over the last few years have indicated increasing Returns on Investments (ROI) in the continent and suggested that several companies based in Africa may soon become world-class contenders in their respective industries.[18]

If ROIs in African business ventures are high and, perhaps, on the rise, it remains difficult to obtain clear data on the percentage of repatriated income against investments, or repatriated income against reinvested earnings. An indicative figure can be provided by those African and OECD countries whose BoP specifies economic relations by geographic areas. Germany, as a matter of example, had in 2009 and 2010 income receipts from Africa for 1.45 and 1.86 billion euros, respectively, against an FDI outflow towards Africa of 927 and 649 million euros, respectively.[19]

Although not a central issue as it was during the 1980s and 1990s, the problem of debt servicing in developing countries, and particularly in Africa, remains at the core of the relationship between developed and developing countries. As of 2009, UNCTAD estimates that Africa as a whole had a long-term outstanding foreign debt of 230 billion USD, which carried long-term interest payments corresponding to 5.52 billion USD for that year only.[20] However, the total amount of debt servicing—which includes interest payments as well as principal repayments—for 2011 stood at 21.77 billion USD, corresponding to 1.15 % of the African GDP for that year.[21] This is a relevant improvement from previous decades: in 2000, debt servicing cost Africa 3.84 % of its GDP; in 1990, this same figure stood at 4.65 %.

The net transfers on debt to Africa (new loans minus debt servicing and principal repayments) have been positive between 1970 and 1989; all in all, Africa was receiving more credit than it was paying back in debt servicing and principal repayments. However, since the early 1990s, and with few and brief exceptions, the loan mechanism has made Africa a net exporter of capital: every year there was more debt-servicing capital leaving the continent than fresh loans coming in.

Isolating debt repayments going to Europe, the USA or China is no easy task as most statistics group lenders by financial mightiness (e.g. the London club) or political affinity (e.g. the DAC OECD) rather than by geography.

Official Development Assistance (ODA)

A relevant voice affecting the Current Account of some African countries is Official Development Assistance (ODA) received from Development Aid Committee (DAC) OECD countries, China and other emerging donors. The OECD DAC—the most authoritative institution in the development aid field—defines ODA as flows to countries and territories on the DAC list of ODA recipients and to multilateral development institutions which are (1) provided by official agencies, including state and local governments, or by their executive agencies; (2) administered with the promotion of the economic development and welfare of developing countries as its main objective; and (3) concessional in character and conveying a grant element of at least 25 % (calculated at a rate of discount of 10 %). In order to be recognized as ODA, contributions towards development countries need to respect the above criteria.

Official statistics suggest that, in 2010, Africa received 50.36 billion USD–worth ODA; DAC bilateral donors alone having contributed 29.34 billion USD. The EU (member states + European Commission) plays a prominent role in global ODA, being the first donor worldwide and to Africa: in 2010, it contributed 25 billion USD to Africa—more than 50 % of the overall flow going to the continent. The USA contribution stood at 7.6 billion USD—being the strongest bilateral donor.

Data on Chinese ODA are sketchy: Beijing does not follow OECD guidelines on ODA, thus limiting the significance of its official data.[22] Former Chinese Premier Wen Jiabao claimed that China had transferred more than 44 billion USD to Africa over the 1955–2005 period (Rotberg 2009, p. 52), although it is unclear how these statistics were compiled. Estimates from think tanks and scholars suggest data in the region of 1–1.5 billion USD a year since 2002. A recent list (Samy 2010) compiled from different scholarly sources estimates Chinese ODA to Africa at around 8.2 billion USD over 16 years (1990–2006), thus suggesting a mid-term trend of 512 million USD/year.

Before analysing these flows, it is interesting to lend attention to how ODA is calculated. Since ODA figures are typically provided by donors rather than by beneficiaries and because donors have an interest in providing inflated figures, available statistics need to be interpreted before a realistic picture can be painted. OECD-complying ODA figures circulated by International Organizations and donor countries do not reflect the financial amounts or value of in-kind goods reaching the final beneficiaries: these figures represent instead the *gross value*. The difference between the publicized amounts (gross value) and the final amounts reaching the beneficiaries (net value) will be referred to here as the "ODA gap".

The "ODA gap" is the result of accounting operations happening at two levels. The first level lies under the sun: the DAC allows its members to count ODA "administrative costs" and "debt relief" as part of ODA itself. Much has been said about the legitimacy of counting non-disbursed funds as ODA.[23] The practice is, however, completely transparent: the openness of these accounting procedures is exemplified by OECD DAC reports clearly indicating the amounts going towards administrative costs and debt relief (OECD 2011). They are no insignificant amounts: between 2000 and 2009, debt relief and administrative costs (which include the voice "other in-donor expenditure", covering items such as "development awareness" and "assistance to refugees and asylum seekers") counted, respectively, for an average of 13.26 % and 10.18 % of DAC bilateral ODA to the world. Together, they weighted 23.44 % of DAC bilateral and 16.57 % of DAC total (bilateral and multilateral) ODA to the world.[24] Regular studies financed by a confederation of European civil society organizations on EU15 ODA suggested a very similar percentage of "inflated aid": debt relief, student costs and refugee costs would account for between 14 % and 18 % of European aid (CONCORD 2008, 2012).[25]

"ODA Gap" operations at the second level happen in a more discreet fashion, protected by a maze of regulations. OECD accounting guidelines use a very restrictive application of the concept "administrative costs", which does not include a number of expenses that are *de facto* costs attached to the disbursement of ODA. At the same time, the DAC adopts an extremely comprehensive list of activities contributing towards the promotion of "economic development and welfare". To exemplify that, it suffices saying that DAC "administrative costs" do not cover the six-figure salaries of development project directors, while OECD governments count the costs of repatriating refugees to their countries of origin as part of their ODA.[26]

A quick overview of OECD DAC auditing rules offers a telling insight on how easily operations at the second level can contribute towards building up the "ODA gap"—and why so many observers cry foul when it comes to quantifying ODA. Here are some of the most significant auditing techniques (1) funds paying donor countries' experts, consultants, teachers, academics, researchers, volunteers and contributing towards public and private bodies for sending experts and consultants in developing countries are computed as ODA (Line I.A.3 or I.A.4.1), (OECD 2010), since "administrative costs" only cover salaries paid to donors' in-house agency staff and contractors; (2) gross financial core support to NGOs, other private bodies and research institutes "[…] for use at their discretion and [contribution] to programmes and activities which NGOs have developed themselves, and which they implement on their own authority and responsibility" (Line I.A.2.1) as well as "payments for NGOs and multilaterals to implement donors' projects and programmes" (Line I.A.3) counts towards ODA; (3) core contributions to multilateral institutions in the form of grants, capital subscriptions and concessional lending—including to IFIs promoting policies with a controversial track record in developing countries such as WB, IMF and WTO—count towards ODA.

There are neither official statistics on the weight of these costs on total ODA, nor on the percentage of disbursements finally trickling down to the beneficiaries. In many cases, the real administrative costs are higher than the value of what the beneficiaries finally get: as a matter of example, the costs of chartering a flight and its crew, fuel, salaries for the project officers handling the operation and distribution logistics on the ground may easily supersede the value of food or medicines contained in that flight, which is what the beneficiaries finally get.

DAC-reported ODA further includes a number of budget lines accounting for funds that were never meant to leave the donor country, the so-called *in-donor expenditures.* While some of these budget lines pertain to the first level (to the extent that they are openly publicized),[27] their full weight can hardly be appreciated by referring to openly audited information only. Current DAC auditing rules allow the following items to be counted as ODA (1) expenditures for the sustenance of refugees in donor countries during the first 12 months of their stay, including payments for refugees' transport to the host country, temporary sustenance (food, shelter and training) and expenditures for voluntary resettlement of refugees in a developing country (e.g. repatriation) (Line I.A.8.2); (2) the sum of scholarships and trainings in donor countries and imputed student costs (Line I.A.5); (3) official sector core contributions to donor country-based NGOs and other private bodies active in development cooperation (e.g. foundations); (4) funding of activities designed to increase public support, that is, awareness in the donor country of development cooperation efforts, needs and issues (Line I.A.8.1); (5) research into tropical diseases and developing crops designed for developing countries even if the research is carried out in a developed country (OECD 2010).[28] This means that the costs linked to assisting—say—a Malian family of refugees arriving in France, sheltering them in public housing facilities, admitting their children into public schools and finally repatriating them, all counts as French ODA towards Africa. If a Paris-based NGO is involved in those processes, the cost of French personnel working for the NGO is counted as ODA towards Africa. If that French NGO publicizes its activities with posters in the Paris underground to promote fund-raising activities or raise public awareness on development cooperation (and pay its own salaries), the bill of the advertising company counts as French ODA towards Africa.

The OECD has a long history of campaigning in favour of "untying aid"—that is, pushing donor countries to avoid attaching conditionalities on their aid by requesting that aid money is spent in cooperation with the donor countries' NGOs, think tanks or universities, employing donor countries' nationals or purchasing equipment from donor countries' companies. However, the normative framework on tied aid remains weak and OECD countries have proved reluctant to report their practices. The OECD claims that between 1999–2001 and 2008, the proportion of untied bilateral aid rose progressively from 46 % to 82 %, thus leaving roughly 20 % of tied aid coming from ODA countries (Clay et al. 2009).

If we take into consideration all the above items, the estimated value of the "ODA gap" is much higher than initially foreseen: grants, loans, goods and services reaching the final beneficiaries are only a fraction of publicized values. How much of a fraction, it remains unclear. Data on overall operating costs are not publicized and those that can be accessed and computed are not uniform. Estimates vary widely, going from burgeoning claims that as much as 85 % of aid flows are used for "other purposes" than what they were originally meant to do, to more conservative figures on overhead costs per development agency.[29] Relying on sketchy data, William Easterly found that the ratio of administrative budget to "Official Development Financing" (ODF) can be anywhere between 1 % and 129 %—a value over 100 % indicating the agency's need for funding on top of its allocated budget just to meet its own expenses (W. Easterly and Pfutze 2008). Multilateral agencies, and, particularly, the UN Development Programme (UNDP), the IMF and the UN Relief and Works Agency (UNRWA) score particularly poorly in efficiency, needing 100 %, 53 % and 52 %, respectively, of their ODF to pay their own salaries and accessory costs.

Regarding the modalities of transfer, the OECD establishes not less than eight modalities through which ODA may be channelled—including those already reviewed above (OECD 2014).[30] Cash transfers into the beneficiary countries' budget, known as *budget support* operations, normally show in the BoPs of beneficiary countries, under the *Secondary Income* heading of their CAs. Other ODA contributions may show in the beneficiary country's budget—and therefore in its BoP—as long as they are channelled on-budget, for example, as long as they transition through the beneficiary country's treasury, independently from the fact that the beneficiary country has any control over them.[31] Such voice represents a relevant component in the BoP of few African countries only. This is visible from the fact that only a few countries heavily rely on ODA to meet their central government's expenses: these include Madagascar (where ODA represents 108.1 % of the central government expenditures), Niger (108.4 %), Mali (97.4 %), Zambia (39.9 %) and, to a lesser extent, Kenya (24 %) and Ghana (26 %) (UNDP 2013, p. 159). This data is confirmed by other statistics: in 2008, only six African countries received ODA in excess of 20 % of their GNI (Burundi, Guinea Bissau, Liberia, Malawi, Mozambique and Rwanda), while ten more received ODA in excess of 10 % (UNDP 2013, p. 160).

Assessing the real significance of Chinese ODA is an even more knotty endeavour than assessing OECD-compliant aid. The financial estimates suggested earlier in this chapter cover grants and concessional loans; both of them come with strings attached, including the obligation to use these funds with Chinese national companies. This phenomenon resembles Western "tied aid" but likely goes beyond because it is only subjected to limited domestic and international scrutiny. Because Chinese ODA does not follow OECD guidelines, it often treats its ODA as a basket that includes all financial operations not following pure market rules. The list of 2006 development cooperation commitments revealed by China during the FOCAC summit includes measures as different (and as unlikely to be considered ODA under OECD definitions) as an equity fund meant to support Chinese investments in Africa (China–Africa Development Fund), cancellation of tariff lines for 440 typologies of African exports (up from 190) and the setting up of three to five trade and economic cooperation zones in Africa.[32]

Whereas ODA represents a relevant amount of certain countries' budgets, ODA generally represents a light entry in African BoPs because it has a limited weight compared with other flows—that is certainly the case when compared with trade (goods and services) and factor income, but more often than not also when compared to other financial entries such as FDI and Foreign Portfolio Investment (FPI), as well as secondary income entries (remittances) and capital flight.

Remittances

Remittances represent household income from foreign economies mainly arising from migration of people to those economies. They include funds that flow through formal (banking, wire transfer agencies) and informal (cash or in-kind goods) channels. Several accounting procedures for remittances are currently in use.[33]

Remittances have come to play an increasingly important role in African BoPs: between 2000 and 2011, there has been a threefold increase of remittances per capita. Total remittances to Africa in 2011 were estimated at 41.6 billion USD, an increase of 5.9 % over 2010 (AfDB et al. 2012). Remittances have also increased as a share of African GDP: between 1995 and 2010, they grew from less than 1 % to over 2 %. These flows are likely under-reported, as a large amount of contributions is sent through informal channels or in-kind. This is particularly the case for Sub-Saharan Africa, where up to 75 % of the total remittances go informally, a figure standing much higher than in other continents (Freund and Spatafora 2005). African countries have developed different dependency levels on remittances: in 2011, Cape Verde was leading the list, receiving 306 USD per capita, followed by Lesotho (291 USD), Morocco (220 USD), Mauritius (193 USD) and Tunisia (175 USD). As a GDP share, this translates into Lesotho receiving 24.8 % of its GDP from remittances, followed by Togo (10.3 %). International Organizations are, however, sceptical about the possibility of drawing detailed regional comparisons within Africa and between Africa and other continents, given the lack of official data in a number of countries, and particularly in central African countries.

The main sources of remittances are different for each African subregion. The USA and Western Europe jointly accounted for nearly 70 % of remittance flows to Sub-Saharan African countries in 2010 (28 % and 41 %, respectively), followed by the Gulf Cooperation Council (GCC) countries (9 %). The Middle East and North Africa, in contrast, received nearly 40 % of their remittances from the GCC in 2010.

Remittances from China still represent a limited amount of total remittances to Africa. Although there are no official statistics, figures reported by Bodomo (2015) through fieldwork in southern China estimate an amount of between 10,000 and 100,000 RMB per person per year. As the number of African residents in China also remains unconfirmed—a large number of them staying illegally—, this range should be multiplied by anything between 200,000 and 500,000 individuals, thus giving a figure included between 2 billion RMB and 50 billion RMB—corresponding to 326 million USD to 8.15 billion USD a year. Although this fork is too large to provide meaningful data, it confirms that remittances from China may also lie in the same order of magnitude of Chinese ODA, as is the case with the relationship between Western ODA and Western remittances.

2.2 Capital and Financial Account

The capital and financial account of the balance of payments represents the alter-ego of the current account: whatever has been consumed or invested in excess of funds generated from current exchanges, must be balanced by borrowing capital on the international market; whatever has been produced or saved in excess of funds used for current exchanges, must be lent to the international market.

The capital and financial account includes capital transfers and acquisition/disposal of non-produced, non-financial assets (capital account part), as well as all components of investment (financial account part): *direct investments* (FDI), *portfolio investments* (equities securities and debt securities), *other investments* (mainly bank loans) and *reserve assets* (operations executed by central banks).

The most important categories affecting this side of the BoP are foreign direct investments and Portfolio Investments.

Foreign Direct Investment (FDI)

A foreign direct investment (FDI) implies the acquisition of a stake in a foreign country's enterprise with (1) lasting interests in developing the enterprise and; (2) a substantial stake in the management of the firm. FDI typically involves the establishment of some physical entity such as a factory or an enterprise in a foreign country, which provides investors with a direct stake in the development of the host economy. According to the OECD definition, the "lasting interest" is evidenced when the direct investor owns at least 10 % of the voting power of the direct invested enterprise (OECD 2009). The OECD considers the 10 % benchmark a condition necessary and sufficient to ensure that the investor has an effective voice and a true interest in the enterprise's management. FDI is generally regarded as promoting stable and long-lasting economic links between investors and investees because investors cannot easily withdraw from their position.

However, stable economic links between the investors and the investees are no guarantee as to the alignment of interests between the two. Private foreign interests are not necessarily in line with public domestic interests and the promotion of the former may be detrimental to the latter. Empirical evidence shows that FDI *can* spur the host economy's earnings, technology acquisition and managerial know-how—*or* simply turn into an exploitative tool in the investors' hands.[34] The key factors in determining the nature and extent of the FDI socio-economic impact are: (1) the investment sector and its level of competitiveness; (2) the host economy's regulatory framework, capacity and development strategies and; (3) the investment's modality (also referred to as "mode of entry": greenfield, merger and acquisitions or brownfield investment). It should also be noted that while incoming FDI is accounted in the BoP as a *positive financial flow*, in the following years it normally generates: (1) very concrete consequences for the hosting country's *real economy* and; (2) a *negative financial flow* for the invested country—for example, a positive financial flow towards the investing country.[35] These mechanisms help explain why African Current Accounts suffer from systematic deficits vis-à-vis the developed world: highly profitable foreign business ventures in Africa (oil, mining, logging, logistics, construction) are often authorized to repatriate the majority of their profits, as will be discussed in Chaps. 5 and 6.

Foreign-financed firms operating in highly protected sectors may contribute in increasing—rather than decreasing—market distortions. Instead of filling the gap between savings and investments, FDI can set up firms that extract rents from non-competitive markets, lower national savings and, if allowed to expatriate profits, eventually drain capital from the invested economy. There is no shortage of examples where foreign investors were allowed to enter a monopoly market and subsequently started extracting monopoly rents, including in public utility sectors providing essential services to the citizens (Sanjaya Lall 2000).

There are also remarkable differences within the group of FDI ventures that positively affect the BoP and/or cause positive social fallouts in the invested economy. Not all investments carry equal benefits to the investees: second and third sector activities are usually more profitable than primary-sector activities; technology- and capital-intensive manufacturing sectors typically entail higher knowledge spillover than labour-intensive sectors; joint ventures (JV), rather than wholly foreign-owned enterprises (WFOE), usually grant better conditions and higher control to the investee economy's shareholders; limits on the repatriation of profits ensure that part of them are spent or reinvested in the market that contributed in generating them and so on.

The host country's regulatory environment and development strategy are vital elements in ensuring a healthy balance between the foreign investors' interests and public interests in the invested economy. Such balance should guarantee the hosting economy with job creation, partial reinvestment of profits, enhanced productivity, technology transfer and best corporate practices to local firms. Where these guarantees are missing, FDI can generate a number of other negative by-products, including driving local competition out of the market ("crowding out effect"); supporting inefficient oligarchies of local partners, workers and/or contractors; and thwarting laws constraining socially undesirable practices, including pollution, health and safety hazards.[36]

Finally, the modality in which FDI is deployed influences its impact over the real economy. FDI is generally divided into three classes by its modality of entry: greenfield investments are made by opening a new branch or making investments into the equity capital of the firm; mergers and acquisitions (M&A) are either outright purchases of existing firms or amalgamations with them; brownfield investments are a combination between the first two, for example, the acquisition of a target company with subsequent heavy investments to upgrade its facilities and production processes. It is generally accepted that M&A—contrary to greenfield investments and recapitalization—do not involve significant changes in the performance of economic variables such as production, employment and turnover. Portfolio investments are not considered part of FDI and are usually computed under a different BoP heading: they will be discussed in the following section.

Africa seems to be suffering from most problems attached to incoming FDI. First, it receives little investments: paraphrasing Joan Robinson (2006, p. 45), it could be said that the misery of being exploited by FDI is nothing compared to the misery of not being exploited at all. Long-term FDI flow trends to Africa are positive in absolute terms (average annual flows to Africa doubled between the 1970s and the 1980s to reach 2.2 billion USD, continued increasing to an average of 6.2 billion USD and 13.8 billion USD during the 1990s and the early 2000s, respectively, and reached 52.6 billion USD in 2010), but the continent is doing poorly when compared with other developing regions of the world. African relative capacity to attract FDI declined during these decades and the total flow of private capital remains today at 5.3 % (3.6 % excluding North Africa) of total world FDI, down from a peak of 6 % in the mid-1970s.[37]

A quantitative analysis of the FDI supply side portrays noticeable differences between the OECD group of countries and China: while Africa-directed FDI originating from OECD countries has remained stable or has known a sluggish growth since the 2000s, Chinese FDI has been growing exponentially. In 2010, OECD countries still accounted for about 40 % of total FDI flows to Africa, but the OECD itself estimates that this share will likely diminish in coming years.

This will have progressively stronger effects on Western FDI stock held in Africa. In 2008, the EU FDI stock in Africa amounted to 153 billion euros (192 billion USD), or 4.7 % of worldwide extra-EU-27 FDI stocks (Xenellis 2010). On the other side, the American think tank, Heritage Foundation, estimates that in the period 2005–2010, about 14 % of China's investment abroad was directed towards Sub-Saharan Africa alone.[38] In absolute terms, this remains comparatively little (77.1 billion USD); yet, it indicates that Africa has become more of a strategic partner for China than it is for Europe or the USA (Scissors 2012).

Second, African inward FDI suffers from sectorial bias. Investments getting into the continent largely go to industries characterized by low value-added content: unprocessed products in the primary sector, including less dynamic agricultural products, minerals, metals and fuels. As seen in the trade section, these industries suffer from periodic profit surges, endemic volatility and limited opportunities for growth.

Inward FDI in the primary sector is also associated with other negative by-products: enclaves of export-oriented primary products typically use imported technology and have limited backward and forward linkages to the rest of the host economy, all phenomena translating into limited job creation in the hosting economy.[39] These industries also show low percentages of reinvested profits, despite the fact that most projects generate healthy returns on their investments. Seen from the hosting societies' perspective, these reasons concur in making FDI in the primary sector a comparatively less advantageous venture than FDI in the manufacturing sectors, and particularly in technology-intensive industries such as mechanics, electronics, communication and IT. Trends are not encouraging as the African dependence on the primary sector to attract investment capital is not improving. On the contrary, the primary sector's share percentage of FDI stock in Africa has been growing in the last decades, a pattern in stark contrast with Latin America and the NIEs of Asia (UNCTAD 2005, p. 9). While both Western countries and China have directed the majority of their FDI towards resource-rich countries, there seem to be relevant differences: Sautman and Hairong (2007) draw attention to the fact that, while roughly 75 % of American FDI to Africa has been concentrated in oil, reported figures on Chinese FDI to Africa between 1979 and 2000 suggest that 64 % of investments went into manufacturing, with only 28 % targeted natural resources.[40]

Sectoral bias also reflects in the geographic distribution of FDI stock, which is unevenly spread across the continent: 24 countries classified by the World Bank as oil and mineral dependent account for close to 75 % of the African FDI inflows between 1990 and 2010—South Africa accounting for a big chunk of the remaining 25 %. All top ten recipients of FDI in Africa in the 2000s have large mineral, gas and/or petroleum reserves. Some of these countries (including Angola) have experienced capital withdrawals after 2010 because of the bearish mineral and oil markets—yet, the long-term correlation between natural endowments and FDI income remains evident (Fig. 4.6).

Third, a large share of investments going into Africa brings little impact to the real economy since it simply reflects change in proprietorship. This is the case of merger and acquisition (M&A) deals, and even more, the case of portfolio investments reviewed in the next paragraph.

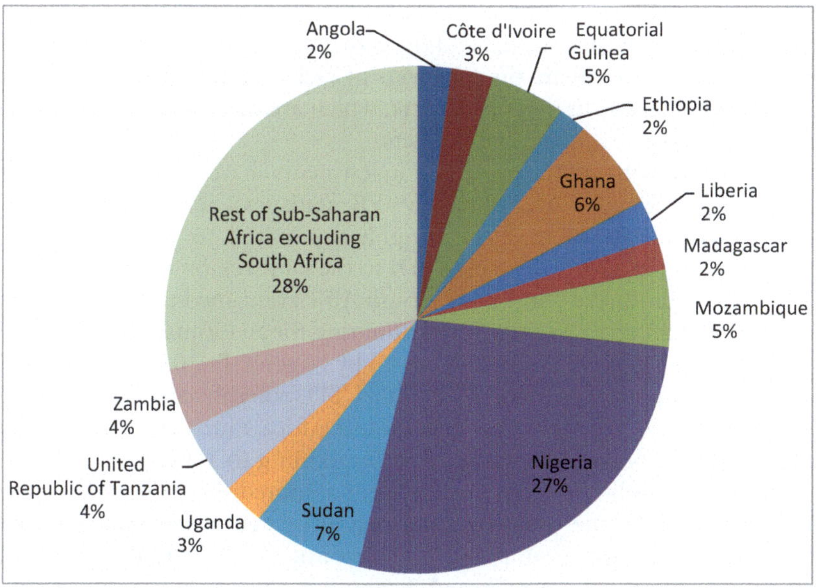

Fig. 4.6 FDI towards Sub-Saharan Africa excluding South Africa: countries having received more than 5 billion USD in FDI stock + rest of Sub-Saharan Africa, excluding South Africa (*Source*: UNCTAD)

Figures from UNIDO show that 2006–2010 M&A operations in Africa shoot off, with a total worth of 120 billion USD recorded compared to 42.5 billion USD for the 2000–2005 period. M&A from the world to Africa in 2010 was valued at 29.6 billion USD, more than doubling the 2009 figure, but below the 2008 peak of 36 billion USD; the average size of deals doubled from 329 million USD (2000–2005) to 664 million USD (2006–2010). The increase in M&A transactions is driven by the emerging economies, with India, China and Brazil representing three out of the five top merger and acquisition deals in 2010.

In particular, Standard Bank estimated that M&A activity between Africa and China rose 90 % in 2011 and is expected to grow further.

Portfolio Investments and Other Investments

OECD defines portfolio investments as international investments where the foreign investor has voting rights of less than 10 %. Although such threshold remains somehow arbitrary, it is considered meaningful in individuating investors with no significant influence or interest in the operations of the invested enterprise. Portfolio investors are, instead, concerned about the safety of their capital and the returns generated on their financial investments: they evaluate the prospects of each investment and shift their capital with changes in these prospects, which are often affected by short-term developments in financial markets.

Compared with FDI, portfolio investments have a secondary but not marginal weight: according to WB statistics, net portfolio flows to Sub-Saharan Africa in 2011 roughly amounted to 8 billion USD, corresponding to 22.4 % of foreign FDI to the same region and 0.72 % of its GDP. Throughout the last decade, South Africa remained the largest portfolio investment receiver in Africa, accounting for an estimated 79 % of the entire African portfolio inflows, followed by Nigeria. In 2011, Nigeria had a bond and equity market of 78 billion USD, roughly corresponding to 16 % of its GDP; in the same year, South Africa's market capitalization stood at 211 % of its GDP, roughly corresponding to 1.18.

Foreign portfolio investments represent a limited share of market capitalization in SSA: the overwhelming majority of African capital is raised in Africa. It is, however, impossible to account for the original source of portfolio investments done through financial hubs such as London, Hong Kong or, on a smaller scale, Mauritius.

A limited foreign portfolio investment is not necessarily bad news. Because portfolio investments do not entail greenfield operations or any direct involvement in management, they are positions from which investors can—and do—easily disengage. As a consequence, portfolio investments are way more volatile than FDI: figures provided by the OECD, exemplifies the volatility of these flows, which peaked at 22.2 billion USD in 2006 to subsequently drop at −27.2 billion USD during the 2008 financial crisis (AfDB et al. 2012). While such volatility is risky for any economy, developing countries are particularly vulnerable to short-term capital outflows: this became clear on several occasions, as in the 1994 Mexican and 1997 Asian crises, following the European crisis of 1992.

Finally, the last major voice of the BoP goes under "other investment" entry, which includes new loans and leasing. These are voices that play a role in the net disbursement of debtor countries.

2.3 *Capital Flight*

Following a distinction proposed in academia, we define *capital flight* as the net unrecorded capital flows leaving capital-scarce countries (illicit capital), and *capital outflows* as the legal and reported flows of capital leaving a country (licit capital) (Epstein 2005). Thus defined, capital outflows from Africa are mainly represented by the repatriation of foreign factor income at the hands of foreign MNCs and SMEs, payments aimed at servicing the foreign debt, African outward FDI, and loss of portfolio capital every time international investors move their capitals from African debt and equities into non-African securities. African capital outflows have been discussed and measured in the previous sections, with reference to official statistics provided by national and international institutions.

African capital flight represents capital that leaves the continent without being recorded; as a consequence, there are no official data on this phenomenon, which can only be estimated through statistical procedures.

There are two main channels through which illicit capital can leave a country: movements on external accounts and mispriced trade transactions. The WB residual model captures the first channel, while the trade misinvoicing model used by the IMF Direction of Trade Statistics (DTS) captures the second channel (Kar et al. 2011). Estimates on the magnitude of capital taking off via the first channel are typically obtained by comparing a country's source of funds with its recorded use of funds.[41] Calculations on the amount of capital siphoned off via trade misinvoicing are carried out by estimating the amount of overpriced imports and underpriced exports on customs documents.[42]

Both methods only provide *estimates*—which are also unable to account for other phenomena contributing towards capital flights, including embezzlement of export revenues and kickbacks on public and private sector contracts. As a consequence, these figures are characterized by a higher level of approximation than the official statistics used so far. Although estimates differ from study to study, they unmistakably point at a disturbingly high order of magnitude.

Boyce and Ndikumana (2012) place the value at 443 billion USD for 33 Sub-Saharan African countries (in 2004 USD) in the period 1970–2004; including imputed interest earnings, this same value rises to 640 billion USD. Earlier on, the same authors had placed the estimate at 606 billion USD (Boyce and Ndikuma 2008). The OECD relies on these studies to estimate the stock of African capital flight at 700 billion USD over the period 1970–2008. Economists at Global Financial Integrity put the estimate at 854 billion USD for the whole of Africa in the years 1970–2008. A simple average of compounded interest values among these different estimates yield a value of 756 billion USD in the 1970–2008 period, corresponding to a 19.3 billion USD/year flow over a 39 year period. These values roughly correspond to the same amount of ODA that went into Africa over the same period (761.2 billion USD): for every dollar that got into Africa via ODA in the last 40 years, there was another dollar that illegally went into Western bank accounts through some other mean.

Thirty-nine billion USD a year is already a significant amount in absolute terms, but this figure is even more relevant when weighted against the total volume of stock capital sitting in Africa, Africa's external debt or Africa's GDP. Several studies found that, as a proportion of these indicators, African countries have experienced much higher capital flight ratios than any other developing region, and particularly Latin America.[43] The most interesting data relate to the capital flight/external debt ratio: development economists have long noticed that the stock of Sub-Saharan African capital flown abroad since 1970 might be larger than the total foreign liabilities of African governments, thus making SSA a net creditor on the international stage. Since these statistics suggest that a tiny minority of African individuals and companies have illegally stacked abroad more money than the total foreign liabilities of their governments, economists Boyce and Ndikumana (2001) suggested changing the term *Severely Indebted Low Income Countries* into *Severely Indebted Low Income governments.*

3 The Bigger Picture

The figures presented in this chapter paint a more detailed representation than the sketch presented in Chap. 1. The key elements are, nonetheless, confirmed:

1. Trade represents an absolutely preponderant part in the Current Account part of African BoPs. With few exceptions, the trade structure of Sub-Saharan Africa suffers from strong imbalances as most African imports consist of consumer manufactured goods and end-user services, while most exports consist of primary sector products;
2. While it remains difficult providing a full picture of the factor income situation, we know that returns on foreign investments in Africa are high. A generous regulation on FDI is allowing foreign companies to repatriate most of their profits to their headquarters, even in this frontier phase of African development. The cost of servicing the international debt in Africa has improved over the last decade; yet, since the early 1990s, the mechanism of international loans has turned African countries into net exporters of capital;
3. OECD-compliant ODA statistics are inflated in terms of weight on African BoPs and, even more, in terms of concrete effects on the final beneficiaries. Once normalized for their real costs and finalities, these financial flows likely represent less than 50 % of the publicized amounts;
4. Remittances have come to overtake ODA flows in many SSA countries. Remittance flows are largely influenced by the migration policies in receiving countries and, therefore, by the stringent criteria that both the West and China more recently impose on migrants from Africa;
5. Long-term incoming FDI trends are positive, but the relative share of African FDI in the world is shrinking: investments in Africa are growing at a slower pace than in the rest of the world. Investments are largely concentrated in the mining industry, with the agricultural and fishery industries representing only a fraction of the first. Investments in the light industry are very limited, while investments in heavy industries are virtually non-existent;
6. Foreign portfolio investments into Africa roughly stand in a relationship of 1 to 5 with FDI and represent only a tiny percentage of total SSA market capitalization;

7. The private external assets of SSA countries measured by cumulative capital flight are greater than their public external debt. Since African private assets abroad surpass the continent's foreign liabilities, the continent has been called a "net creditor" to the rest of the world.

The two following chapters will analyse the processes, interests and social organizations that, in the Western world as in China, contribute in shaping this type of economic relationship between Africa and its key economic partners.

Notes

1. The balance of payment is defined as a statement summarizing the economic transactions of a national economy with the rest of the world for a specified time period.
2. Ironically, while most Westerners think to know that the Chinese live their everyday life in a world where the Chinese Communist Party (CCP) decides what is true and what is not, they are almost perfectly reciprocated by the mainstream Western narrative among Chinese nationals, which portrays Western consciences as brainwashed by an instrumental use of concepts such as "democracy" and "human rights".
3. The figures proposed in this chapter fall short of representing the full picture of the African trade structure since they do not provide (1) intra-African exchange data, which, particularly in the case of South Africa/rest of Sub-Saharan Africa exchanges, may reach important quantities; (2) for certain items, figures with countries other than the OECD and China. However, Africa's most sizeable exchanges remain with the EU, the USA and China.
4. For practical reasons, the data and analyses contained in this chapter will be restrained to Europe–Africa and USA–Africa relations as a proxy for Western–Africa relations. Some of the data refer to Europe–ACP (Africa, Caribbean and Pacific) group of states relations rather than Europe–Africa relations.
5. In 2011, exceptions include Algeria, Angola, Botswana, Gabon, Libya since 1994, Namibia, Nigeria, South Africa, 1985–1995. Some nuanced results are obtained by Ivory Coast, Egypt, Equatorial Guinea, Djibouti, Gambia, Lesotho, Morocco and Swaziland.

6. UNCTAD's selected petroleum exporters in Sub-Saharan Africa: Angola, Chad, Congo, Equatorial Guinea, Gabon, Nigeria, South Sudan and Sudan. UNCTAD's selected mineral exporters in Sub-Saharan Africa: Botswana, Democratic Republic of the Congo, Eritrea, Guinea, Mauritania, Namibia, Sierra Leone, Zambia.
7. EU data from DG trade are in EUR. Data reported as recorded by Europe; discrepancies with data recorded by Africa are typically due to error, misinvoicing and "creative" accounting.
8. Since neither the WTO nor other international institutions provide China–Africa statistics, the only available sources are the Chinese government and private sources analyzing Chinese government data.
9. Source: Global Trade Information Services, data retrieved in 2011.
10. Within a country, the relationship between trade and the national economy is a bi-univocal, cause–effect relationship: the state of the economy affects the country's exports and imports, while the country's position vis-à-vis the world economy affects what it is going to produce (and, as a consequence, what it is going to import).
11. SITC Revision 3, published by the United Nations Statistics Division. In 2011, the African, Caribbean and Pacific (ACP) group of states includes Angola; Antigua and Barbuda; Belize; Cape Verde; Comoros; Bahamas; Barbados; Benin; Botswana; Burkina Faso; Burundi; Cameroon; Central African Republic; Chad; Republic of Congo; Democratic Republic of Congo; Cook Islands; Côte d'Ivoire; Cuba; Djibouti; Dominica; Dominican Republic; Eritrea; Ethiopia; Fiji; Gabon; Gambia; Ghana; Grenada; Republic of Guinea; Guinea-Bissau; Equatorial Guinea; Guyana; Haiti; Jamaica; Kenya; Kiribati; Lesotho; Liberia; Madagascar; Malawi; Mali; Marshall Islands; Mauritania; Mauritius; Micronesia; Mozambique; Namibia; Nauru; Niger; Nigeria; Niue; Palau; Papua New Guinea; Rwanda; St. Kitts and Nevis; St. Lucia; St. Vincent and the Grenadines; Solomon Islands; Samoa; São Tome and Principe; Senegal; Seychelles; Sierra Leone; Somalia; South Africa; Sudan; Suriname; Swaziland; Tanzania; Timor Leste; Togo–Tonga; Trinidad and Tobago; Tuvalu; Uganda; Vanuatu; Zambia; Zimbabwe. Hence, the group of ACP African countries includes all Sub-Saharan African countries except, at the time of writing, South Sudan.

12. ACP processed exports to the EU included manufactured goods classified chiefly by material (SITC 6) and machinery and transport equipment (SITC 7), totalling 20.1 % of the overall value.
13. While certain categories of goods are traded in both directions, these often have different processing levels: an important chunk of "mineral fuels" exported by Africa is crude oil and gas, while its imports falling in this category mainly consists of refined oil products. Same goes for the food and live animal sectors, with European imports largely relying on crop and exports mainly consisting of processed food. These differences fail to show in the overall summary: the already imbalanced situation would be even more skewed if the statistics would take into consideration processing levels within the same SITC categories.
14. Both these elements have been analyzed in the IPE literature (Toussaint 2005); suffice to note here that a number of economists have consistently argued that official accounting measures of national wealth—including GDP, GNI and the BoP—are fictitious, as they do not account for resource depletion and costs entailed by environmental degradation, two voices that would have a strong negative weight in the balance sheet of commodity-dependent economies.
15. See Robert Wade's introduction (Wade 1990).
16. "Countries importing commodities from Africa add value to these products through manufacturing and trade back higher value products to African countries, thus creating jobs abroad and draining foreign exchange reserves from Africa" (Yumkella 2010).
17. As defined by the WB, MVA expresses the value added in industries belonging to International Standard Industrial Classification (ISIC) codes 15 to 37.
18. See studies from Boston Consulting Group (Aré et al. 2010), McKinsey (Leke et al. 2010) and Goldman Sachs (Goldman Sachs 2007).
19. German balance of payment, 2009 and 2010, Deutsche Bundesbank.
20. Only interest repayments are counted in the Current Account under the factor income voice.
21. Source: UNCTAD. All measures in current prices and current exchange rate.
22. China allegedly keeps these figures confidential in order to avoid creating tensions with its domestic stakeholders.

23. Forgiven debt is usually recorded at its nominal value instead of its market value, which is necessarily lower, since part of the principal might not be reimbursable anyway. More generally, counting debt relief as ODA is a rather dubious accounting practice: since several highly indebted countries (HICs) do not stand any chance of repaying these debts, it is standard business practice to write off bad debt as a matter of course and not as a matter of charity.
24. Administrative costs include costs computed under the voice "other in-donor expenditures"; author's calculation.
25. The European NGO Confederation for Relief and Development (CONCORD) brings together 1800 NGOs across Europe.
26. "Temporary assistance to refugees from developing countries arriving in donor countries is reportable as ODA during the first 12 months of stay, and all costs associated with eventual repatriation to a developing country, are also reportable as ODA" (OECD 2008).
27. OECD DAC openly acknowledges that its members count refugee and scholarship costs as ODA.
28. A donor country-based NGO is an NGO organized at the national level, based and operated either in the donor country or another developed (non-ODA eligible) country.
29. Dambisa Moyo claims that a WB study found that "[...] as much as 85 % of aid flows are used for purpose other than that for which they were initially intended, very often diverted to unproductive, if not grotesque ventures" (Moyo 2009, p. 39). No details about the study are provided.
30. These are traditionally divided into "bilateral" and "multilateral" ODA and may consist of budget support, bilateral core support and pooled programmes and funds, project type interventions, experts and other technical assistance, scholarships and student costs in donor countries, debt relief, administrative costs, other in-donor expenditures and multilateral contributions.
31. For example, the trust funds of development banks may manage 100 % of the funds destined to country A through companies and service providers which are not from country A; nonetheless, these funds are usually computed as country A's budget revenues (as ODA) and expenses.
32. In this same package, China also added more orthodox ODA measures, including the cancellation of all interest-free loans owed by

heavily indebted poor countries (HIPCs), the provision of 3 billion USD of preferential loans and 2 billion USD of preferential buyer's credits.

33. According to the International Monetary Fund's interpretation, remittances are recorded in three different sections of the balance of payments (1) compensations of employees are the gross earnings of workers residing abroad for less than 12 months, including the value of in-kind benefits (in the current account, sub-category "income", item code 2310); (2) workers' remittances are the value of monetary transfers sent home from workers residing abroad for more than one year (in the current account, sub-category "current transfers", item code 2391); (3) migrants' transfers represent the net wealth of migrants who move from one country of employment to another (in the capital account, sub-category "capital transfers", item code 2431) (IMF 2010).
34. By reviewing dozens of projects in different countries and industries through a cost-benefit analysis, several studies carried out in the 1970s and the 1980s already showed that, while a majority of FDI projects have a positive effect on aggregate economic growth, there is a sizeable minority of FDI projects that result in a net reduction of the hosting country's national income, even though these projects remain profitable to the foreign investor. Lall and Streeten (1977) examined 88 foreign-owned and locally owned projects operating in six countries; only two-third of them had positive outcomes for national wealth. Encarnation and Wells (1985) examined the contribution of 50 proposed FDI projects to national income to conclude that a sizeable minority comprised between 25 % and 45 % contributed in reducing the host country's national income. More recent analyses on the quality of FDI include Lall (2000) and Lall and Narula (2004), classifying FDI into two categories: "low quality" FDI (e.g. FDI seeking natural resources, expanding market access for consumer goods manufactured abroad, restructuring existing foreign production), which is asset-exploiting and generating economic rent by using existing firm specific assets and "high quality" FDI (e.g. seeking new strategic assets), which is asset-augmenting and aimed at acquiring new assets that protect or enhance existing assets. They argue that often, developing countries attract the "low-quality" FDI. For a meta-bibliography of

articles dealing with the issue of positive/negative FDI's impact, see Gallagher and Zarski (2006) and Sumner (2005).

35. Inward FDI is audited with a "plus" in a country's Capital Account; however, after the initial investment, any non-reinvested profit accruing from FDI flows back to investor countries and is, therefore, audited in the host country's Current Account with a "minus".
36. Many real-life case scenarios prove that FDI can give rise to socially distorting consumption patterns. Brand names with high advertisement budgets have crowded out local competitors in many developing economies: in African countries, food produced under FDI has often supplanted cheaper and more nutritious local products. For a meta-bibliography of articles dealing with the issue of positive/negative FDI's impact, see Gallagher and Zarski (2006).
37. Data from UNCTAD (2005) and updated statistics from UNCTAD (2012).
38. Part of these investments go through Hong Kong, a phenomenon that helps exemplify why UNCTAD statistics on official Chinese FDI to Africa are lower.
39. UNCTAD measures the significance of enclave production through the difference between a country's GDP (value of output generated within national boundaries) and its GNP (income earned by national citizens), by the ratio of earnings to value added and by the presence of a large informal economy. See also, Todaro (2009, p. 357).
40. A more in-depth discussion of Western and Chinese FDI in Africa is carried out in Chaps. 5 and 6.
41. Sources of funds—a country's inflow of capital—include cash transfers (ODA and remittances), increases in net external indebtedness of the public sector and the net inflow of FDI. Use of funds includes financing the current account deficit and additions to central bank reserves. According to the model, whenever a country's source of funds exceeds its recorded use of funds, the residual comprises unaccounted-for, and hence illicit, capital outflows.
42. To estimate trade misinvoicing, the IMF compares a developing country's exports to the world with what the world reports as having imported from that country, after adjusting for insurance and freight. Additionally, a country's imports from the world are compared to what the world reports as having exported to that country; discrepancies in partner-country trade data, after adjusting for insurance and freight, indicate misinvoicing.

43. Chang and Cumbi (1991) found that between 1976 and 1987, 36 African countries had higher flight capital to GDP and flight capital to debt ratio than Latin American countries. Similarly, Hermes and Lensik (1992) placed the capital flight to GDP ratio at 61 % for a Sub-Saharan sample of countries against 22 % for Latin America. Collier et al. (2001) found that in 1990 about 40 % of the African private capital was held abroad, the highest ratio across countries in the developing world.

References

AfDB, ADB, OECD, UNDP, & UNECA. (2012). *African Economic Outlook 2012. Promoting youth employment.* OECD Publishing.

Aré, L., Chabenne, S., Dupoux, P., Ivers, L., Michael, D., & Morieux, Y. (2010). *The African challengers: Global competitors emerge from the overlooked continent.* Boston, MA: Boston Consulting Group.

Bodomo, A. (2015). Africans in China: Guangzhou and beyond—issues and reviews. *The Journal of Pan African Studies, 7*(10).

Boyce, J. K., & Ndikumana, L. (2001). Is Africa a net creditor? New estimates of capital flight from severely indebted sub–Saharan African countries, 1970–96. *Journal of Development Studies, 38*(2), 27–56.

Boyce, J. K., & Ndikumana, L. (2008). New estimates of capital flight from Sub-Saharan African countries: Linkages with external borrowing and policy options. In *PERI Working Papers, 144.* Amherst, MA: Political Economy Research Institute.

Boyce, J. K., & Ndikumana, L. (2012). Capital flight from Sub-Saharan African countries: Updated estimates, 1970–2010. PERI Research Report, October 2012. Amherst, MA: Political Economy Research Institute.

Broadman, H. G., & Isik, G. (2007). *Africa's silk road: China and India's new economic frontier.* Washington, DC: World Bank.

Chang, K. P. H., & Cumby, R. E. (1991). Capital flight in sub–Saharan African countries. In I. Husain, J. M. Underwood & B. Mundial (Eds.), *African external finance in the 1990s.* Washington, DC: World Bank.

Clay, E. J., Geddes, M., & Natali, L. (2009). *Untying aid: Is it working? An evaluation of the implementation of the Paris declaration and of the 2001 DAC recommendation of untying ODA to the LDCs.* Copenhagen: Danish Institute for International Studies.

Collier, P., Hoeffler, A., & Pattillo, C. (2001). Flight capital as a portfolio choice. *The World Bank Economic Review, 15*(1), 55–80.

CONCORD. (2008). *No time to waste: European governments behind schedule on aid quantity and quality.* Brussels: Concord.

CONCORD. (2012). *Aid Watch Special Report.* Brussels: Concord.
Easterly, W., & Pfutze, T. (2008). Where does the money go? Best and worst practices in foreign aid. *Journal of Economic Perspectives, 22*(2), 29–52.
Edoho, F. M. (2011). Globalization and marginalization of Africa: Contextualization of China–Africa relations. *Africa Today, 58*(1), 102–124.
Encarnation, D. J., & Wells, L. T. (1985). Sovereignty en garde: Negotiating with foreign investors. *International Organization, 39*(01), 47–78.
Epstein, G. A. (2005). *Capital flight and capital controls in developing countries.* Northampton: Edward Elgar.
Freund, C., & Spatafora, N. (2005). Remittances: Transaction costs, determinants, and informal flows. *World Bank Policy Research Working Paper*, No. 3704. Washington, DC: World Bank.
Gallagher, K. P., & Zarsky, L. (2006). Rethinking foreign investment for development. *Post-autistic Economics Review, 37*, 28.
Goldman Sachs. (2007). *BRICS and beyond.* The Goldman Sachs Group/Global Economics Department.
Hermes, N., & Lensink, R. (1992). The magnitude and determinants of capital flight: The case for six Sub-Saharan African countries. *De Economist, 140*(4), 515–530.
IMF. (2010). *Balance of payments manual* (9781451986167). Washington, DC: International Monetary Fund.
Kar, D., & Freitas, S. (2011). *Illicit financial flows from developing countries over the decade ending 2009.* Washington, DC: Global Financial Integrity.
Lall, S. (2000). *FDI and development: Research issues in the emerging context.* Adelaide: Centre for International Economic Studies.
Lall, S., & Narula, R. (2004). Foreign direct investment and its role in economic development: Do we need a new agenda? *The European Journal of Development Research, 16*(3), 447–464.
Lall, S., & Streeten, P. (1977). *Foreign investment, transnationals, and developing countries.* London: Macmillan.
Leke, A., Lund, S., Roxburgh, C., & van Wamelen, A. (2010). What's driving Africa's growth. *McKinsey Quarterly, June.*
Lu, Y. (2011). China's trade rush with Africa. *Capital Week 25.4.2011.*
Moyo, D. (2009). *Dead aid: Why aid is not working and how there is another way for Africa.* London, New York: Allen Lane.
OECD. (2008). *Is it ODA?* Factsheet: OECD Publishing.
OECD. (2009). *OECD benchmark definition of foreign direct investment 2008 fourth edition.* OECD Publishing.
OECD. (2010). *DAC statistical reporting directives.* OECD Publishing.
OECD. (2011). *Development Co-operation report 2011 50th anniversary edition.* OECD Publishing.
OECD. (2014). Type of aid tab in worksheet.

Robinson, J. (2006). *Economic philosophy*. Piscataway, NJ: Transaction Publishers.
Rotberg, R. I. (2009). *China into Africa: Trade, aid, and influence*. Washington, DC: Brookings Institution Press.
Samy, Y. (2010). China's aid policies in Africa: Opportunities and challenges. *The Round Table, 99*(406), 75–90.
Sautman, B., & Hairong, Y. (2007). Friends and interests: China's distinctive links with Africa. *African Studies Review, 50*(03), 75–114.
Scissors, D. (2012). Chinese outward investment: Accelleration Features the USA. *Issue Brief 3656 on Asia and the Pacific*. Washington, DC: The Heritage Foundation.
Shen, X. (2013). Private Chinese investment in Africa: Myths and realities. *World Bank Policy Research Working Paper* No. 6311. Washington, DC: World Bank.
Sumner, A. (2005). Is foreign direct investment good for the poor? A review and stocktake. *Development in Practice, 15*(3/4), 269–285.
Todaro, M. P. (2009). *Economic development* (10th ed.). Boston: Pearson Addison Wesley.
Toussaint, E. (2005). *Your money or your life: The tyranny of global finance* (Updated edition). Chicago: Haymarket Books.
UNCTAD. (2005). *Economic development in Africa – Rethinking the role of Foreign Direct Investment*. New York and Geneva: United Nations Publications.
UNCTAD. (2012). *World Investment Report*. Geneva: United Nations Publications.
UNDP. (2013). *Towards human resilience: Sustaining MDG progress in an age of economic uncertainty*. New York: United Nations Publications.
UNIDO. (2012). *Africa investor report 2011: Towards evidence-based investment promotion strategies*. Vienna: UNIDO Publications.
Wade, R. (1990). *Governing the market: Economic theory and the role of government in East Asian industrialization*. Princeton, NJ: Princeton University Press.
Xenellis, G. (2010). *Africa-EU: Economic indicators, trade and investment*. Luxembourg: Eurostat.
Yumkella, K. (2010). Keynote address: Energy Justice Conference, October 23, 2009. *Colorado Journal of International Environmental Law and Policy, 21*(2), 277–285.

CHAPTER 5

A Qualitative Analysis of Africa–West Economic Relations

Econometrics provides a picture of African BoPs, along with past trends and patterns. Yet, it does not answer the question of how and why contemporary African BoPs are structured the way they are. Part of the story certainly lies with the specific domestic dynamics of each African state. However, since these countries are characterized by different national political systems, economic organizations, cultures, traditions, geographic positions and national endowments, something independent from domestic policies must also have contributed in channelling their economic histories towards a similar fate. That "something" is unlikely to account for the whole story, but is certainly part of it.

Africa's economic relations with Western countries are not very different from what they were during the colonial era. Trading patterns have not evolved much: developing countries have always exported primary goods and imported services and manufactured products. The nature of international income and FDI entering Africa has not evolved much either: the international oil-based economy and the discovery of new oil and mining fields has modified size and destination of FDI flows, but, by and large, investments in Africa continue to be concentrated in the primary sector. ODA and remittances represent a relatively new variable, partially caused by the political and legal frameworks established after de-colonization; as suggested in Chap. 4, the scale of these flows has, however, a limited impact upon the core features of West–Africa economic relations.

S. Raudino, *Development Aid and Sustainable Economic Growth in Africa*, DOI 10.1007/978-3-319-38936-3_5

Contemporary relations between Western and African countries can, in fact, be seen as partially relying on a set of rational and long-tested pragmatic policies devised by the former and largely accepted by—or imposed on—the latter. Beyond the rhetoric of Western developmental efforts, there is also little empirical evidence to suggest that contemporary international economic policies are aimed at reforming the fundamental mechanisms of politico-economic relations between OECD and G90 countries. The reading proposed here is based on a historical and interpretative analysis of the interests and processes that shape the relations portrayed by the quantitative analysis of the African Balances of Payments.

1 The Players: Who the Actors Are

Existing political, economic, financial and trading provisions affecting Africa's international relations with Western countries emanate from different actors and instruments. For clarity of presentation, they can be organized under three headings (1) the supranational level; (2) the national level; and (3) the subnational level.

Global intergovernmental organizations (e.g. the UN, IMF, WB, WTO) and agreements/negotiations emanating from these institutions (e.g. Uruguay Round, Doha Development Agenda, Structural Adjustment Policies, Millennium Development Goals, etc.) are considered as being part of the supranational or systemic level (first level). Region-to-region institutions (e.g. the ACP-EU Joint Institutions) and agreements (e.g. the Economic Partnership Agreements, Cotonou Agreement) as well as bilateral institutions (e.g. bi-national commissions) and agreements (e.g. bilateral treaties) are treated as part of the supranational level. Nation states are the key actors of the national level (second level). Domestic players (e.g. national political parties, trade and labour unions, civil society organizations) and policies (e.g. migration laws, trade subsidies, trade defence measures, health and safety standards) are classified as pertaining to the subnational level (third level).

All three levels interact in a seamless fashion and contribute in shaping the nature of political and economic relations between Western and African countries, in the same way they contribute in defining relations between any other two countries or regions of the world, including the China–Africa relations discussed in Chap. 6. Yet, the essence of sovereignty and the main source of bargaining power lie with a specific level: the nation state. A review of the role of ten actors pertaining to one of the three levels in influencing global business norms across 13 regulatory fields has found that states (national level) have, by far, been the most important players (Braithwaite and Drahos 2000).[1] Among nation states, the USA, the UK, France and Germany have been found to be the most influential players. In economic matters, International Organizations (systemic/intergovernmental level), and particularly International Financial Institutions, represent little more than appendixes of these same governments and other OECD countries. In liberal democracies, national economic constituencies (subnational level) are largely influential in shaping their governments' positions on international political economy issues.

1.1 The Supranational/Systemic Level

International Organizations are today full-fledged members of the international community. All major global (e.g. UN, IMF, WB, WTO), regional (e.g. EU, Council of Europe, Organization for Security Cooperation in Europe, Organization of African Unity and then AU) and thematic (e.g. OECD; North Atlantic Treaty Organization, Organization of Petroleum Exporting Countries) International Organizations contributing to the relationship reviewed in this chapter (Africa–West) were founded after 1945 and came to play a significant international role in the following decades. Today, few countries dare to take steps at the international level without a direct or indirect backing of these organizations: for hegemonic countries, International Organizations represent a way to legitimize and "multilateralize" their policies and interests; for second-tier countries, they often represent a useful leverage tool on the international scene; for third-tier countries, they provide an institutional setting where their positions can be voiced. Clearly, not all of these institutions exert the same influence upon G90 countries, their economies and their relations with the developed world: the UN, WB, IMF and WTO arguably represent the most influential organizations.

By representativeness and competency, the UN system is the closest example we have to an international governance system. When the international community reunited in San Francisco in 1945, it mandated the UN with the task of achieving "[…] international co-operation in solving international problems of an economic, social, cultural, or humanitarian character"[2]; against this mandate, the UN seemed to be in a privileged position to address structural imbalances in the global economic system.

Yet, its agenda was also to be shaped by its governance structure, and a restricted oligarchy within the Security Council (UNSC) quickly relegated the General Assembly (UNGA) to a secondary role. Within the UNSC, permanent members (P5) enjoy an exclusive right of veto, including in the process leading to the selection of the Secretary General (SG). Traditional geopolitical, economic, ideological and military opposition among P5 members has allowed the UN to play a balancing role—but also a very limited one. Confrontation during the Cold War meant immobility for an intergovernmental organization that had two bitter foes sitting in the same board. Many constituencies within the UN—including the UN bureaucracy itself, G8 countries that had lost the war, and rising powers in Asia, Latin America and the Muslim world—have been sidelined for decades by entrenched opposition and also by *huit clos* agreements among P5 members.

Within this scenario, most of Sub-Saharan Africa and other Least Developed Countries (LDCs) did not have much chance to influence the international governance agenda and contented themselves with the strong developmental mandate the UN granted to many of its agencies and programmes. Such mandate was, however, interpreted by promoting development assistance (distribution of grants, concessional loans and technical assistance) rather than by redressing skewed international economic mechanisms (redistribution of value-creating capacity). This clearly shows from the contributions of UN member states towards the UN budget: mandatory and voluntary budget allocations towards UN programmes and agencies with a "contingent welfare" mandate (UNDP, UNICEF, FAO, UNHCR, etc.) are significantly higher than budget allocation towards UN agencies with a "structural redressing" mandate (UNCTAD, UNIDO, ECA, etc.).[3]

It was further understood that the institutional structure of the UN would not have authorized any decision against the core common interests of P5 members. To this extent, the UN "constitutional" set-up was born with a restrained capacity to intervene upon North–South structural economic imbalances.

One year before the San Francisco conference, the Allied nations reunited in Bretton Woods had mandated two International Financial Institutions (IFIs) with creating a framework of international economic cooperation for the after-war era: the IMF was tasked with the promotion of monetary cooperation and assistance to countries with BoP imbalances, while the WB was asked to look after long-term development and poverty reduction.

It is interesting to note that, while the IFIs' mandate and structure could be agreed upon in a fairly loose and cooperative way among the 44 states represented at the conference,[4] decisions on power-sharing arrangements turned out to be a contentious exercise: quota negotiations between the American and the Soviet delegations trailed for several weeks and an agreement could only be reached on the very last day of the conference.[5]

Diplomatic efforts naturally focused on a power-sharing agreement that was meant to fix the decision making mechanism of two powerful financial institutions—and the political and economic nature of the projects these institutions were to finance.[6] The power-sharing mechanism to be used by the IFIs finally created a substantially different balance of power than in the UNSC, where the two parties to the Cold War were represented on an equal standing. Instead, all the influential countries within the IMF executive board and the WB board of directors pertained to the Western block and shared a remarkably homogeneous set of political and economic interests. Both the IMF and WB governance structures were engineered around a quota system that reflected their members' financial standing: the member countries' weight in total voting power was proportional to the size of their economies.[7] This meant the absence of an effective counterweight to the Western block of nations: within the IMF executive board and the WB board of directors, the Soviet Union and China were unable to exert the same influence they had within the UNSC. The industrial heavy-weights instead benefitted the most from this system: aside from the USA—which in 1948 had almost 35 % of the IMF quotas alone—, Western Europe and Japan acquired a disproportionally strong capacity to influence the "hard-wiring" of the international economic system. The alignment of interests and powers within the IMF and the WB effectively meant the capacity to influence the work of these institutions right from the beginning.

Seventy years after Bretton Woods, this is arguably still the case. In 2013, the USA maintains a 16.75 % share of total votes within the IMF, the EUR area controls 20.19 %, Japan 6.23 % and the UK 4.29 %—at the other extreme, 23 member countries representing francophone Africa weight together 1.55 % of total IMF votes. The WB has similar power-sharing arrangements: the USA controls 15.62 % of total votes, while 20 among the least developed Sub-Saharan African countries weigh together 1.82 % of total votes.[8] The presidencies of both the organizations have firmly been in OECD countries' hands, with an informal rule attributing the WB presidency to a USA citizen and the IMF presidency to a European national.

Much has been said about the shortages of the IFI's governance system, highlighting the disproportional power held by the USA, Japan and Western Europe. Even in its own corporate governance logic—one share, one vote—the system remains unbalanced: despite having undergone 14 reviews since the 1950s to provide increased representation to NIEs, the quota system has constantly fallen short of creating a fully proportional system.[9] Several authors have also drawn attention to the difference between voting weight and voting power, noting how the IMF governance system is particularly distorting on the latter's scale as a result of indirect provisions granting special rights to the USA voting share as well as to specific voting blocs (Paloni and Zanardi 2006). For example, veto thresholds allow the USA to exert an exclusive unilateral capacity to freeze proposals on 18 sensitive matters, while veto on other 21 issues can be exerted by a coalition of the five biggest shareholders: USA, Japan, Germany, France and the UK.[10]

Key IFI's structural imbalances seem, however, to lie elsewhere. Countries like China and India may ultimately manage to get a quota that is truly proportional to their economies' size—yet, this would not make the system any fairer to weaker members. As ultimate guarantors of the short- and long-term viability of the *entire* financial system, the IMF and WB governance structures should have provisions guaranteeing smaller economies' interests to feed into the decision-making process. Unbalances are not about the position of specific disadvantaged economies; they are more about recognizing that relative poverty is intrinsic to the system and deciding which role these disadvantaged members of the international community should play.

Countries "qualifying" to higher quota shares within the IFIs have typically achieved (or are in the process of achieving) a position in the international economy that provides them with a set of structural incentives to transform their behaviour (and identity) from "poachers into gamekeepers": from low-income countries scrambling against the international rules that contribute in keeping the *status quo*, into high-income countries upholding those same rules they were fighting few decades before. The international behaviour of some Asian NIEs is emblematic of such U-turn: after having built their own development upon ISI, SOEs, public subsidies and market imperfections, they are today part of that group of states pushing for early liberalization and advanced privatization in G90 economies. Such a trend has already been visible among the four Asian tigers and, if the theory holds water, it will not take long before countries like Thailand, Vietnam and, even, China will hold similar stances.[11]

The General Agreement on Tariffs and Trade (GATT)—which became a full-fledged international organization with the setting up of the WTO in 1995—had an independent genesis from Bretton Woods institutions, a peculiarity that is reflected today in a seemingly democratic governance structure: unlike the IMF and the WB, the WTO grants equal voting rights to each of its member states, while not recognizing the right of veto. However, the WTO conducts negotiations on the basis of *consensus* rather than *majority voting*, meaning that votes are seldom taken into consideration: decisions are, instead, left to the outcome of bargained negotiations. Different WTO members carry different bargaining powers and weaker members often need accepting suboptimal negotiation outcomes: stances they do not like but which represent the best or only outcome available to them. The praxis of negotiation over nine major multilateral rounds from 1947 to today (eight successful rounds plus the stalled Doha Round) has clearly shown the dominance of OECD countries. This has become evident since the Tokyo round, with the practice of restricted negotiations in "green room" meetings, small gatherings of representatives from up to 30 member countries invited by the WTO Director-General (DG) and invariably attended by the EU and the USA. Such meetings are largely seen as a way for larger and more powerful countries to maintain control over the bargaining process (Jones 2009).

Given their governance structure, global intergovernmental organizations are largely led by the most influential national actors among the OECD group of countries, including in their delicate task of promoting development among G90 countries.

1.2 The National Level

Nation states are the longest-established and less ambiguous actors of the international system. Despite long-standing debates among different international relations schools, it is generally accepted that states behave in their self-interest, generally understood as the advancement of their own relative wealth and power vis-à-vis the wealth and power of other members of the international community. The key variable of states' behaviour does not relate to their goal (which invariably consists in promoting self-interest), as much as to the states' *capacity* to achieve largely predetermined goals. Different actors can afford different means, human resources and technical expertise in dealing with the international arena.

Differences in the capacity of state actors here reviewed vary enormously. In 2011, the USA roughly dedicated 3.6 trillion USD (24 % of its GDP) to its federal budget: these resources pay the USA Department of Defence's military procurement needs, the USA State Department's capillary diplomatic network, the USA Department of Commerce's subsidy policies, thousands of research and development grants across the most disparate sectors, and the many other federal budget lines that contribute in making the USA government an informed, omnipresent and all-powerful actor on the international scene.[12] The USA federal budget adds up to another 2.4 trillion USD of public money administered at the state level; these funds take care of expenses that contribute in creating the basis of a safe, healthy, active and knowledgeable society by paying for its schools, hospitals, police and the alike. The EU's four major economies (Germany, France, UK and Italy) had a 2011 cumulated budget of 5.5 trillion USD—the European Union also having an independent federal-like budget of 184 billion USD.

On the other hand, the cumulated state budgets of 47 African states whose 2011 accounts were readily available roughly amounted to 450 billion USD—slightly more than the public budget of Australia alone. The interests of 22 million Australians are represented on the international stage by a government whose budget equals the financial resources of 47 African governments representing 1 billion people. These gaps obviously show in government resources and negotiation capabilities.

From an institutional perspective, the lobbying capacity of national delegations to International Organizations varies from nil—more than 20 LDCs have no diplomatic representation in Geneva—to overwhelming: the USA has four diplomatic missions (and respective Ambassadors) in Geneva: to the UN, to the WTO, to the Conference on Disarmament and to the UN Human Rights Council. From a capacity perspective, imbalances start from the basis of the pyramid: among the non-OECD groups of students that made it to the list of world top students ranked by the PISA (Program for International Study Assessment) in 2012, nine were from European countries (including Russia), nine from Asia, six from Latin America and three from the Middle East and Maghreb.[13] No Sub-Saharan African country made it to the PISA list; Ghana and Botswana participated in TIMSS (Trends in International Mathematics and Science Study), having been ranked last and third last, respectively, in the 2007 survey. The same trends are to be found at graduate level: among the 500 best Universities in the world, 128 are from North America, 229 from

Europe and four from Africa.[14] The European Commission's DG Trade, largely responsible for designing and implementing the EU trade policy, currently counts 518 staff, mostly hired from among graduates of the world's first-tier universities.[15] These professionals add up to the thousands of officers that work in national ministries of economy and trade in the 28 member states. Among the 47 Sub-Saharan African countries there are only two whose ministries of trade have comparable levels of resources and skills to Western administrations: South Africa and Nigeria.[16]

Old boys' club networks in the Western world have enabled the establishment of symbiotic relationships between the most powerful state bureaucracies and the "referees" of supposedly neutral international global organizations. Pascal Lamy, the 2005–2013 WTO DG, is a former European Commissioner for Trade, as was Pether Sutherland, who also headed the GATT/WTO in 1993–1995. All IMF managing directors have been European nationals, mostly coming from the ministerial ranks of Western European governments (Christine Lagarde is a former French Minister of Trade, Dominique Strauss-Kahn is a former French Minister of Finance, Rodrigo Rato is a former Spanish Minister of Economy, Horst Köhler is a former German Deputy Federal Minister of Finance, etc.), while all WB presidents have been American nationals, mostly coming from the ranks of the USA government or from investment banks closely associated with the USA Treasury and the Federal Reserve (Robert Zoellick is a former Deputy Secretary of State and a previous Vice Chairman at Goldman Sachs, Paul Wolfowitz is a former Deputy Secretary of Defence, Lewis Thompson Preston is a former CEO of J.P. Morgan, Alden W. Clausen was President and CEO of Bank of America, etc.). As emerging economies—including those of Brazil, Russia, India, China and South Africa (BRICS)—move into positions that make their trade and investment preferences more similar to those of the G20 than those of the G90, they gain top appointments in International Organizations traditionally dominated by nationals of Western countries: 2002–2005 WTO DG Supachai Panitchpakdi from Thailand and current DG Roberto Azevêdo from Brazil are among the few non-Western top appointments in the history of global IFIs.

Quantitative studies on WTO members' institutional behaviour confirm the rather obvious intuition that a country's legal capacity is directly proportional to its capacity to promote national trade interests—whether this is measured in the number of disputes initiated or successfully settled.[17] Empirical studies further confirm that legal capacity and economic size positively correlate to trade's defensive[18] and offensive[19] capability. This simply reflects the all-natural principle that countries can only take advantage of international norms if they have the legal and economic resources to do so.

1.3 The Subnational Level

In democratic countries, public officials are accountable to the constituencies that elected them into office. In the highly industrialized countries of the OECD group of states, political power is scattered among different actors, including political parties, state bureaucracies, trade and business unions, MNCs, SMEs, NGOs and churches. Such actors have divergent economic interests, political vision and support bases. Their interests are often at loggerheads, so much so that political, economic and ideological competition within Western democracies is generally fierce. When it comes to be represented on the international scene, several of these actors have enough capacity and financial leverage to intervene directly; most, however, try to enrol the support of their governments. On their side, governments have an active interest in supporting the national actors that voted them into office. When acting on the international scene, governments translate their constituencies' preferences in national positions by channelling divergent stances into a single position that, in those governments' eyes, maximizes the national interest. In such mechanism, it would be unusual for a democratic government to forge its position on the basis of academic theories, bureaucratic self-interests, ideology or altruism. National delegations defend the interests of the constituencies that elected them into office: this is what they are elected and paid for. In a democratic system, governments guided by other principles are destined to be short-lived.

What are these constituencies interested in? Political parties are interested in votes, a variable that crucially depends upon their capacity to improve their citizens' conditions. Since the end of World War II, improving citizens' conditions in OECD countries has essentially translated into increasing income and expanding welfare services. Several studies show that political incumbents have much higher chances of being re-elected when macroeconomic performances during their term in office were satisfactory. For example, by coupling economic data with 16 USA presidential elections (1948–2008), American statistician Nate Silver found that the Institute for Supply Management (ISM) manufacturing index and changes in non-farm payrolls can explain almost half of presidential election results in post-war America.[20]

Economic constituencies are typically interested in expanding their businesses: acquiring new markets and increasing profit margins. A corporation's first priority is to please its owners; since the managers' (and sometime employees') salaries are also linked to the dividends gained by the company's shareholders, it is safe to assume that all interests within a corporation are normally aligned behind the goal of increasing turnover and profitability. To do so, Chief Executive Officers (CEOs) follow their own specific strategies, but also request industry-wide support from their governments. A *Wall Street Journal* poll bringing together 100 American CEOs found that what American CEOs want most from their government is to (1) improve workers' skills to foster export growth; (2) encourage the immigration of the best and brightest from around the world and encourage foreign students educated in the USA to stay; and (3) welcome foreign investments to create businesses and jobs (WSJ 2011). This essentially translates into asking their government to assist in deepening/broadening foreign market access, poaching international talents and attracting inward FDI.

Labour constituencies are chiefly interested in improving their working conditions: crucially, this depends not only on their bargaining power with capital owners but also on the economic conditions of their employers: successful companies usually offer better working conditions than struggling companies. Twenty-first-century globalization has brought the historical antagonism between capital and labour under further strain: delocalization can be profitable for corporate capital but costly for national labour. This also remains one of the most controversial issues for OECD governments on the international stage, since favouring globalization can potentially hurt their own workforce. Economic constituencies in OECD countries seem to have been more successful than labour constituencies in lobbying their governments in favour of free trade, to the extent that industrial relocation has become the norm in most of the Western world; welfare measures have, however, contained some of the negative side effects.

2 The Stage: Western Policies Towards Africa

How do western players' structure, underlying interests and relative power contribute in shaping Western international economic policies towards Africa and G90 countries?

Data in Chap. 4 suggest that Africa largely relies on commodity-led economies: export of primary products, import of services and manufactured goods, running of current account deficits and systemic lending on the international market. This structure is well-established: such an economic, trading and financial model has prevailed since the colonial days and is largely acknowledged by the international economic literature. What instead represents a controversial position is the claim that governments of Western countries do not have plans in place to assist Africa evolving from this situation. More radical versions of such a claim include the idea that the West purposefully misleads developing countries' economic, financial and trading policies for its own benefit.[21] These claims rely, by and large, on the analyses of existing international agreements and ongoing negotiations on issues relating to the international financial and monetary system, trade and capital liberalization, property right regimes, foreign investments and ODA. To assess them, it is necessary to verify whether Western foreign and development policies in G90 countries are promoting or hampering those same developmental public policies that in the past have been successfully adopted by Western countries and NIEs.

Ideally, a pro-development international policy should allow developing countries to accumulate capital by reaping maximum benefits from primary products export, facilitate seed investments and technology transfer in progressively more dynamic sectors of the economy, and allow developing countries' manufactured products and services the opportunity to earn hard currency in highly profitable OECD markets. Are these principles guiding Western policies in Africa?

2.1 *International Trade*

Throughout modern and contemporary history, relatively powerful countries have sought to guarantee a safe supply of cheap primary products, while expanding market access for their services and manufactured products—this, as was argued in Chap. 3, appears to be the single most important international economic policy that OECD countries have used to grow their own economies. The world order established after World War II marked no relevant discontinuity: developed countries have continued pushing for market access in third countries, while securing their supplies of cheap primary products.

Translated into policies, this has meant that countries with highly competitive manufacturing industries and service providers have promoted an international normative regime that forbids or limits other countries to adopt (1) import duties or non-tariffs barriers, such as regulatory legislation and quota, on services or manufactured goods; (2) export tariffs on commodities and raw materials; (3) cartels among commodity exporters; (4) public subsidies to national manufacturing industries. Such agenda is pursued through different modalities: multilateral negotiations within the GATT/WTO institutional framework, bilateral and regional negotiations aimed at establishing preferential trade agreements (PTAs), including free trade agreements (FTAs), as well as diplomatic pressures, economic coercion and unilateral military threats.[22] At the same time, these same countries seek to protect their domestic and international market shares in those sectors where they have little capacity or competitive edge vis-à-vis foreign competitors, also by resorting to public subsidies and trade defence measures.

Since 1945, developed countries have invested a tremendous amount of efforts in pursuing the neoliberal agenda. These diplomatic efforts paid off: between 1947 and 2001, the GATT/WTO held eight successful trade liberalization rounds before getting stuck on the Doha Development Round, with the result of cutting down manufactured goods tariffs on a most favoured nation (MFN) basis, from an average of over 50 % to between 5 % and 10 %. When the multilateral liberalization process began trailing in the 1990s, OECD countries pursued the same agenda on a regional and bilateral basis, an endeavour that sent skyrocketing the number of new preferential trade agreements (PTAs): between 1995 and 2005, WTO members notified an average of 20 PTA per year, with many more bilateral and regional agreements currently negotiated in all parts of the world. The share of world trade now covered by PTAs is well over 50 % (Manger 2009).

PTAs are negotiated between all countries; analysts estimate, however, that most of them are sealed between developed countries and developing countries.[23] This trend clearly shows in the lists of EU and USA PTAs.

Brussels has concluded Association Agreements with most of its Mediterranean partners, which will likely lead to a Mediterranean free trade area[24]; established an Association Agreement with the Central American region, which effectively establishes a free trade area between the EU and six Central American countries[25]; established bilateral FTAs with Colombia, Peru, Mexico, South Africa and Ukraine. An even larger number of agreements, covering most of the developing world, is under negotiation: the Economic Partnerships Agreements (EPAs) with ACP countries, aiming at establishing full FTAs between the EU and a total of 76 developing countries divided into seven regions[26]; regional negotiations aimed at establishing a free trade area with the Association of South-East Asian Nations (ASEAN), currently stalled[27]; regional negotiations aimed at establishing a free trade area with the *Mercado Común del Sur* (MERCOSUR)[28]; bilateral negotiations with India; and contacts to reopen negotiations with Ecuador and Bolivia.[29]

The USA has free trade agreements in force with 20 countries, including 13 countries classified as middle-income by the WB, but none with any Sub-Saharan African country.[30] It has also promoted Trade and Investment Framework Agreements (TIFAs) in 47 countries/regions of the world, mostly pertaining to the group of WB-classified mid-income countries.[31] While falling short of creating any PTA, TIFAs establish, nonetheless, bilateral institutions ("Council on Trade and Investments") tasked with holding "consultations on specific trade and investment matters of interest to the Parties and the enhancement of trade and investment flows [and the] removal of impediments to such trade and investment flows".[32] The USA has also ratified bilateral investment treaties (BITs) with 42 countries, mostly pertaining to WB-classified low-income and middle-income countries. BITs impose favourable conditions for American investments abroad (ostensibly on a bilateral basis; the FDI flow between these countries is, however, largely unidirectional); as such, they are only accessorily related to the free trade agenda and will be treated in the FDI section. A number of OECD-backed proposals that never saw the light of the day equally testify to the continuous efforts that developed countries have dedicated to advancing the free-trade agenda with low and mid-income countries.[33]

What do these agreements entail or promote? By and large, a lower level of tariff and non-tariff barriers on manufactured goods and services, sometimes on a fully reciprocal basis, sometimes through concessional terms that typically grant a longer transition period to the weaker party. The final result remains, however, the same for all ratifying parties: over the mid-term, both developing and developed countries are asked to liberalize.

Consideration on OECD Trade Policies

Advocates of trade liberalization largely rely on neoliberal theories to argue that open competition leads to economic specialization and optimization in the allocation of resources. On that basis, OECD governments maintain that opening up to international trade is intended to allow people to access higher-quality and cheaper products, thus pushing inefficient producers out of the market, while substituting them with competitive companies.

On the basis of pure economic modelling, the theory holds: looking at the Ricardian model, the reform creates value for the consumers by taking rents away from inefficient producers. However, implementation has always been problematic, since the “inefficient producers” are often the very same companies that provide jobs to the consumers. In many real-life cases, inefficient national producers have not been substituted by efficient national producers: their market shares have simply gone to leaner and more efficient foreign companies. Even where alternative jobs have been created through inward FDI, these have remained dependent upon the strategies of foreign MNCs or SMEs with several alternative investment opportunities and a set of interests purely driven by corporate logic.

Among well-known examples quoted in the literature, Malawi and Zambia have vigorously pursued the Structural Adjustment Program (SAP) agenda promoted by international institutions from early 1980s onwards, till becoming two of the most liberalized economies in the region. Trade liberalization allowed these countries to achieve some gains in non-traditional export earnings, but these were not enough to offset losses given by the contraction of output of previously protected industries (de Córdoba and Laird 2006, p. 92). The World Bank also admitted that Zambia “[…] saw significant progress in the area of structural reforms during the 1990s but full macroeconomic stability and sustainable growth proved elusive. All the social and education indicators deteriorated. Infant mortality rates, adult illiteracy, malnutrition and poverty remained very high” (Jaffee et al. 2003, p. 8). Allegations that trade liberalization hit particularly hard among labour found confirmation in numerous studies, including econometric analysis suggesting that in Ghana “[…] a decrease in an industry tariff tends to be associated with lower welfare being earned by households employed in the industry […] this negative effect of trade liberalization is disproportionately greater for low-skilled labour households” (Ackah 2006). Econometric analysis aimed at investigating the interrelationship between trade liberalization, employment and poverty alleviation in Nigeria during the period 1985–2010, found that the overall expansion of the Nigerian economy was accompanied by a rapid rise in unemployment and poverty (Balogun and Dauda 2012).

The neoliberal model maintains that lack of open trade contributes in keeping Africa in the grip of poverty. The proof of this would be the fact that Africa and other G90 countries are overprotected when compared to OECD countries and NIEs. Current data confirms that G90 countries have relatively closed economies: developing countries maintain higher tariff rates than developed countries: the simple average Most Favoured Nation (MFN) tariff rate for 43 African countries is 13.21 % on non-agricultural products and 12.83 % on all products, trade weighted (WTO 2010).[34] This tariff level is sensibly higher than what is applied by developed countries today: the EU's simple average MFN tariff rate on non-agricultural products stands at 4 %, while its trade weighted average on all products is 3.2 %. Other OECD countries apply equally low average tariff levels: the USA stands at 3.3 % on non-agricultural products and 2.1 % on all products; Japan at 2.5 % and 2.7 %, respectively (WTO 2010).[35]

Comparing today's African trade protection levels to today's European trade protection levels is, however, a misleading exercise: Africa has today the same stock of capital, technology and expertise that Europe had centuries ago. A more reasonable comparison should look at tariff levels between Africa today and the industrialization phases of OECD countries. The average tariff rate on imported products during the UK's early stages of development (1820) was between 45 % and 55 %; in the USA, between 1875 and 1913, the average tariff index has consistently stayed above 40 %; in France, it went from roughly 15 % in 1875 to 30 % in 1931; in Japan, it grew from 5 % in 1875 to 30 % in 1913 (H.-J. Chang 1996). As a matter of fact, most OECD countries during their industrialization phase maintained substantially higher tariff rates than Africa has today.

Does this mean that Africa would automatically gain from introducing higher tariff and non-tariff protections on imported goods and services? Not necessarily, and perhaps not on the short run—neoclassic economics has a number of proven arguments against high tariff protection. For example, tariffs make the domestic market more lucrative, thus creating an extra-incentive for national companies to concentrate on national buyers rather than seeking hard currency through exports. Openness, by leading to lower prices, better information and newer technologies, often has, under specific circumstances, a catalyst role in promoting growth. In fact, comprehensive reviews of studies on the link between trade liberalization and economic growth have concluded that the literature is largely uninformative and admitted a significant gap between the conclusions derived from theory and the "facts" on the ground (Rodriguez and Rodrik 2001).

However, history shows that all of today's developed countries had consistently stronger protection levels than Africa has today. There is no regression or algorithm in the neoclassic toolbox that can explain why such a strategy could have worked in the 600 years of economic policies reviewed in Chap. 3 and cannot possibly work, *mutatis mutandis*, for Africa today.

There is, on the other hand, strong evidence that corporations based in OECD countries invest large financial amounts in convincing their political representatives and the public opinion of the contrary, suggesting, for example, that taking down tariff and non-tariff barriers in G90 countries is in the very interest of these economies. The most influential among these economic actors are organized in transnational pressure groups, including the *European Roundtable of Industrialists* (ERI), the *European Employers Federation* (UNICE) or the *Competitiveness Advisory Group* (CAG), which brings together European-based MNCs with turnovers above 1 billion USD. In America, the *USA Industry Coordinating Group*, the *USA Chamber of Commerce* and the New York-based *Global Business Forum* have proved powerful players in lobbying the USA administration. More specialized international business organizations have been instrumental in shaping the global regulatory agenda within specific sectors; this is the case of the *International Federation of Pharmaceutical Manufacturers Associations* among others. The sophistication level of OECD corporate interest groups has reached the point to which they set up front groups which present themselves as NGOs rather than as business organizations: *Consumers for World Trade*; *Citizens for Sensible Control of Acid Rain* and the *National Wetland Coalition* have been presented in the specialized literature as puppet NGOs effectively representing the interests of, respectively, a pro-WTO industry coalition, a coal and electricity industry front, and a heterogeneous coalition of USA oil companies and real estate developers (Braithwaite and Drahos 2000, p. 489). EU and USA-based MNCs have also created ad-hoc industry coalitions to push for the inclusion of punctual issues during GATT/WTO negotiations. In several instances, well-organized interest groups have even managed to exert direct rather than indirect influence on their political representatives: the USA State Department has often allowed members of the corporate world to constitute the backbone of their WTO delegations. The PR industry in Washington and Brussels caters to the needs and interests of smaller or less organized players, providing services ranging from "lobbying consultancy" to "perception management" among public decision-makers. Many of these public affairs firms also work for "heterodox" interests—including humanitarian organizations and trade unions; their services are, however, mostly hired by corporate interests.

The USA corporate world reportedly spent 1.86 billion USD in 2011 alone to lobby the USA government.[36] A European-based NGO laments that the current European regulatory environment in matter of lobbying—which is based on a voluntarily register of activity—is completely inadequate as it reflects unrealistically low lobbying budgets: in 2008, the 50 top European-based MNCs have only declared a total of 14 million euros in lobbying expenses. This figure is incompatible with the profile of these companies in their own industry sectors, their overall presence in Brussels circles and their lobbying expenditure in the USA.[37]

2.2 *International Investments*

Data in Chap. 4 suggest that oil and mining play the lion's share among OECD FDI in Africa. Oil and mining reserves represent assets with a terrific potential to kick start or further boost development; countries like the United Arab Emirates (UAE), Qatar and Venezuela are also examples of how oil resources can be used to successfully diversify and grow national economies. Other Gulf States—including Saudi Arabia, Bahrain and Kuwait—have been less successful in diversifying their economy but have at least ensured a consistent and well managed flow of revenues deriving from oil resources.[38] In Africa, Botswana, Namibia and South Africa in their early days represent relevant examples of how mineral endowments can be exploited in the interest of the national economy at large.

However, for most parts of Africa, mineral resources have represented a curse rather than a blessing, fuelling civil wars and social unrest: Sierra Leone, Liberia, Central African Republic, Chad, Ivory Coast, Nigeria, Angola, Democratic Republic of Congo, Republic of Congo, Zimbabwe, Uganda and Sudan are all cases in point. Revising the political and social implications of mineral wealth is a task that goes beyond the scope of this book—besides, the issue has already been extensively researched (Cilliers and Dietrich 2000; Ross 2012). This review will instead try to understand whether OECD development policies have favoured an investment regime that allowed Africa to fully harness the potential benefits deriving from operations on its soil.

Just as for trade, the history of past FDI policies traces a roadmap of what is "good" FDI from the host country's perspective. A basic observation relates to the fact that, during the early stages of their development, all successful economies have (1) specialized in attracting FDI geared at setting up manufacturing and service capacity rather than primary-sector activities; (2) maintained refining capacities even if foreign capital was needed to launch oil and mineral exploitation; (3) discriminated between national and international investments, applying more stringent conditions on the latter than on the former; (4) moved towards a relaxation and removal of these rules—and even promotion of an international ban on them—as soon as their economy allowed them to move from a "defensive" into an "aggressive" investment position.

As detailed in Chap. 3, since the early stages of their development, OECD countries and NIEs have put in place legal provisions aimed at reaping maximum benefits from foreign investments: in certain sectors these worked through plain bans on investments in sensitive sectors, while in others the hosting government requested joint ventures or ceilings on foreign shares. Hosting countries also had informal mechanisms aimed at preventing hostile acquisitions and takeovers by foreign investors. SOEs played a vital role in advancing the most technology-intensive sectors; when these same companies were privatized later on, the state often maintained a controlling stake, either directly or through friendly shareholders. Where the investments were led by foreign entrepreneurs, the local government maintained significant minority shares. Other strategies aimed at favouring national interests included provisions on corporate governance: national citizenship as a condition to sit on the boards of directors and withdrawal of the right to vote to all foreign, non-resident shareholders. Other rules included performance requirements explicitly geared at maintaining a healthy balance of payments, including minimum export requirements, local content requirements, foreign exchange balancing requirements and ceilings on licensing fees. Hosting governments ensured that FDI entailed technology and expertise transfer to local businesses, either directly or through indirect spillovers. Some countries, including Taiwan, explicitly required foreign investors to assist local suppliers in upgrading their technological and competitive hedge. This roadmap is in stark contrast with what OECD countries have consistently asked from G90 countries since the late 1970s onwards, at least in the major African investment sectors: mining, oil and gas, and agriculture and fisheries.

Mining, Oil and Gas

Since the 1980s, the WB and IMF have pushed for deregulation in the African mining sector under Structural Adjustment Program (SAP) reforms. This represented a major shift with respect to the traditional World Bank's support to activities of exploration and production towards the privatization of SOEs. The normative effects of these programmes were evident: the UN estimates that between the beginning of the 1980s and 1995, 35 countries had published new mining codes with strengthened contractual stability, favourable regimes for the incorporation of foreign companies, reduced tax levels, eased migration laws for expatriate workers, tax exemption for imported capital goods, strong concessions in profit repatriation and free access to foreign exchange (UNCTAD 2005, p. 41).

Although these measures are often considered "monolithic" reform packages aimed at improving the sector's efficiency and streamlining FDI processes, they often contain regulations that are very different in nature. For it is one thing to ensure certainty of the investment by providing guarantees against expropriation, and another thing to decide the corporate structure of investing entities or the fiscal regime applying to them: the former lays essential conditions for FDI to happen; the latter establishes how the cake is to be divided between investors and investees. It is the opinion of many economists that IFIs have endorsed investment codes that heavily advantaged investors over investees. For example, UNCTAD reports that the 1998 Tanzania code allowed for 100 % foreign ownership, unrestricted repatriation of profits and capital, waiver of any requirement for local procurement of goods and services and a pre-established maximum royalty rate of 3 %. In Ghana, the mining companies were allowed to retain, on average, about 58 % of their export earnings in offshore accounts.[39] None of these conditions would have been acceptable to any of the countries part of post-war success stories: not Singapore, which aggressively attracted FDI only in high-technology content industries hand-picked by the government; not China—which for a long time only allowed joint ventures, while enforcing strict conditions on the purchase of local inputs; certainly not Taiwan or South Korea, which barred foreign access altogether in a number of industrial sectors considered strategic and left to their own SOEs, while imposing local content and subcontracting rules to allowed FDI. These governments also had regulations limiting the repatriation of profits accruing to foreign firms: a trickle-down economy already has slim chances of contributing towards social development, but these chances are brought to nil if foreign companies are allowed a full repatriation of their profits and expatriate wages.

The result of SAP-induced mineral-sector reforms was a shift from the development of partially autonomous national industries—with all the implications in terms of control on the value-adding components of the productive processes, employment policies and management of resources—towards a strategy aimed at generating tax revenues by privatizing national enterprises. In the IFIs' narrative, tax regimes were to become the central piece of the reform: against the extremely favourable investment environment that was set up for international FDI, hosting governments were meant to receive a "fair" slice of the increased revenues accruing to foreign investors (World Bank 1992).

The literature dealing with the overall efficiency of new tax regimes reveals, however, that African governments have not been able to optimize mining tax revenues—not even during boom periods.[40] According to these studies, this was due to excessively generous tax subsidies and to the high incidence of tax avoidance by mining companies through a number of techniques, including secret mining contracts, corporate M&A and "creative" accounting mechanisms. This fully reflects in the BoP of most African mining countries, which sensibly worsens in the 1980s.

SAPs-induced mining sector reforms also did little to improve the loose linkages between the mineral industries and the rest of the economy. A far-telling indication is provided by the fact that none of these reforms touched upon the all-important issue of domestic processing, which has the potential to add value, foster local use of the mineral sector output and limit the drainage of potential gains away from Africa. After the SAP reforms, most raw ore and crude oil continued being exported for processing or refinement elsewhere; in 2011, the continent's total active distillation capacity was about 3317 thousand barrels daily against a production of 8804 thousand barrels daily: only 37 % of African crude oil is refined in Africa. The same proportion (refinement/production) for USA, Eurasia (except Russia) and Latin America stands, respectively, at 226 %; 268 % and 89.2 % (BP 2012).[41] Higher percentages indicate control of the downstream sector ("manufactured" sector): refining more oil would put Africa in a stronger market position and help African oil producing countries to exit the awkward situation of suffering from fuel shortages.[42]

SAP reforms, if anything, worsened the situation: out of the 48 African oil refineries existing in Africa until 2005, most of them had been established in the 1970s and 1980s, with reportedly only two built in the period 1990–2005, in Sudan and Egypt. On the contrary, market liberalization in the refining sector put further strain on small refineries, pushing some of them out of business (AfDB 2009, p. 50). SAPs reforms envisaged no systematic approach to technology and expertise transfer; as a consequence, the extractive industry continues importing foreign mechanical equipments along with the technical, financial and managerial services needed to run wells and mines.

Chapter 4 suggested that several factors likely contributed in placing intrinsic limits to the development potentialities of economies relying on mining and oil. Commodity volatility is a notorious problem marring the mineral sector. Boom years in international commodity prices have allowed exceptional expansions in the past: Zambia's GDP in 1969 exceeded that of South Korea and Brazil, largely thanks to a bull mineral market. The other side of the story is that slump periods have entailed diminishing margins, foreclosing operations and growing debts—as it happened during the 1980s and the late 1990s. These bear waves have truly destructive effects on the non-diversified economies of oil-producing countries, in Africa as elsewhere: Saudi Arabia's GDP per capita shrunk from 16,650 USD in 1981 to 6960 USD in 2000 while the 2014/15 slump in oil prices forced the oil Kingdom to engineer a major overhaul of its economy.[43]

These problems are inherent to the mining sector; their economic mechanisms work independently from the actors involved and the profit-sharing structure between investors and investees. Since the bull–bear cycle in commodities is well known to economists and politicians, a meaningful way for the primary sector to contribute towards long-term and sustainable national growth is to use its capital-generating capacity during boom years to nurture countercyclical economic activities. Another way is to create market imperfections aimed at maximizing profit margins in the upstream petroleum sector, as countries pertaining to the Organization of the Petroleum Exporting Countries (OPEC) have done with crude oil.[44] Countercyclical economic activities have never been proposed by donor countries; where economic diversification in developing countries has worked, including in the UAE and Qatar, this came as a result of purely endogenous policies and home-grown development strategies. Oil-consuming countries have obviously done whatever was in their capacity to break or weaken cartels among mineral and oil-producing countries. The striking element to retain is the fact that Western ODA policies have done little to address the problem of revenue instability; on the contrary, SAPs have pushed mining countries in relying on increasing mineral exports, arguing that comparative advantages and free trade were key to access foreign markets and hard currency. This argument does not make any basic distinction between primary commodities and manufactured export, nor does it differentiate between short-term reliance on commodity export as a *mean* towards development into higher-profit products and commodity export as an *end* in itself.

Agriculture and Fisheries

Agriculture and fisheries represent the second sector by inward FDI size in Africa. Relatively high-value added activities in this sector can result from two different dynamics (1) exporting commodities with intrinsic higher market value than agricultural staples/crops: these include fresh vegetables, flowers, fish, seafood, exotic and dry fruits and; (2) processing raw agricultural products and fisheries and exporting the final product to consumer markets. In the 1980s, a number of African countries successfully diversified their production towards agro-goods with intrinsic higher values; although there are indications of a positive FDI role played in this sector, it is difficult to find relevant statistics (UNCTAD 1999).[45]

Concurrently, it remains to be ascertained whether most FDI going towards agriculture is still concentrated in the production of raw goods—including crops and staples—which arc subsequently processed elsewhere. FDI in the processed agricultural sector of the market, and particularly in products earning higher profits such as tobacco, chocolate and sugar, is still limited in quantity and destination. Not only has the processing level of agro-food products remained low, but UNCTAD also laments that in Africa, as elsewhere across the developing world, a few MNCs purchase from a multitude of local producers by simple contractual agreements and without any structured business cooperation model. The number of players in the agro-food industry is currently shrinking, with fewer firms controlling the purchase, processing and distribution phases (UNCTAD 2005).[46]

Such a structure, with few strong and well-organized purchasers, on the one side, and fragmented suppliers, on the other, has been detrimental to the bargaining capacity of the latter, which have seen their profit margins shrinking since the 1980s (UNCTAD 2005). This situation is not a casual development: SAPs have asked for the dismantlement of national marketing boards that previously negotiated commodity prices on behalf of national growers, thus, effectively shielding producers from divide-and-rule tactics. These developments have resulted in an asymmetry in the production chain, with enhanced bargaining power in the downstream end (processing and distribution, in the hands of MNCs) and reduced power in the upstream end (local producers). As a consequence, agricultural producers have been moved closer to being classical price-takers, being unable to do much aside from accepting market prices.

Considerations on OECD FDI Policies

Were "market logic" reasons solid enough to justify SAPs reforms as purported by IFIs policy papers? Likely not: UNCTAD carries out an "if not" scenario, arguing that less MNCs-friendly policies in the mining sector would have limited inward FDI, maintained relatively low production, reduced global extraction levels and, eventually, caused an upsurge in commodity prices. This would have enticed investors and led them to reconsider the profitability of their business ventures despite the lack of business-friendly regimes. A second "if not" scenario could be carried out with countries that choose a different regulatory environment: countries that did not undergo mineral and agricultural reforms along the lines suggested by the IMF and the WB, including UAE, Russia and Venezuela. These countries did not show lower profit margins or higher inequality rates than commodity-rich African countries.

Since the mid-2000s, many low- and mid-income countries felt they had large room for improving their stakes in inward FDI and sought a new regulatory approach. Several of them have implemented divestment requirements, increased government stakes in key mining companies and raised—to different degrees—taxes and royalties in the extractive industries, sometimes following negotiations with the mining business associations (UNCTAD 2012, p. 90). This trend has been on the rise, fuelled by governments' desire to benefit from the soaring global commodity prices and a general dissatisfaction with the SAP-induced FDI regime.[47] Newly introduced measures are part of a global trend that touches African countries like Ghana, Zambia, Central African Republic, Eritrea and Zimbabwe, but also spans beyond the black continent: Russia, Colombia, Guatemala, Honduras, Peru, Argentina, Chile and Venezuela have all moved away from SAP FDI requirements.[48] More radical measures undertaken so far include nationalization and expropriation.[49] Other signs of malaise with SAPs in these countries include the collapse of the Doha Development Agenda (DDA) negotiations, as well as cold reactions towards European efforts in pushing region-to-region FTAs through the European Partnership Agreements (EPAs).

Is Africa bound to automatically benefit from similar counter-Washington Consensus policies? Just as it is simplistic to group all SAPs-induced reforms in all countries under the same umbrella and put a label on them, so it would be reductionist to label the "new course" as exclusively positive or negative. Since the late 1990s, Zimbabwe squandered its foreign reserves in botched economic policies and lavish public expenses, while managing to scare off most of its foreign investors and local white entrepreneurs through a land seizure programme; it unlikely represents a successful example of counter-liberal policies. Mozambique, on the contrary, had a way more balanced approach to FDI reforms, which, combined with the discovery of new gas and mineral resources, bodes well for its future public revenues. What emerges is, therefore, the impression that debates around SAP reforms in the FDI sector are unnecessarily politicized: historical successful cases of FDI have been extremely pragmatic and unmistakably point at the plain necessity of strong developmental governments, able to negotiate favourable international deals on their national economies' behalf.

3 Washington Consensus Demystified

In the 1990s, the trade and investment policies reviewed above were identified as part of the "Washington Consensus" or "Structural Adjustment Program" package. This included, according to the American economist John Williamson, ten policy areas geared at achieving macroeconomic stability, increased FDI, increased trade and—eventually—increased economic growth (Williamson 1990).[50] The term became extraordinarily popular in the following years, particularly among those of its detractors who used it as an umbrella concept for free market fundamentalism. As usual, having a much-publicized tag attached to a complex phenomenon does not help in its understanding. Much confusion and prejudice has arisen on the substance of these policies, which should be addressed before proceeding to a general evaluation of OECD policies in developing countries.

When the term was coined in 1989, "Washington Consensus" indicated a set of policies that had been used since the late 1970s by global IFIs in dealing with countries in need of their assistance. However, the term identified policies whose origin stretched way back in history. We have seen how, since achieving a strong competitive position, today's OECD countries have been interested in accessing international markets, liberalizing international capital flows, stabilizing the macroeconomic and political environments in the invested economies, and limiting the tax burdens and redistribution policies in whichever country they were operating.

The strategies beyond these policies were even older: pushing commodity-led economies to build logistic infrastructure, accept foreign investments in the primary sector and increase exports in these same sectors essentially meant to access cheaper primary goods. We have seen how the OECD "import raw and export manufactured" strategy has long existed; scholarly texts in the Western economic tradition refer to it since the fourteenth century at least. This strategy is a simple variation of the "buy cheap—sell expensive" principle that has informed trade since it was invented. Incentives towards deregulation and privatization essentially meant the opportunity of getting a foot into highly profitable foreign industries—including the utility sectors. Looking at the history of economic praxis, we know that efforts at acquiring stakes in profitable and strategically important sectors of foreign economies were common since the existence of early joint-stock companies in the thirteenth century. Similar policies had long been sought by state actors in their own foreign policies. Several Western European countries adopted them since the Renaissance: the USA emulated Europe from the end of the eighteenth century onwards, while Japan began at the end of the nineteenth century—earlier in the chapter, we have seen how the institutional structure of the IFIs entrusts these very same countries with setting the trade and finance normative agenda. Seen from this perspective, the Washington Consensus simply represented a repackaging of centuries-old practices.

Since the early 2000s, the Washington Consensus terminology has been progressively phased out in governmental and academic circles, while several of the "made-in-IFIs" concepts that contributed in identifying them have decayed. Some authors have started talking of a post-Washington consensus: we do not talk anymore—or not as much—about "liberalization"; "deregulation"; "privatization"; "decentralization of wage bargaining"; "relaxation of labour market regulations"; or "reduction of unemployment benefits". We have instead assisted to the rising of a new vocabulary: "civil society", "social capital", "governance", "transparency", "new international economic architecture", "institution-building", "safety nets"—but also the "human security"; "sustainable development"; "ownership"; and "partnership" concepts seen in the world of ODA; today, they all form part of what has been labelled the "post-Washington consensus".

Does this mean that the substance of OECD policies has changed? This is unlikely. Just as "Washington Consensus" policies were not born in the late 1970s, most they unlikely died when IFIs started introducing the "Poverty Reduction Strategy Papers" (PRSPs) approach. Writing in the sixteenth century, British author and politician Henry Wotton called diplomats "men of virtue sent to lie abroad for the good of their country". *Mutatis mutandis*, the concept remains relevant to today's public diplomacy. The reader will find stable guidance in her interpretation of IFIs and OECD countries' development policy position papers, by keeping in mind that rhetoric is part of what International Organizations do for a living. Many research centres and public affairs agencies are on MNCs and governments' payrolls; these organizations work in that window-dressing business that is sometimes referred to as the "public affairs" industry. These actors are often better prepared and better financed than those scrutinizing their policies, including genuinely independent civil society organizations, think tanks and academics. There is no conspiracy-theory pathos in the simple remark that it would be naive to believe that the ontological essence and normative ethos of the Washington Consensus has changed just because the wording that describes it has changed.

To be sure, PRSPs introduced some changes, to the extent that, *within the scope of ODAs projects and loans*, social spending has gained relevance, while market conditionalities attached to them were loosened. However, institutional and corporate actors remain capable of pursuing their objectives through multiple venues. Limiting conditionalities on concessional multilateral lending or using more development money for social projects tells us of a change of direction in the use of ODA money—which we estimated to represent 4 % to 6 % of financial exchanges between the West and Africa. Negotiations on items affecting the remaining 96 % to 94 % of financial exchanges are done on other items and through other institutional settings: WTO, bilateral PTAs, Paris and London clubs negotiations, bilateral and regional international agreements on trade, investments and migration, multilateral institutions and so on. What we see in these fields is little change. Discussions around the PRSPs and the so-called post-Washington consensus positions they allegedly reflect, have—if anything—strengthened the faulty assumption that the public should concentrate on the 4 % to 6 % of West–Africa exchanges, while forgetting about the core of their economic, financial and trade relations.

4 An Evaluation of OECD International Policies in Africa

Have "Washington Consensus" policies—before, during and after the term was coined—been detrimental for Africa? These policies were inspired by economic interests in OECD countries; does that automatically turn them into "bad policies" for the others? Just like a seller does not automatically harm a buyer simply because he pressures him into a purchase, or a bachelor does not automatically harm a woman because of his insisting advances, so SAPs did not automatically harm the countries that accepted them. A few of them found these policies quite fitting with the problems they had: in the 1980s, several Latin American countries—including Brazil and Argentina—had uncompetitive national manufacturers extracting rents from their overprotected markets (Baer 1972). Several of these governments did have structural budget deficiencies, highly inefficient welfare spending and currency instability; these countries did benefit from some years of "shock therapy". However, these were experiences limited in time and space: they hardly provided a model for mid or long-term development. Countries that indulged too long in these policies approached the collapse—including Argentina and Peru in the early 2000s. On the other hand, countries that moved out of the neoliberal paradigm, including Brazil, found a more viable path. The point is that there is no discernible pattern because SAPs—as well as the larger policy categories that encompass them, including ODA and foreign economic policies—are shaped around the interests of the countries promoting them (the "donors" of ODA) and not around the interests of the countries accepting them (the "beneficiaries" of ODA).

Many countries found SAPs—as well as comparable economic policies introduced through the ODA conditionality mechanisms—to be counterproductive, even when measured against their self-imposed goals. The stated rationale of SAP-induced policies was to accelerate growth, even at the expenses of inequality and poor service delivery. The logic was to react to low productivity suffered by national companies, remedy the lack of investment capacity to keep up with international competition, and expand primary exports; there is, however, evidence that these results were not achieved. The macroeconomic fundamentals of G90 countries have not improved; on the contrary, BoP imbalances worsened in the 1980s and 1990s, GDP per capita shrank and trade further moved away from the "virtuous cycle" model. At the same time, there is strong evidence as to the fact that, while the world economy was growing at an average of 2 % to 3 % a year, large OECD-based corporations were typically growing by 8 % to 10 % annually.

Washington Consensus policies were also met with increasing hostility worldwide—first in the developing world and, subsequently, in OECD countries. In developing countries, anti-liberalization manifestations started in the 1980s, when SAP-induced reforms cut down welfare assistance. In the Western world, a turning point came in November 1999, when job losses among blue-collar workers and concerns over the developing world brought 50,000 workers, students, environmentalists and human rights advocates to protest against the WTO Ministerial in Seattle. The following years saw the world public opinion passing from a general disinterest towards OECD-led trade negotiations towards an increasing awareness of the economic consequences entailed by the neoliberal agenda. Albeit for different reasons, there is today a heterogeneous coalition of people opposing further trade liberalization: for the right or the wrong, American steelworkers losing jobs and Ghanaian peasants losing social welfare protest against the same economic processes, perceived as transferring value from labour towards capital.

5 Contextualizing ODA: What Is It Really About?

If it is the case—if OECD foreign policy efforts are geared at capturing the profits of those 94 % to 96 % of financial flows, why do they engage in ODA then? Would not such behaviour be schizophrenic—giving with one hand and taking back with the other? More generally, why do citizens of sovereign states spontaneously decide to renounce part of their public budgets in favour of people in faraway countries? A number of studies have posited such a question as a puzzling phenomenon in international relations: if states live in a self-help system dominated by logics of relative power, why do they decide to engage in spontaneous and unilateral cooperative behaviour—for example, by providing donations for which they do not receive anything in exchange?

Some elements collected so far already provide a partial answer. Even if ODA does not incentivize structural change, it still contributes in saving and improving lives in beneficiary countries; this is sufficient to create a moral justification among donor countries' citizens. Other elements help put Western aid into perspective: the 4–6 % of total quantifiable exchanges between Western and African countries channelled in ODA are partially recovered through the mechanisms discussed in the previous chapters, including tied aid and public diplomacy. The ODA industry also maintains a professional community of over 60,000 people, mostly OECD citizens, who have by now acquired their own class interests, social identities and agenda. The most sophisticated mechanism, however, still needs to be discussed, and is the one that allows avoiding conflicts of interest between ODA and donor countries—thus permitting rich countries to exercise charity without building competition. Such mechanism can be best understood by looking at the content of development projects as well as the conditions attached to budget support.

A close look at ODA by typology of intervention shows an interesting phenomenon: a very limited percentage of this money is channelled towards the setting up of manufacturing or non-public services capacity, and almost none is invested with the intention to strengthen the capacity to export capital goods, finished goods or private professional services. Most of the projects are instead concentrated in public service delivery, distribution of consumable goods and infrastructure development. Where there is support for productive activities, this is usually restrained to the primary sector, typically with a view to increase commodity exports or to supply local and unprofitable markets with low-capital and low-technology intensive products.

Let us take World Bank's development activities as generally representative of the ODA activities performed by the community of donors: out of the ten fields and 73 subfields chosen by the WB to classify its projects, only one field and five subfields deal with manufacturing industries.[51] At closer inspection, there is, however, little that relates to the setting up of productive capacities. As a matter of example, the first three projects in the subfield "general industry and trade sector" are: (1) national initiative for human development project aimed at improving access to participatory local governance mechanisms, basic infrastructures, social services and economic opportunities in Morocco; (2) a loan to support the Brazilian state of Bahia's programme to reduce social inequality; and a (3) project in Cape Verde aimed at providing vocational training and improving the efficiency and transparency in the use of public resources.[52] The subfield "agro-industry marketing and trade" sports among its first three entries: (1) a rural livelihood project in the Indian province of Bihar, aiming, *inter alia*, at federating the capacity of the women managed community, improving health and nutrition, social protection, rural employment and agriculture through demand-side interventions; (2) an agriculture productivity programme in West Africa, aimed at enhancing the generation, dissemination and adoption of agricultural technology (also by facilitating access to "improved genetic material"—no mention of the agro-processing industry); and (3) an agricultural development policy operation in Ghana, aiming at improving on-farm productivity, skills training and education in agricultural sciences and farm management, market and value chain development, irrigated agriculture and other infrastructure services.[53]

The classification of these same projects by theme does not enlist "industrialization" among its 11 theme categories.[54]

All these projects likely have a positive social impact—but they hardly contribute in generating economic activities and tax revenues. They may facilitate economic growth by contributing towards the creation of enabling conditions, but they do not tackle the core issue of production. The same goes for most other projects financed by Western development agencies: the list could go through hundreds of projects that are oblivious of the historical role played by industrial production and exports in any empirical process of socio-economic development.

A second remarkable feature is the fact that some of these programmes seem to be facilitating exactly those activities that fall at risk of incentivizing "vicious cycle" dynamics seen in Chap. 3. A number of these projects are aimed at fostering the extractive industry by supporting beneficiary governments in creating policies and institutional frameworks that can promote a process of rapid and large-scale FDI in the oil and mining sectors. Incentivizing FDI in the primary sector is not bad in itself: the development of oil extraction and mining has been an enabling condition for capital accumulation in many developing countries. However, none of the ODA-financed projects in the energy sector envisage the setting up of an extractive or processing capacity owned by the beneficiary country.[55] Nor, for that matter, do they envisage capacity development and coordination among oil and mining producing countries for the setting up of an international regulatory framework or a common industrial development plan—two tools that have proved extremely efficient in the past.

It is universally recognized that developing countries lack skills in dealing with MNCs, including on the all-important issue of fiscal oversight; yet, no ODA project assists them in creating the necessary expertise and international coordination to extract maximum benefits from hosting FDI.

Other projects look at fostering public–private partnerships (PPP)—a lofty word covering heterogeneous economic and financial policies. As understood by many governments in low and mid-income countries, PPPs are state contributions to incentivize greenfield investments in sectors that would otherwise be considered too risky, thus, following the Asian NIEs model. However, the WB has often used PPPs for fostering brownfield investment of OECD capital in companies operating across utility sectors—the very same sectors that have usually been managed by state companies in today's NIEs and OECD countries, including the production and distribution of basic services, such as water and electricity.

World Bank projects also facilitate the processing of low-capital, low-technology manufacturing goods in export processing zones (EPZs). Just like mining, EPZs may represent a necessary step in climbing the technology ladder and an enabling condition for backward and forward integration of manufacturing activities in the hosting economy, along the EPZs and special economic zones (SEZs) strategies devised by China and India. However, there is little indication in these projects as to the existence of any progressive vision, since their finality is usually limited to building public facilities and to facilitate access to employment opportunities within the EPZs.[56] Although some of these projects allow for increased percentages of local inputs and labour, these remain at a typical modest level of 35 %, while there is no mention as to the establishment of mechanisms allowing technology and expertise spillover to local firms, or of a regulatory framework guaranteeing the hosting country with a minimum percentage of reinvested earnings on its national territory.

Why does ODA money not finance the most direct, straightforward and empirically proven way of creating productive capacity, jobs, economic growth and, ultimately, sustainable poverty reduction? The development aid industry's regulatory framework does not prevent donors from classifying as ODA any support towards the strengthening of productive capacity in the secondary and tertiary sectors. There is no international norm under WTO regulations or any other trade agreement prohibiting financial support towards industrial development in third countries. Yet, this does not happen. The EU's Country Strategy Papers (CSPs) and Multi-Annual Indicative Programmes (MIPs); the World Bank's Poverty Reduction Strategy Papers (PRSPs) and the IMF Country and Regional reports regularly mention the centrality of private sector development (PSD) as a leading force towards economic growth. Yet, there are little specifications as to the nature of involved actors, their ownership structure, the nationality of their majority shareholders and directors, their field of activity, their market and financial strategies and so on. Finding a clear OECD ODA commitment to support the national companies of beneficiary countries in producing mid- and high-value added goods and services for export towards hard-currency markets is like looking for the Holy Grail: blurred signs are everywhere, but no conclusive evidence can be found.

Instead, what can be found is clear evidence that ODA projects promoting productive activities are typically restrained to industries with limited value-added, domestic-oriented marketing strategies and limited distribution capacity. Projects promoting basic agro-food processing are, as a matter of example, financed through EU and United Nations Industrial Development Organization (UNIDO) funds across Africa: they cover activities aimed at producing conserved fish, dried fruits and vegetables, juices, milk and dairy products. Activities in a typical project include identification, sourcing and technical training on available technologies for food processing, market studies, setting up of supply networks, registration and abidance to national regulatory frameworks, training, and capacity building.[57] These projects are typically targeting local or regional distribution networks with limited production capacity; consequently, they have little chances to operate as competitive import substitutes or to develop the potential for export towards profitable OECD markets. The same fact that these projects are always financed on a small scale bears witness to the absence of any real intention to develop an endogenous agro-processing industry with strong potential for competition with OECD agro-industrial and food conglomerates.

Neither the World Bank nor the European Union or any other traditional donor uses—or allows the use of—ODA money for the setting up of productive capacity aimed at export, particularly in capital and technology intensive sectors. After all, the broader cooperation framework is negotiated at the Ministerial level and politicians in the Western liberal world are accountable to constituencies that have no stomach, intention or sufficient lack of common sense to voluntarily nurture aggressive competition.

Notes

1. The ten players individuated by Braithwaite and Drahos are: (1) organizations of states, (2) states, (3) international business organizations, (4) national business organizations, (5) corporations, (6) international NGOs, (7) national NGOs, (8) mass public, (9) individuals and (10) epistemic communities of actors. The 13 fields reviewed are: (1) contract and property right, (2) finance, (3) corporations and securities, (4) trade and competition, (5) labour, (6) environment, (7) nuclear safety, (8) telecommunications, (9) drugs, (10) food, (11) sea transport, (12) road transport and (13) air transport.
2. Article 1 of the Charter of the United Nations.

3. As a matter of example, the UNDP budget in 2014 amounted to 9.5 billion USD (UNDP 2013) and UNICEF budget to an yearly average of 6.21 billion USD (UNICEF 2013) over the period 2014–2017; in comparison, resources for UNCTAD programme budget in the biennium 2012–2013 were in the region of 219 million USD (UNGA 2011), while UNIDO's total operation costs budgeted for 2012–2013 were in the region of 605 million USD (455.1 million euros) (UNIDO 2011).
4. "[…] During the extensive preliminary negotiations prior to the Bretton Woods conference, officials from the participating states had already accepted the basic structure of the fund and the bank" (Schild 1995, p. 112).
5. Animosity and resentment towards quota concessions finally granted to Russia reportedly run high among members of the British delegation. All along the conference, the Soviet delegation did not take even minor steps without the green light from Moscow, thus betraying the importance that this negotiation covered for Stalin (Schild 1995, pp. 113–122).
6. In July 1944, World War II was still more than a year away from its closure—yet, frictions within the allied camp were already surfacing: the Soviets and the Anglo-Americans suspected each other of delay tactics in the war to achieve the strongest possible position on the ground at war end. The term *Cold War* was to be mentioned for the first time only one year after the Bretton Woods conference.
7. The IMF and WB have broadly similar governance systems. All countries have representation at the Board of Governors, but the management of the institutions is done by the organizations' respective executive boards. For the IMF, the Board of Governors consists of one Governor and one Alternate Governor for each of the 188 member countries; most functions are delegated to the executive board, composed by 24 full-time executive directors selected on a quota system. Currently, each of the eight countries appoints an executive director (the USA, Japan, Germany, France, the UK, China, Russian Federation and Saudi Arabia), while the remaining 16 directors represent constituencies consisting of 4– 22 countries.

   Within the WB, the Boards of Governors consist of one Governor and one Alternate Governor appointed by each of the 188 member countries; the executive board is composed by 25 executive directors (the president is the presiding officer, and ordinarily has no vote except a deciding vote in case of an equal division) selected on a different quota system: each of the five members having the largest number of shares appoints an Executive director, and the remaining members elect the other twenty Executive directors.

8. Data refer to IMF 2008 Amendment on Voice and Participation (in effect since March 3, 2011) and WB shares as assigned in August 2012.
9. Current quotas are not proportional to the relative weight of member countries' GDPs.
10. The Articles of Agreement stipulate that some decisions require a qualified majority of cast votes. The result is that decisions on 18 subjects require 85 % of the total vote, and can thus be vetoed by the USA alone; 21 other questions must be decided by a 70 % and can thus be vetoed by the five countries with the most voting power. Among the issues that the IMF executive board must resolve by qualified majority are decisions on quota size, rates of charge, exchange-rate arrangements, matters related to special drawing rights (SDRs), policies on access to IMF resources, payments to the IMF, use of the IMF's gold holdings and reserves, management of the IMF's investment accounts, publication of reports, remuneration of creditor positions, and temporary suspension of IMF operations. Thus, according to Ariel Buira, "[…] all significant decisions, those related to the size of the IMF and the use of its resources, to SDRs, gold, and the international monetary system are subject to the will of one or a few countries" (Buira 2004, p. 6).
11. All these countries, as a matter of example, after having been a large source of labour export, apply today stringent limitations on incoming labour. China, in particular, has recently toughened working visa requirements and cracked down on illegal migrants from developing countries.
12. Considering the total spending at the state and local government, the 2011 USA public spending figure goes up to 6.13 trillion USD.
13. PISA assesses the competencies of 15-year-olds in reading, mathematics and science (with a focus on reading) in 65 countries and economies (OECD 2013).
14. QS World University Ranking 2011.

15. http://ec.europa.eu/civil_service/about/figures/index_en.htm
16. With 1300 staff, the South African Department of Trade and Industry (DTI) is the best-staffed ministry of trade in Africa.
17. "[...] legal capacity is the main constraint limiting [member countries'] access to dispute settlement; more legal capacity would allow [member countries] to participate in all aspects of WTO dispute settlement". Scholarly debates on the best way to operationalize the concept of legal capacity have, so far, concentrated on three proxies (1) per capita income or GDP; (2) the number of professional staff in a country's delegation to the WTO in Geneva; and (3) existing indexes of bureaucratic quality or governmental efficiency. Beyond the academic debate, it remains beyond doubt that a country's capacity to defend its interests on the international scene is directly proportional to its wealth.
18. "[...] [countries] abundant in legal capacity are more likely to challenge anti-dumping (AD) duties brought against them, and less likely to be targeted by AD duties in the first place" (Busch et al. 2008, p. 30).
19. "[...] trade volume and economic size of the complainant and target country have consistently positive effects on the probability of dispute initiation" (Sattler and Bernauer 2008, p. 28).
20. Data were taken in the January to September period of election years (Silver, 18 November 2011). The ISM index is based on surveys of more than 300 manufacturing firms, by monitoring employment, production inventories, new orders and supplier deliveries.
21. Korean economist Ha-Joon Chang and Norwegian economist Erik Reinert pertain to this group: "Today there are certainly some people in the rich countries who preach free market and free trade to the poor countries in order to capture larger shares of the latters' markets and to pre-empt the emergence of possible competitors" (H.-J. Chang 2009, p. 16).
22. For a selection of techniques used by OECD countries in fostering globalization, see chapter 22 of Braithwaite and Drahos (2000).
23. Mark Manger estimates that out of 170 PTAs in force in 2008, 100 of them were "North-South" PTA, where a 15,000 USD GDP per capita represents the threshold between developing and developed countries (Manger 2009).

24. Association Agreements have been concluded with Libya, Algeria, Egypt, Jordan, Israel, Morocco and Tunisia, between 1995 and 2005. They grant associated countries immediate duty free access to the EU market for manufactured goods and preferential treatment for agricultural and fisheries products, while phasing out all duties for EU exports to the Mediterranean region by 2017. These agreements have replaced non-reciprocal Cooperation Agreements signed in the 1970s.
25. The EU–Central America Association Agreement covers Panama; Guatemala; Costa Rica; El Salvador; Honduras; Nicaragua. Negotiations were concluded in May 2010 and the trade pillar entered into force in 2012.
26. EPAs cover all Sub-Saharan African countries (five regions) plus the Caribbean and Pacific regions. Most EPAs negotiations are still ongoing at the time of writing.
27. Negotiation with the ASEAN group of countries (Burma, Brunei, Cambodia, Indonesia, Laos, Malaysia, Philippines, Singapore, Thailand and Vietnam) were initiated in 2007 and interrupted in 2009. Since then, the EU has initiated bilateral negotiations with Singapore and Malaysia.
28. Negotiations with MERCOSUR countries (Argentina, Brazil, Paraguay, Uruguay and Venezuela) for a region-to-region Association Agreement were launched in 1999, suspended in 2004 and reopened in 2010.
29. In 2006, the EU opened negotiations for an Association Agreement with the Andean Community of Nations (Bolivia, Colombia, Ecuador, Peru), subsequently suspended in 2008. In 2009, negotiations between the EU and three Andean countries—Colombia, Ecuador and Peru—restarted, aiming at a multi-party trade agreement; a successful conclusion was reached with Columbia and Peru in 2010. This agreement preserves its region-to-region approach in the hope of attracting other countries. Discussions are currently ongoing between the EU and the Ecuadorian and Bolivian authorities.
30. The middle income countries are Chile, Colombia, Costa Rica, Dominican Republic, El Salvador, Guatemala, Honduras, Jordan, Mexico, Morocco, Nicaragua, Peru and Panama.

31. In Africa: Angola, COMESA, East African Community, Ghana, Liberia, Mauritius, Mozambique, Nigeria, Rwanda, South Africa, West Africa Economic and Monetary Union. In Americas: CARICOM and Uruguay. In Europe and the Middle East: Algeria, Egypt, Georgia, Iraq, Kuwait, Lebanon, Libya, Tunisia, Turkey, Ukraine, Yemen. In Asia and the Pacific: Afghanistan, Central Asia (Kazakhstan, Kirgizstan, Tajikistan, Turkmenistan and Uzbekistan), Nepal, Pakistan, Sri Lanka, ASEAN, Cambodia, Indonesia, Malaysia, the Philippines, Thailand, Vietnam.
32. USA–Ghana TIFA. Source: Office of the USA Trade Representative.
33. Among others, the 1995 EU proposal for a Multilateral Agreement for Investment (MAI) asking would-be-signatories to significantly reduce their economic regulations. In a 1995 European Commission communication entitled, "A level playing field for direct investment world-wide", Brussels suggested the abolition of economic measures that were not in line with MAI's financial and performance requirements, including positive discrimination programmes for minorities or fiscal incentives for businesses located in impoverished areas. These proposals were to raise eyebrows in OECD countries—let alone in the developing world: Africa and Southern Asia rejected the proposal.
34. This average has been obtained by doing the simple average of two indexes collected in 42 African countries: "trade weighted average of agricultural products" and "trade weighted average of non-agricultural products". Author's calculation.
35. The EU average has been obtained by doing the simple average of two indexes collected in EU Member States: "simple average MFN applied in non-agricultural products" and "trade weighted average total products". Author's calculation.
36. *Lobby Spending Database* at www.opensecrets.org
37. See Friends of the Earth–Europe (FEE 2010).
38. On the different patterns towards economic diversification in the Gulf Cooperation Council (GCC) countries, see Ugo Fasano and Zubair Iqbal (2003).
39. Source: Akabzaa Thomas, *Boom and dislocation: environmental impacts of mining in the Wassa West District of Ghana* in (SAPRIN 2004). Author's calculations.

40. Aside from the literature issued by "engaged" actors—including Lambrechts et al. (2009)—a number of econometric studies underline the limits of SAP-induced tax reforms. For a comprehensive study of mining tax regimes, see Otto et al. (2000).
41. Author's calculation on the basis of refinement/production data.
42. African crude production (8804 thousand barrels a day [tbd]) largely covers its consumption needs (3336 tbd); however, the refinement capacity (3317 tbd) is below such need continent-wide, and even more at the country level (BP 2012). This creates the paradoxical situation of countries like Angola, a major international oil producer, suffering from shortages of refined gasoline.
43. Incidentally, it is the first of these bear waves that forced many resource-dependent countries to accept SAPs in first instance.
44. OPEC was founded in 1960 and has effectively established a cartel of oil-producing countries. OPEC currently has 12 members, out of which two are African: Islamic Republic of Iran, Iraq, Kuwait, Saudi Arabia, Venezuela, Qatar, Libya, United Arab Emirates, Algeria, Nigeria, Ecuador and Angola.
45. In 2005, UNCTAD identified three MNCs dominating trading in the coffee industry and a total of nine cocoa grinders, with three of them accounting for more than 50 % of the market (UNCTAD 2005, p. 53).
46. This trend started in 2005 and was immediately picked up by observers: Andrew Sumner estimates that "[…] in 2005 one in five FDI policy changes were less favourable to FDI. In contrast, in the mid-1990s one (or two) in a hundred policy changes were less favourable to FDI" (Sumner 2005, p. 239). The 2014 and 2015 oil slump is likely to impact the capacity of investee economies to re-negotiate favourable terms on their incoming FDI in the mining sector.
47. Among the examples of countries taking action: in 2005, Russia increased government stakes in the gas and oil sector by a seizure leading to a majority share in Gazprom and, shortly after, seized a majority stake in Royal Dutch Shell's oil and gas holdings in the Stakhalin-2 project; the Central African Republic suspended indefinitely permits for gold and diamond mining, while curtailing foreigners' entry to mining zones; Eritrea closed its FDI promotion agencies, suspended private import-export licences and limited the free transfer of foreign exchange; Chile introduced new taxes in

copper mining; Nigeria's re-nationalization of natural resources became an electoral issues (Sumner 2005).

48. In May 2006, the Bolivian Government first nationalized oil and gas activities and, subsequently, extended this to all natural resources; in 2005, Venezuela began a wave of nationalization in various sectors—including oil, agriculture, finance, industry, gold, steel, telecommunications, power, transport and tourism—proceeding to establishing new state companies from 2003 onwards, Argentina renationalized postal services, railways, shipyards, water and sanitation utilities, while renegotiating contracts and tax rises with foreign investors (Sumner 2005). In 2012, Argentina also proceeded to nationalize the country's biggest oil company, YFP.
49. (1) Fiscal policy discipline, with avoidance of large fiscal deficits relative to GDP; (2) redirection of public spending from subsidies toward broad-based provision of key services like primary education, primary health care and infrastructure investment; (3) tax reform, broadening the tax base and adopting moderate marginal tax rates; (4) interest rates that are market determined and positive (but moderate) in real terms; (5) competitive exchange rates; (6) trade liberalization: liberalization of imports, with particular emphasis on elimination of quantitative restrictions; any trade protection to be provided by low and relatively uniform tariffs; (7) Liberalization of inward foreign direct investment; (8) privatization of state enterprises; (9) deregulation: abolition of regulations that impede market entry or restrict competition, except for those justified on safety, environmental and consumer protection grounds, and prudential oversight of financial institutions; (10) legal security for property rights.
50. Projects & Operations classification provided by the WB on-line database.
51. World Bank Projects ID P116201; P126351; P122669, accessed in July 2012.
52. World Bank Projects ID P130546; P129565; P122808, accessed in July 2012.
53. Categories enlisted by theme in the WB online database include: economic management, environment and natural resources management, financial and private sector development, human development, public sector governance, rule of law, rural development,

social development and gender inclusion, social protection and risk management, trade and integration, and rural development.

54. Most projects in the WB's "Energy and Mining" category—and particularly in the sub-category "oil and gas"; "coal mining"; "other mining activities"—are mainly aimed at (1) accessing mineral resources and efficient management of upstream activities (extraction); (2) extending the role of the private sector in enhancing extractive and exporting capacity; (3) updating and simplifying legal and regulatory frameworks with a view to secure increased private sector investment. Among the many examples with budgets over 30 million USD: WB project ID P118925 in Afghanistan; WB project ID 124648 in Burkina Faso; and WB project ID 122153 in Cameroon.
55. WB projects ID 114841 and ID 120843 in Bangladesh.
56. UNIDO programmes for SMEs in agricultural activities represent a good set of examples of this typology of projects.

References

Ackah, C. (2006). *Who gained from trade liberalisation in Ghana? Unskilled vs. skilled households.* Paper presented at the IZA/CEPR European Summer Symposium in Labour Economics ESSLE 2006.

AfDB. (2009). *Oil and gas in Africa.* Oxford: Oxford University Press.

Baer, W. (1972). Import substitution and industrialization in Latin America: Experiences and interpretations. *Latin American Research Review, 7*, 95–122.

Balogun, E. D., & Dauda, R. O. (2012). *Poverty and employment impact of trade liberalization in Nigeria: Empirical evidence and policy implications.* Akoka: University of Lagos.

BP. (2012). Statistical review of world energy, June 2011. *embp.com/statisticalreview.*

Braithwaite, J., & Drahos, P. (2000). *Global business regulation.* Cambridge: Cambridge University Press.

Buira, A. (2004). The Governance of the IMF in a Global economy. *G24 Research Paper.* Washington, DC: Intergovernmental Group of Twenty Four.

Busch, M. L., Reinhardt, E., & Shaffer, G. (2008). Does legal capacity matter? Explaining patterns of protectionism in the shadow of WTO litigation. *Social Science Research Network.*

Chang, H.-J. (1996). *Liberalization in the developing world: Institutional and economic changes in Latin America, Africa, and Asia Why developing countries*

needs tariffs: How WTO NAMA negotiations could deny developing countries' right to a future. London, Geneva: Routledge, South Centre.
Chang, H.-J. (2009). *Bad Samaritans: The myth of free trade and the secret history of capitalism*. New York: Bloomsbury Press.
Cilliers, J., & Dietrich, C. (2000). *Angola's war economy: The role of oil and diamonds*. Pretoria: Institute for Security Studies.
de Córdoba, S. F., & Laird, S. (Eds) (2006). *Coping with trade reforms: A developing country perspective on the WTO industrial tariff negotiations*. Houndmills: Palgrave Macmillan.
Fasano, U., & Iqbal, Z. (2003). *GCC countries: From oil dependence to diversification*. Washington, DC: International Monetary Fund.
FEE. (2010). *Lobbying in Brussels – How much do the top 50 companies in the EU spend?* Brussels: Friends of the Earth Europe.
Jaffee, S., Kopicki, R., & Tyler, G. (2003). *Zambia: The challenge of competitiveness and diversification*. Washington, DC: World Bank.
Jones, K. (2009). Green room politics and the WTO's crisis of representation. *Progress in Development Studies, 9*(4), 349–357.
Lambrechts, K., Darimani, A., & Kabemba, C. (2009). *Breaking the curse: How transparent taxation and fair taxes can turn Africa's mineral wealth into development*. Johannesburg: Open Society Institute of Southern Africa.
Manger, M. S. (2009). *Investing in protection: The politics of preferential trade agreements between North and South*. Cambridge: Cambridge University Press.
OECD. (2013). *PISA 2012 assessment and analytical framework mathematics, reading, science, problem solving and financial literacy: Mathematics, reading, science, problem solving and financial literacy*. OECD Publishing.
Otto, J., Batarseh, M. L., & Cordes, J. (2000). *Global mining taxation comparative study*. Golden: Colorado School of Mines and UNCTAD.
Paloni, A., & Zanardi, M. (2006). *The IMF, World Bank and policy reform*. London: Routledge.
Rodriguez, F., & Rodrik, D. (2001). Trade policy and economic growth: A skeptic's guide to the cross-national evidence. *NBER Macroeconomics Annual 2000* (Vol. 15, pp. 261–338). Cambridge, MA: MIT Press.
Ross, M. (2012). *The oil curse: How petroleum wealth shapes the development of nations*. Princeton, NJ: Princeton University Press.
SAPRIN. (2004). *Structural adjustment: The SAPRI report: The policy roots of economic crisis, poverty, and inequality*. London, New York: Zed Books.
Sattler, T., & Bernauer, T. (2008). *Litigation in the World Trade Organization: Power of gravity or power of discrimination?* Paper presented at the Conference on the Political Economy of International Organizations, Monte Verità, February 3–8, 2008.
Schild, G. (1995). *Bretton Woods and Dumbarton Oaks: American economic and political postwar planning in the summer of 1944*. London: Macmillan.

Sumner, A. (2005). Is foreign direct investment good for the poor? A review and stocktake. *Development in Practice, 15*(3/4), 269–285.
UNCTAD. (2005). *Economic development in Africa – Rethinking the role of Foreign Direct Investment.* New York and Geneva: UNCTAD.
UNCTAD. (2012). *World investment report.* New York and Geneva: UNCTAD.
UNDP. (2013). UNDP integrated budget estimates for 2014–2017 (DP/2013/41).
UNGA. (2011). Proposed programme budget for the biennium 2012–2013.
UNICEF. (2013). UNICEF integrated budget, 2014–2017. (E/ICEF/2013/AB/L.4).
UNIDO. (2011). Programme and budgets 2012–2013.
Williamson, J. (1990). What Washington means by policy reform. *Latin American Adjustment: How Much Has Happened, 7*, 7–20.
World Bank. (1992). Strategy for African mining. *World Bank Technical Paper No. 181.* Washington, DC: World Bank.
WSJ. (2011). The CEO's top priorities. *Wall Street Journal* 21.11.2011.
WTO. (2010). *World tariff profiles 2010.* Geneva: World Trade Organization.

CHAPTER 6

A Qualitative Analysis of Africa–China Economic Relations

1 Context

Two reasons likely contribute in making an analysis of China–Africa relations a more straightforward exercise than the analysis of West–Africa relations.

The first is that, for a long time, China had a less intense relation with Africa than any Western power.[1] Chinese rhetoric has it that links with Africa pre-date Europe–Africa relations. This is historically true, as archaeological findings place the first contact between Sub-Saharan Africa and China at the Sung dynasty (960–1279 AD), while trade relations commenced as early as 1413 AD, a few decades before the Portuguese sailed for the first time South of the Sahara. China–Africa trade remained, however, sporadic and migratory flows were weak for a long time: South African historian Karen Harris suggests that at the beginning of the twentieth century there were as few as 5000 Chinese in the whole country (Shinn and Eisenman 2012, p. 24). Chinese migration to Africa was to change dramatically in the following years[2]—yet, Chinese political, economic and cultural influence remained largely marginal. Political relations staid at an unofficial level until the end of the nineteenth century, when the first diplomatic knots were tied via a Chinese consulate in Cape Town (1897). When, in 1912, the new National Government of China begun by Sun Yat Sen and later led by Chiang Kai-shek replaced the Qing/Manchu Dynasty, Africa continued remaining a secondary preoccupation.[3] It was only in the years following

S. Raudino, *Development Aid and Sustainable Economic Growth in Africa*, DOI 10.1007/978-3-319-38936-3_6

World War II that communist China, realizing the potential for political cooperation with the African continent, boosted diplomatic relations: first, with the Bandung conference in 1955 and the African foreign assistance programmes initiated to support socialist leaders and subsequently expanded to advance more direct political goals; then, with a more intense, albeit irregular, engagement in the 1960s and 1970s, which brought diplomatic cooperation on a number of issues, and notably on Beijing's bid to the United Nations Security Council (UNSC); and finally, with a skyrocketing number of business and international agreements from the early 1990s onwards. All in all, the list of China–Africa politico-economic relations remain, nonetheless, far less conspicuous than the West–Africa dossier, which is charged with over five centuries of growing trade and investment flows, direct political and economic management during the colonial experience and privileged relations since decolonization.[4]

The second reason is that, until recently, China had a limited influence upon the international governance system and, as a consequence, upon the international norms regulating many aspects of the international economy—including Africa's relations with third countries. Such impact is limited when compared to Europe, but almost inexistent when compared to the West, considering Washington's role within international organizations, and particularly within international financial institutions. China was a founding member of the League of Nations in 1919; yet, throughout the organization's lifespan, it only yielded limited political influence.[5] At the end of World War II, the Kuomintang Party was among the United Nations' founding members and successfully secured a Chinese permanent seat at the UNSC, which the Republic of China (ROC) managed to defend until 1971, when it was transferred to the People's Republic of China (PRC). However, in the following years, Beijing only had limited scope in using its veto power; marred by Cold War logic, the UN institutional setting remained locked and incapable of much deliberation until 1989. Even within the communist camp, Beijing was long overshadowed by Moscow: Mao considered all post-Stalin Soviet leaders his junior, but crucially depended on them for economic and military aid (Dikötter 2010).

Chinese influence in the international financial system was even more limited than in the political sphere: bogged down by a centralized planned economy until 1979, marred by unrealistic, poorly thought-through economic plans (great leap forward) as well as outright paranoid social reforms (cultural revolution), the PRC's GDP stood long at pair with Canada, a country of 21 million people, representing 2.4 % of the then Chinese population.[6] Nor did the 1970s Chinese structural reforms yield immediate results: at the beginning of the 1990s, 15 years into Deng Xiaoping's economic policies, China was not yet among the world's ten biggest economies, scoring well below trouble-ridden (but recently privatized) Russia and mid-sized countries like Spain or Italy. Constrained by poor economic performances, China had limited leverage in international economic and financial institutions: Beijing's IMF and WB quota long stood at meagre levels.[7] Entering the WTO as late as 2001 allowed Beijing to deflect external pressures at early trade liberalization, but it also meant political incapacity to influence the world trade regime for more than 50 years.[8] A limited domestic GDP throughout the 1980s also meant that Chinese domestic economic policies (including agricultural and industrial policies) had little impact on the economic development of Africa—or any other developing nation for that matter. Trade relations between China and Africa were fairly limited and Chinese domestic regulations had little scope for influence upon them.

This situation radically changed early in the 1990s, when bilateral trade and investment flows between the two regions began growing steadily. Not only was China becoming a prominent economic actor in Africa, but it was also devising sophisticated political and diplomatic strategies bound to initiate one of the most vigorous and discussed love affairs in contemporary international relations. Has such relationship proved healthy and fulfilling for both parties?

2 The Players: Who the Actors Are

Compared to OECD African policies, China's Africa policy is rather peculiar. Beijing does engage Africa through standard international practices—including bilateral relations, strategic partnerships and institutional cooperation fora; promotion of development cooperation initiatives; participation in international business biddings; and co-sponsoring of peace-keeping operations—, but seems to stand out from the group of Western players in many other respects. Part of these differences can be explained by the nature of the policies and engagement strategies; part is, however, explained by the different nature of the player itself: compared to Western liberal democracies, China is a different political animal altogether.

2.1 *The National Level*

Differences between OECD and Chinese activities in Africa relate, in first instance, to capabilities. On the one hand, China suffers from structural limits when measured through Western standards, on the other hand, Beijing has made significant steps in establishing an alternative cooperation framework with Africa.

China is not part of regional or security organizations comparable to the European Union or the North Atlantic Treaty Organization (NATO), and is also out of more traditional regional intergovernmental organizations (except the Shanghai Cooperation Organization); as well as from ODA leading institutions—including the Development Aid Committee (DAC) of the Organization for Economic Cooperation and Development (OECD)—and their private financial counterparts such as the London and Paris clubs. China has a number of bilateral military agreements with African countries and several military attachés deployed on the ground, on top of being a strong contributor to peacekeeping operations; however, unlike the USA, France and, to a lesser extent, the UK, it neither has a stable military presence in Africa, nor a track record of overseas military operations. Beijing has been playing an increasingly important role in the IFIs, particularly following the 2008 international financial crisis, but majority stakes within the boards of directors and executive jobs in the World Bank, International Monetary Fund and World Trade Organization firmly remain in European and American hands. The RMB has made clear steps towards international convertibility but is still far away from becoming a fully convertible tender, let alone from representing a credible USD alternative as an international reserve or a fall-back currency.

This modest record assessed through Western-led standards needs, however, being balanced with China's alternative institutional framework for cooperation with Africa. Since 2000, the Forum on China–Africa Cooperation (FOCAC), a multilayered institutional framework providing for governmental meetings at different levels (Summit; Ministerial; and Senior Official Meetings) and regular meetings between delegations of their legislative assemblies, has provided an institutional home to a political and economic relationship that had already thrived for over a decade.[9] With representatives from 44 African countries, agreements reportedly running to the tune of 5 billion USD in loans and credits and 1.9 billion USD in business deals, the first FOCAC Ministerial, in 2000, already looked more successful than any other conference organized by European and Asian competitors before.[10] The conference has been pursued ever since, with the sixth Ministerial meeting being successfully held in December 2015. Such an ambitious framework for political and economic dialogue has been substantiated by a matching institutional presence at technical level: since 1990, Beijing has multiplied its embassies in Africa to reach full diplomatic relations with 48 countries, representing by 2010 the most extended diplomatic network on the continent.[11] The cultural campaign to gain the hearts of Africans has not been less impressive: since 2004, China has opened 38 Confucius institutes in Africa and has increased the number of government-sponsored programmes to reach the staggering figure of 30,000 vocational trainings and 18,000 scholarships offered in the 2013–2015 period only.[12]

Extensive institutional cooperation between China and Africa has become possible also because the Chinese government has made resolute steps to substantiate its economic presence overseas. Since the 1980s, Chinese State Owned Enterprises (SOEs) have undergone a number of reforms which are part of a broader effort aimed at ferrying a centrally planned system into a fully market-driven economy; yet, the Chinese government still masters China's largest companies' business strategies, in Africa as elsewhere. According to the Ministry of Commerce of the PRC, state-owned enterprises accounted for as much as 69.6 % of the Chinese outward FDI stock in 2008 (MOFCOM 2008). Chinese SOEs, along with the multitude of SMEs receiving credit facilities from government-backed financial institutions, represent a more closely knit community than most Western business communities, which typically rely on a fairly loose consular support from their countries. These peculiar and inherent features of Chinese companies influence their business policies: Chinese SOEs, for example, are sometimes willing to operate at a loss or in highly unstable environments because business strategies are not only influenced by market imperatives but also by political directives.[13] In other words, these firms often respond to the economic interests and political needs of a machine whose operations span beyond specific industries, specific countries or specific revenue targets.

These elements concur in determining a situation in which, for the good or the bad, China mainly engages Africa unilaterally rather than through multilateral frameworks or in coordination with other international players. This *modus operandi* seems to represent a good fit with the country's history and administrative structure: the Chinese government has traditionally relied on a highly centralized bureaucratic system, which today takes the shape of a republican autocracy with limited political accountability towards civil society and a direct influence upon the country's industrial and financial texture. Such a politico-administrative structure entails a number of consequences on China's international relations. Reflecting its internal outlook, China is keen to establish government to government relations, while distrusting the role of civil society and multilateral organizations: whereas a consistent share of Western outbound financial flows goes—directly or indirectly—to civil society organizations, International Organizations or private companies, Chinese FDI and ODA funds are mostly channelled through national SOEs or directly injected in the state budgets of beneficiary governments. Relying on a centralized administrative system, Beijing is generally capable of passing decisions and disbursing funds with extraordinary efficiency, a phenomenon that helps to explain the sustained pace of Chinese advances in Africa. This is particularly true when compared to most OECD governments, which rely on governance systems regulated by strong checks and balances, not only raising their accountability standards but also lowering their effectiveness and efficiency. Freedom from strong democratic checks and balances entails other consequences: one that is often discussed in the West is China's availability to work with pariah governments that are stigmatized in Western public opinions, including Al-Bashir in Sudan and Mugabe in Zimbabwe. As suggested in Chap. 3, Western institutional narratives often forget, at their own turn, to mention their cooperation agreements with authoritarian and gruesome African administrations.

All in all, it could be said that China's mixed picture in terms of capabilities and alliances seemingly makes the China–Africa marriage a somewhat less skewed power relationship than the West–Africa marriage. Beijing knows this and has been keen to play on a strong South–South rhetoric dense of references to their common past as colonized nations and their common future as allied antagonists of the Western leadership.[14] Social indexes confirm that Africa has more to share with China than with the West.[15]

However, a China–OECD institutional and power comparison should also be contextualized against African governmental capabilities. Faced with booming Chinese activism and the waning influence of the West on its territory, Africa's negotiation capabilities seem to have evolved little. To external observers, most African national and international institutions continue to appear fractured and poorly organized. This reflects in scholarly articles representing Chinese actors as dominating the agenda and acting in a highly organized way, while Africans are portrayed as reactive and lacking agency.[16] Such approach is so common in the China–Africa scholarship that it has been compared to the 1960s Dependentist literature on West–Africa relations: "[…] contemporary analyses of China in Africa have much in common with earlier debates about dependency, where African developments were seen as determined by external capitalism" (Mohan and Lampert 2013, p. 95). Similarly, African diplomats refer to a number of Chinese practices betraying how the Chinese government treats African governments as junior and economically dependent partners.[17]

Double-digit growth rates in certain regions of Africa continue hiding a strong reliance upon resource extraction and an apparent incapacity to channel fiscal surpluses away from consumption and into value-adding investments, as not only Asian NIEs—but also Middle Eastern countries such as the UAE and Qatar—have done in the recent past. Several analysts have noted that the continent seems to be repeating many of the mistakes it has committed since independence, particularly by failing to bridge socio-economic fractures between peoples and their elites, as well as political fractures among African governments. Most African countries continue to play on their own, with weak institutional cooperation and sporadic political coordination at the regional and continental level. The African Union (AU) seems to suffer from the same internal divisions[18] that have long allowed OECD countries to play *divide et impera* tactics, while African Regional Economic Communities (RECs) have seldom propelled growth.

These same gaps have long provided fertile ground for unbalanced economic agreements between the West and Africa and seem to continue playing a role in today's China–Africa agreements: many of the China–Africa deals scrutinized by international analysts are not any more transparent or conducive towards sustainable growth than OECD–Africa deals (Raine 2013; Strange et al. 2013). Whatever *systemic* favourable economic conditions the West could extract from past international agreements with Africa—also by nurturing privileged relationships and a shared culture with its elites—seem to be replicable today by China through its appealing business offers, in a process that is also showing signs of increasing refinement.[19] This situation is unlikely to change until Africa's domestic and regional gaps are addressed.

Differences in macroeconomic and institutional capabilities between China and Africa are also remarkable. Against grim public budget figures on the African side,[20] the Chinese national expenditure in 2012 reached 12.79 trillion RMB—corresponding to 2.08 trillion USD. Out of this, 5.61 trillion RMB (915 billion USD) went to central level–expenditure, including diplomacy and foreign aid, the largest budget line remaining however military spending with 650.6 billion RMB (106 billion USD). According to journalistic sources, the number of higher education institutions in China has more than doubled in ten years, passing from 1022 in 2000 to 2263 in 2010, with 5 million students enrolled in degree courses in 2011 (Economist 2011b). The 2013 QS World University Rankings placed 48 Chinese universities in the world's top 200 for at least one subject. A sample of Chinese students from Shanghai have also performed remarkably well in PISA, ranking at the top in mathematics, science and reading, ahead of more than 60 countries worldwide (OECD 2009).[21] Competitive Universities, a large base of fresh domestic graduates and increased efforts at attracting Overseas Chinese Professionals (OCP) (Biao 2011) translate in strong state capabilities. Also, if China only participates in a few regional organizations, it is nonetheless well represented bilaterally and globally by a well-staffed and professionally trained diplomatic corps: aside from being a UNSC permanent member, Beijing's embassies are capillary distributed in world capitals and International Organizations headquarters alike, and have long proven their capacity to lobby African governments.

These figures contribute in picturing a relevant capability gap between African and Chinese institutions. At similar population levels, China retains a stronger economic, political, institutional and diplomatic capability than the whole of Africa. China also has a defined foreign and economic policy towards the black continent, whereas African governments have so far fallen short of forging a common strategy towards China.

2.2 The Subnational Level

Power emanating from the Chinese Communist Party (CCP) and the subsidiary government it controls is shared among a number of state administrations whose interests and agenda are not necessarily aligned.

At policy level, the most relevant players in China's foreign policy, in general, and China's Africa policy, in particular, are the Politburo

Standing Committee, the Leading Group on foreign affairs within the China Communist Party (CCP), and the International Department, which runs a Sub-Saharan Africa bureau. At executive level, the key governmental players are the State Council with its overseeing capacity upon Chinese ministries, the Ministry of Foreign Affairs (MOFA), the Ministry of Commerce (MOFCOM), the Ministry of Finance, the China's Export-Import Bank (and to a lesser extent the China Development Bank, the China–Africa Development Fund, the China Investment Corporation and the China Africa Business Council)[22] and a few major State-Owned Enterprises and trading companies involved in key sectors, with a particularly relevant role played by the three National Oil Companies (China National Petroleum Corporation, China Petroleum and Chemical Corporation and China National Offshore Oil Corporation). Since the state often holds strong minority equity in most Chinese "private" companies, a number of private companies can also be assumed to be under state influence, either directly through the state's shareholder capacity or indirectly through its role as a financier, customer and tax authority.[23] The provincial level also plays an important role: Chinese provinces, cities and regional offices of national agencies maintain an extended network of direct relations with foreign countries. While the largest Chinese SOEs are accountable to the State Council, it is estimated that provincial SOEs constitute almost 90 % of Chinese firms investing abroad (Broadman and Isik 2007, p. 305).

If all these actors are somehow influenced by the Chinese government and therefore subordinated to the general political direction imparted by nation-wide agencies—including the National Development and Reform Commission (NDRC) and the State Assets Supervision and Administration Commission of the State Council (SASAC)—the ensuing dynamics are not always clear-cut: not all these actors can be taken as working in a coordinated and organic fashion. Obstacles to the setting up of a consistent strategy towards Africa arise from tensions and rivalries among central ministries as well as among Beijing and the provincial capitals. Ministerial mandates are often poorly delineated and overlapping, thus facilitating rivalries between different administrations; also, while Beijing decides on the general imprint of international agreements, it is often up to the provincial governments to execute them. Reportedly, the central government and its agencies also experience problems in passing their policies down the hierarchical chain, the culture of "*guanxi*" or policy connection often allowing senior officials to bypass standard policy channels and hierarchical rules to enforce their own agenda (Raine 2013).

As the line between public and private in China is blurred, so are differences in the nature, business strategies and practices of public and private companies, which have become increasingly similar. Distinctions between official, quasi-official and unofficial Chinese economic players have become particularly difficult to draw.[24] In the 2000s, most Chinese SOEs have stopped fulfilling the social welfare role they were assigned until the 1980s: they now pursue profit maximization for their shareholders, also by undergoing painful restructuring processes which have already laid off millions of workers in an attempt to become leaner organizations and more competitive international players. This means that SOEs can become unresponsive towards state indications to invest in politically motivated but market-unattractive projects. Similarly, today, the ownership structure seems to weigh less than general performances in assuring state support: in general terms, it could be said that SOEs cannot take public support for granted anymore. As it will be discussed, the practice of engaging in unfruitful investments in pursuit of larger domestic or foreign policy goals remains, however, ingrained in Chinese FDI culture, particularly among Chinese National Oil Companies (NOCs) and other selected corporate champions. These companies are mostly free from accountability to private shareholders, can leverage state capitals and scale economies by building their businesses on the back of a vast and booming domestic market, and are free from labour and environmental standards: it is natural that they come to enjoy considerable freedom of manoeuvre and a higher appetite for risk (Alden and Davies 2006).

Conversely, most Chinese small entrepreneurs and traders and some Chinese SMEs can be assumed to behave independently from Chinese governmental strategies, policies or connections, except perhaps from the indirect benefits these companies enjoy from Beijing's groundwork in opening business ties with African countries. These companies uncoordinatedly pursue market interests, which can, at times, be at loggerheads with the Chinese government's long-term interests in the continent.[25] Researchers have also suggested that some of these companies see advantages at keeping distance from the Chinese government and that, in several instances, have deliberately sought such distance (Raine 2013).

3 The Stage: Chinese Policies Towards Africa

There is little doubt about the role that the Chinese hunger for commodities has played in shaping China's Africa strategy: Beijing's policies in Africa are chiefly dictated by its concern to stabilize energy and mineral supplies, while diminishing its reliance on international markets. However, China was a minor player in African commodity markets until the 1990s, and since then, it has graduated into a world-class player, becoming for several African countries a more vital ally than the USA or the European Union. Such results could not be achieved if Beijing was to limit its role to being a customer paying market prices against increasingly scarce natural commodities. Instead, Beijing has shaped a comprehensive economic, trade, financial and human resources African strategy. In general terms, this strategy focuses on energy and mineral resource acquisition, by offering bilateral preferential loans against the beneficiaries' commitment to devise amortization payments in natural resources and use the credit provided by these loans to contract Chinese companies and purchase Chinese goods. Typically, China also added to the package a number of collateral aid programmes, including training, university scholarships and technical assistance.[26] Since these financial commitments are offered at competitive interest rates and unbound from political conditionalities, they undoubtedly contributed in expanding Chinese SOEs' activities in Africa, while also reinvigorating diplomatic relations between Beijing and most African capitals.[27]

To this extent, explaining China–Africa economic relations by analytically dissecting its multiple vectors (trade, FDI, ODA and migration) is an artificial step to exemplify the working mechanisms of this relationship. In reality, these vectors work in an integrated fashion and could hardly be understood if isolated one from another—an exercise that was instead meaningful in analysing West–Africa relations.[28] For example, since the bulk of China's purchases in Africa consists of oil and minerals through SOEs, China–Africa trade growth cannot be understood in isolation from the Chinese SOEs' FDI policy in African oil fields. Similarly, how, early in the 1990s, Beijing managed to convince a number of African countries to include Chinese SOEs among the few fortunate partners that were granted new exploration and exploitation rights, is something that can hardly be explained without looking at China's "assistance" policies—and, in ultimate instance, at China's foreign policy. Categories of financial flows between China and Africa are therefore not as neatly defined as between West and Africa; as a testimony put it to the USA—China Commission, "[…] China comes to Africa with what one analyst has called the "complete package": money, technical expertise, and the influence in such bodies as the UN Security Council to protect the host country from international sanctions" (Lyman 2005). Hence, China's Africa policy is better understood as an imperfectly coordinated, multivector strategy rather than as the sum of independently waged initiatives: the role, scope and results of Chinese trade, investments, diplomatic efforts and ODA-like policies in Africa could not be explained without looking at their close interaction.

The results of this "complete package" strategy have been hailed in Chinese institutional discourse as a new era of South–South cooperation. These same results are also well known to Western chancelleries, which have grown increasingly distrustful and jealous of Beijing's successes. At the same time, China's Africa "complete packages" have also entailed a number of drawbacks for African societies and economies. Thousands of Chinese privately owned SOHOs and SMEs have opened up in Africa in a time span of two decades, providing Africans with the opportunity to purchase goods they could never afford before, but also flooding local economies with cheap imports that have driven local competitors out of the market. Tensions have been growing over the years: Zambia, Kenya, the Democratic Republic of Congo and Ghana have, among others, witnessed a number of violent incidents between Chinese entrepreneurs and traders, on the one side, and African authorities and labour, on the other. Several studies have confirmed that growing exports of poorly manufactured Chinese goods, concurrent with frequent trade dumping practices, are operating to seriously disadvantage a number of African industries, including apparel and textile.[29] It is, however, important to notice that African traders and small entrepreneurs had also opportunities deriving from Chinese competitive advantages in capital and finished goods, by entering the African markets as retailers of Chinese products or as small manufacturers.[30]

The review below presents the main vectors of Chinese economic policies in Africa and outline how they are contributing to a common Chinese strategy in Africa.

3.1 International Trade

An article circulated on the Chinese Ministry of Foreign Affairs' FOCAC page candidly remarks that "China's import of natural resources from Africa is the driving force behind China–Africa trade boom. China's imports from Africa are dominated by primary products" (Lu 2011). Figures presented in Chap. 4 are in line with this statement: China's staggering growth of trade flows with Africa is mainly—albeit not exclusively—related to its imports of natural commodities and exports of capital and consumer goods. The main tools China used to promote this trade structure are what we called "complete packages": investment offers coupled with assisting business measures and development aid. Other instruments included diplomatic pressures, promotion of normative measures aimed, *inter alia*, at reducing tariffs, as well as reliance upon the comparative advantages created by Chinese economic, trade and monetary policies. In 15 years, these policies contributed in creating and structuring a trade flow worth more than 200 billion USD in 2014.

"Complete packages" proposed to resource-endowed African countries have largely been geared at acquiring oil and minerals. Among the most studied examples, the case of Angola provides telling insights on this commercial strategy. In 2002, the Chinese's Construction Bank provided a first funding for infrastructure development, followed by a framework agreement in 2003 and a first ExIm Bank 2 billion USD finance package the year after. Two additional ExIm Bank loans of 500 million USD and 2 billion USD were approved in 2007 and financing from Chinese state banks continued till reaching, according to the Chinese Ambassador to Angola, 14.5 billion USD in credit by 2011 (Mohan and Lampert 2013, p. 98). The Angolan case has also been defined as exceptional because of the unusually large existence of a secondary unofficial financing channel, in this case, going through a Hong Kong–based private company.[31]

ExIm Bank loans are normally denominated in RMB, have lower-than-market interest rates and/or longer grace periods than commercial loans; it remains, however, unclear whether their concessional component would be large enough to make them OECD ODA compliant.[32] Loans are structured in such a way that there is a revenue stream to support debt repayments: Angola, for example, can use the export of oil to China to repay the loan.[33] At the same time, decisions on how to use Chinese credits go through a Sino-Angolan technical group (*Gabinete de Apoio Tecnico de Gestão de Crédito da China*, Technical Support Office for the Management of the Chinese Credit Line), of which the Chinese MOFCOM is also part, and which is tasked in selecting infrastructure projects to be financed. For each project tendered, the Chinese Government proposes a number of Chinese firms: once the tender has been assigned to a construction company, payments are done directly by the China ExIm Bank, which maintains full control of project disbursement.

China's provisions on infrastructure financing are often linked to Chinese mining and oil companies' access to exploitable resources. This has obviously been the case in the first phases of the China–Angola relation, and particularly in 2004 when China Petroleum and Chemical Corporation (Sinopec) bought a 50 % stake of block 18 in exchange for 725 million USD, corresponding to the first tranche of China Exim Bank's financing. The subsequent intensity of Chinese NOC's engagement in other Angolan oil wells has followed an erratic path, which owes much to variables as different as international competition at times of bidding, Chinese limited technical capacity in oil exploration and exploitation, and concurrent negotiations on other dossiers (Corkin 2011).[34]

Since equity stakes in African natural resources were acquired against concessional loans to be used with Chinese contractors, and because Chinese contractors display a strong preference for Chinese labour, equipment, material and technology, these policies have also been positively linked to a rise in the export of Chinese capital and consumer goods towards Africa, as well as to increasing levels of labour migratory flows. Most capital goods used by Chinese companies in Africa appear to be imported from China rather than locally sourced; these imports have also enjoyed tax breaks, which have reportedly been exploited to illegally import and resell goods at zero import duty rate (Raine 2013). These dynamics partially result from the particular industrial texture of involved countries—most African countries do not produce any of these capital or consumer goods, thus leaving Chinese entrepreneurs with little option but importing them—but are also the result of intentional Chinese trade and diplomatic policies geared at creating international market opportunities for their national manufacturers. ExIm Bank concessional loans, for example, usually require that at least 50 % of the contracts' procurements come from China; research shows, however, that most projects are implemented at closer to 70 % (Power et al. 2012, p. 77) Several indicators suggest that African governments have grown increasingly aware of the importance of integrating FDI projects into the national economic texture, including by adding local content and hiring provisions to contracts signed with Chinese SOEs.[35] However, it is likely that most of these imbalances will remain unaltered for decades to come, as it has already happened with the West–Africa trade structure.

The key features of China's "complete packages" can therefore be found in four elements: (1) Chinese commodity-backed loans are often denominated in RMB and always channelled off-budget[36]; (2) since these loans must obligatorily be used with Chinese contractors, from the Chinese Government's standpoint, they represent Keynesian expansionary fiscal policies: these are Chinese state-owned banks indirectly contracting Chinese construction companies to carry out works outside of China, which means that money never leaves China; (3) these loans also imply a fundamental opportunity for Chinese State-Owned mining companies to become competitive in a bidding market in which they would otherwise lag much behind their OECD competitors; (4) because both construction and mineral extraction activities often rely on Chinese capital goods and labour, and because Chinese state banks loans contain provisions on minimum Chinese procurement rules, "complete packages" also represent export opportunities for linked industries in China, as well as oversee job creation opportunities for a government in constant need of generating employment for its 1.4 billion population.

On top of the "complete packages", Chinese diplomatic pressure has reportedly played a role in many instances of China–Africa trade frictions, ultimately contributing towards the shaping of today's trade structure. Several accounts refer in particular to China's negotiating efforts in acquiring natural commodities at the lowest possible processing level, destining value-adding activities to China-based companies. This has been particularly true for oil, minerals and wood, three sectors that contribute towards strong refining and processing industries in China, which are responsible for millions of jobs and billions of value-adding activities.[37] Chinese trade diplomacy is also known to be at work in all instances where China trade with Africa has hurt local industries—such as the textile and garment industries of Nigeria and South Africa—and resulted in trade defence measures.

Another set of tools that likely contributed in promoting China–Africa trade consisted of trade liberalization measures, including Chinese unilateral tariff reductions. Since the establishment of FOCAC, China has largely followed in the footsteps of the EU and the USA by reducing or voiding import duties on a large selection of African goods: in 2010,

Xinhua claimed that the Chinese Ministry of Commerce had stopped levying tariffs on 60 % of imports from 26 least developed African nations. Similarly, the Chinese Minister of Commerce was quoted reporting that tariff exemptions between 2006 and 2008 already amounted to 680 million USD.[38] In principle, these duty concessions were granted across the manufacturing spectrum and should, therefore, allow greater market access to African exporters; however, the extent to which these tariff reductions can advantage industries where Africa has a real comparative advantage remains unclear. It is doubtful, in particular, whether these measures represent anything innovative with respect to initiatives, such as the European Everything but Arms (EBA), where non-existent or uncompetitive G90 producers were given free access to developed, mature and highly competitive consumer markets.

Finally, China–Africa trade relations should be read in the larger context of the Chinese role in world economy. Since the early 1990s, China has built a consistently positive and steadily growing current account, reflecting economic, trade and monetary policies deliberately aimed at turning China into the world's manufacturing hub. China maintains a positive balance of trade with all African countries, except oil exporters, a data mirroring the success of a trade policy aiming at over-exporting and under-importing through a heterogeneous set of measures, including a monetary policy that has long kept the RMB undervalued. China can also maintain a positive trade balance with virtually all non-oil and mineral exporting countries—as well as limited trade deficits with commodity exporting countries—because it obliges exporters, including foreign MNCs operating in China, to surrender foreign currency earnings to the Central Bank, which subsequently hoards them while artificially setting the RMB value at below-market rates (Rosefielde 2011). This policy has a number of consequences, including low domestic consumption levels: Chinese people are accepting to consume way less foreign goods than they could afford; in so doing, not only do they sacrifice a portion of their individual rights to the Chinese national interest as understood by the Chinese government, but they also restrain Western commercial penetration in China and cut the competitive edge that African (and other G90) exporters could have in China.

A skewed trade structure (import raw material and export manufactures), a strong geographic concentration of trade partners (importing mainly from commodity-producing countries), overly positive trade balances and current accounts with non-commodity exporting countries (reflecting over-imports and under-exports), as well as collateral policies aimed at maintaining the current trade structure (whether trade defence measures or use of foreign capital goods and technology for all FDI projects) are all features of West–Africa trade: to this extent, Chinese trading policies in Africa represent little novelty. What may represent a change with the past is the much-discussed availability of Chinese firms in creating manufacturing capability in Africa, while including Africa-based companies in Global Value Chains (GVCs). Is that what is happening? This aspect can be better analysed by looking at Chinese investments and migratory policies.

3.2 *International Investments and Migration*

Statistics in Chap. 4 outlined how Chinese official FDI flows to Africa and stock in Africa are relatively small when compared to Western FDI figures; yet, statistics since the early 2000s concur in suggesting that China is set to quickly erode the OECD leadership. The African-bound FDI to total FDI ratio has showed for several years how Africa has become more of a strategic partner for China than for the West, an element that complements trends seen in political and diplomatic cooperation. Here as well, results were made possible by a multifaceted policy recipe. The leading tools of such policy are still to be found in the "complete package" agreements; however, there are also strong institutional and normative aspects at play—including measures aimed at encouraging and protecting Chinese private investments in Africa ("economic cooperation agreements" giving rise to non-concessional loans and agreements on the avoidance of double taxation); as well as structural complementarities between the Chinese economy and the Chinese government's go-global FDI policy. The following paragraphs analyse the nature and effects of both official FDI—mainly channelled through SOEs and quantifiable in 1.7 billion USD of flows and 16 billion USD of stock (2011)—and unofficial FDI, mainly represented by fully private SMEs and single entrepreneurs and traders, for which there are no official figures but whose size is understood to be relevant.

The "complete package" model has largely been seen as allowing Beijing to obtain key investment objectives in Africa: (1) procuring natural resources; (2) finding outlet markets for Chinese enterprises, products and workers (particularly unskilled); (3) diversifying investments towards markets that have the potential for high returns on investments (also taking into consideration that, as the Chinese economy matures and reaches more sustainable growth levels, Chinese enterprises will witness progressively shrinking domestic ROIs) and; (4) extend China's diplomatic outreach. Disentangling the concessional part of loans conceded through these agreements from the non-concessional part or from other non-ODA, non-OOF financial instruments—including preferential buyer's credits—is no easy task. Rather, what should be retained of the Chinese "complete package" strategy is the increased bargaining power that Chinese institutional investors have received from acceding such a large spectrum of offers through government-to-government agreements. Reportedly, Chinese managed to outbid Western commercial offers on several occasions, exactly because of the vast set of tools Chinese negotiators could accede.[39]

Aside from resource exploration and exploitation, FDI figures in Chap. 4 suggest that China has been heavily involved in infrastructures and transportation; these projects complement Chinese needs in securing access to natural commodities through investments in railways, highways, harbours and airports. Chinese FDI to Africa is, however, not limited to oil and mining-related industries: a consistent portion goes towards manufacturing, particularly labour-intensive industries such as textile, apparel, household appliances and toys (Cheung et al. 2012, p. 8). A review of Chinese FDI by sector in 20 SSA economies indicates that most of these investments were concentrated in the textile, garment, shoes, leather and agro-processing sectors, and were using African operations both as an exporting platform and as a base to serve local markets (AERC 2008). This class of investments has an ambiguous effect upon the invested economies. On the one side, it holds a significant potential for favourably impacting the local industrial texture because of the backward and forward links it nurtures with the local economy, the technology spillover as well as the potential for joint ventures with local entrepreneurs and subsequent spin-offs generating local competition. On the other, it has also proved harmful to local competitors by taking away shares of both domestic African markets and Africa's preferential market access in the USA and the EU. Balancing the pros and cons on the African side would require an econometric analysis by sector; on the other side, it is safe to say that, since the 1990s, Chinese entrepreneurs have successfully acquired new profitable market shares across Africa.

All that glitters is not gold: the picture for Chinese SOEs in Africa is not fully rosy. Part of the remarkable success story of China's African bids against Western competitors is explained by the low profitability margins Chinese firms operate on—a further indication of China's readiness to postpone consumption and enjoyment of returns on investments. Chinese SOEs—as many Western companies operating in publicly sponsored African projects—win public procurements sponsored by their own government. However, the Chinese government can put forward such competitive offers to African governments and sustain so many of them because Chinese SOEs have extremely low operating costs: whereas typical profit rates for Western firms run in the 15 %–25 % range, Chinese firms typically operate at 3 %–5 % profit rates (Raine 2013; Sautman and Hairong 2007). Similarly, Kaplinsky (Kaplinsky and Morris 2009) reports that a number of African projects are voiced to be carried out by Chinese construction companies at 25 % of the costs budgeted by OECD national companies. This also reflects on salary levels: in a 2009 poll, researchers found that Chinese workers in Africa receive the lowest international salaries on the continent, roughly standing at 50 % of the Indian level, 19 % of the Western level and 15 % of the South African level (Henley et al. 2009).

Another remarkable element is the Chinese government's willingness to back Chinese companies in risky or unprofitable business ventures. With few exceptions, most official Chinese FDI in Africa is channelled through large-scale projects managed by SOEs that have access to cheap credit lines backed by governmental financial guarantees. These companies are keener than Western companies to engage in long-term, high-risk projects. Reportedly, Chinese companies are used to bidding at a loss in a number of projects, from oil to real estate: Taylor (2007), for example, quotes a SOE's general manager being instructed to keep the profit margins of large construction projects in Ethiopia at 3 %—a level easily entailing losses—because Beijing's finality is to consolidate its presence in the country rather than maximizing its SOEs' profits. Being freed from the logic of maximizing profitability at the unit level, Chinese SOEs effectively work as state agents in furthering multiple foreign policy goals that may consist, at different times and in different places, in political, geostrategic, business or public relations outcomes.

Finally, it is important considering the role of Chinese private sector investments that are mostly unrecorded. This FDI segment largely corresponds to small trading, light manufacturing and logistic services. In principle, it holds the potential for a positive socio-economic impact upon African economies; in practice, it has also stirred competition with African traders and entrepreneurs. As suggested above, these investments do not follow policies intentionally promoted by Chinese authorities and cannot, therefore, be directly ascribed to Beijing's responsibility.

The phenomenon of increasing Chinese FDI in Africa—both state-promoted and private—has been linked to changing migratory trends. Institutional and academic observers have levelled criticisms towards Chinese migratory policies in Africa. These concentrate on Chinese companies' tendency to fill most of their labour needs with Chinese nationals, even in job positions where no particular skills are required. These migratory flows are complemented by a large number of Chinese nationals reaching Africa individually and overstaying their short-term visas; they represent the bulk of people running small businesses and capitalizing on their access to Chinese products and capital, making profits in industries where Africans used to run the show, including petty trading, agriculture, manual mining and building works. Available data support these allegations: between 2000 and 2010, Chinese migration towards Africa has been estimated at anything between 270,000 and over 1 million, a flow that has multiplied by three to ten, the total estimated Chinese presence in the early 2000s (French 2014; Mohan and Tan-Mullins 2009). The Chinese government has also a tradition of venting excess labour into foreign markets, in an effort to establish durable linkages with outlet markets and ease the political, demographic and sexual pressure created by rural poverty, urban unemployment and gender imbalances. There are nuances worth mentioning: Raine (2013, p. 1007) and Mohan and Lampert (2013, p. 104) quote scholars, practitioners and punctual field work studies suggesting that Chinese companies have been keener in hiring locals where skilled labour was available at comparable conditions.

3.3 Official Development Assistance

Data from Chap. 4 reveal that there is much uncertainty around Chinese ODA: Beijing does not follow OECD guidelines on ODA auditing, thus limiting the significance of any comparison with Western countries. Interestingly, while Beijing justifies secrecy on ODA figures on several accounts—including the potential dissatisfaction it could stir among China's own population living below the poverty line and the risk of attracting pressures from partner countries that are benefiting less than others—there is no shortage of propagandistic declarations on Chinese commitments in Africa. Aside from overblown figures resulting from a conscious public relations exercise, ODA rhetoric also reflects the Chinese government's intention to portray its cooperation model as profoundly different from Western ODA, being geared towards creating business opportunities rather than promoting assistentialism.[40]

Most Chinese ODA is channelled through policies strictly entangled with the other vectors of Chinese economic and political involvement in Africa: FDI and trade.[41] The Chinese Department of Foreign Assistance's location within the Ministry of Commerce (MOFCOM) already speaks loudly as to ODA's role in Chinese foreign policy: the concessional part attached to loans is regarded by the MOFCOM as an investment to promote Chinese sales and industrial presence overseas. In fact, the largest share of these funds likely consists in the interest subsidies attached to concessional and zero-interest loans destined to commercial ventures: to a certain extent, Chinese ODA can be seen as a start-up cost built into the country's FDI policy.

Relying on Chinese primary sources, Paul Hubbard (Rotberg 2009, p. 217) indicates that bilateral framework agreements are typically signed between China's ExIm Bank and the borrowing country; although the details of such agreements remain secretive, available data indicate that the loans' average size (and, therefore, its concessional element) has been growing from 8.2 million USD in 1998 to 28 million USD in 2007; that the grant element is variable in size and therefore does not always technically qualify as OECD ODA (otherwise qualifying as OOF or Private Flows); and that beneficiary Chinese firms are requested to purchase from China as much equipment, technology and services as possible. The Chinese ExIm Bank typically finances these projects by raising the principal on international markets and by providing a concessional term, which at its own turn is normally sponsored through the public budget. Aid coming from ExIm, the MOFCOM and other government agencies is also used to directly finance projects, training and technical assistance, including the Africa medical programme that China has initiated during the Cold War.

3.4 Political and Diplomatic Cooperation

China has long maintained strong diplomatic relations with Africa. This began—and continues—also as a result of Chinese ODA and FDI policies: from 1961 to 1971, when Beijing successfully bid to the UNSC, China extended aid to 16 new African countries, winning official diplomatic relations with them. Since the 1990s, this trend has found new energy in the trade and financial exchanges between the two regions. As a consequence, Beijing was able to erode diplomatic influence in Africa not only from Taipei, but increasingly also from Washington, London, Paris, Brussels, Lisbon and Rome.

China's diplomatic ascendant over Africa has, however, also been possible because of its principled positions in foreign policy and economic aid. China is a staunch supporter of non-interference, and, as a country with its own sovereignty issues in Tibet, Xingjian and Inner Mongolia, it avoids any involvement with foreign conflicts—in Africa as elsewhere. Thousands of miles away from the East African coast, China maintains as little involvement as possible with African peace and security affairs, limiting its actions to the protection of Chinese economic interests and to the fulfilment of international informal requirements for a nation with world power ambitions. In 2008, the Chinese navy joined international anti-piracy operations off the Somalian coast, thus marking the PRC's first engagement in an operational mission outside its claimed territorial waters; similarly, in 2011, the Chinese air force participated, for the first time, in a civilian evacuation mission overseas when it chartered four military planes to evacuate its nationals from war-spiralling Libya. China has also long been a strong contributor towards UN peacekeeping operations: as of July 2013, it was contributing a total of 1700 troops, out of which over 1400 were stationed in Africa (they were 1300 in 2007).[42] These are considerable efforts, yet they are more related to Beijing's bid to promote its image of world power and good international citizen rather than an attempt to project its military power. Despite its global aspirations, China prefers, for the time being, to limit its geopolitical and military focus on the Asia-Pacific region.

On the other side, Beijing's newly acquired African diplomatic reach has clearly shown in a host of international cases. From influence on African delegations within the UNGA and the UNSC[43], to the promotion of the one-China policy through aggressive "purchase campaigns" towards African governments recognizing Taiwan[44], to reported dissuasion in supporting the Japanese bid to a permanent seat within the UNSC, to search for critical support in hosting international events, China has been perceived as a skilful player in leveraging its African contacts in multilateral issues and settings. As the continental (African Union)- and regional (Regional Economic Communities [RECs])[45]-level influence on their member states grows, China has also intensified diplomatic efforts to reach out to the headquarters of these institutions. Such influence has also worked in the interest of a number of African states, with a number of them avoiding UN resolutions or sanctions thanks to Beijing's veto option within the UNSC.[46]

4 Considerations on Chinese Involvement in Africa

How should Chinese economic, trade, financial and migratory policies in Africa be assessed? The "complete package" policy has allowed Beijing to win investment bids in an extremely competitive environment by leveraging its different vectors and obtaining from them increased bargaining power with its negotiating counterparts. China has also skilfully taken advantage of its institutional structure, which allows flexible negotiation and fund disbursal capacity, to outbid competitors and close sizeable deals in unusually short time frames. This short-term strategy contrasts with Western business and diplomatic habits, which have instead sought influence by resorting to long-term processes and soft-power outreach, exemplified by the instrumental use of conditionality and the institutionalization of African elites to the neoclassic theories underpinning SAPs-like reforms.

China is likely to have an impact upon African economies through two major venues (1) its governmental resources and; (2) its large population autonomously seeking better opportunities abroad. Because of their different nature and finalities, it is useful to divide the assessment on Chinese presence in Africa following the cleavage between institutional or state-led involvement and private or people-led involvement.

4.1 State-Led Involvement

It is difficult establishing whether Chinese SOEs in Africa are getting similar rates of ROIs as Western MNCs, and whether the Chinese government is benefiting from similarly cheap commodity imports, high primary income and favourable value-adding opportunities. What is clear is that an exclusive focus on the low profitability margins many Chinese firms operate on would provide a misleading picture, as these contracts are the results of much larger business deals (the "complete packages"), in which China has multiple sources of income or strategic advantages, including using its outward FDI for Keynesian-type expansionary fiscal policies, accessing competitive mining and oil markets despite the relative backwardness of its technology, accessing export opportunities for linked industries within China, and creating overseas job opportunities for its 1.4 billion population, including 100 million rural poor. Official data also show that West–Africa and China–Africa trade structures are not very different. Differences in the FDI trade structure may be accounted for by the relatively larger and more stable presence of Chinese national communities in Africa when compared to national communities from Western countries. This analysis is supported by the fact that China, despite displaying a broader spectrum of industry investments in Africa, has a strong FDI geographic concentration, thus following Western trends. China might be investing in different sectors, but it does so only in countries where it sources its primary commodity needs and where it envisages long-term interests. Beijing could, therefore, see its contribution towards Africa's manufacturing capability as a spillover effect from its expanding extractive operations, its large outflow of Chinese migrants, and the constant seeking of opportunities to serve a burgeoning manufacturing and services domestic market. We can also say that Chinese ODA compared to Western ODA has a limited weight in absolute terms and is largely understood as an integral part of FDI and trade policies.

Similarly to Western ODA, Chinese financial assistance does not seem to be used to create an Africa-owned manufacturing capacity able to export capital or consumer goods and services to OECD countries or even to China. A review of 20 "Chinese megadeals" between 2003 and 2011 (Strange et al. 2013, p. 32), including seven ODA and OOF-like projects, as well as 13 purely commercial projects, reveals that none of these is geared at setting up Africa-participated manufacturing plants.[47] Considerations on these projects largely overlap with considerations on World Bank projects in Chap. 5: while they might be contributing in creating the underpinning conditions for allowing Africa to climb the value-adding ladder, as well as provide social relief during the first stages of development, they may also serve the purpose of strengthening a trading and financial system that sees Africa at a structural loss. Some analysts go further and read in China's FDI policies with Africa, an attempt to emulate the Japanese strategy of keeping home as much profitable operations as possible, while delocalizing only those activities whose profitability would not justify domestic labour cost.

Similarly, it remains unclear whether Beijing has serious intentions to integrate Africa in those Global Value Chains, where China plays a pivotal role. China has reportedly exploited Africa's export concessionary terms in trading with the EU and the USA to delocalize some of its state-owned facilities that would otherwise be barred from exporting in developed markets—something that Western-based companies have never done. These investments were mainly targeted at the apparel and textile sectors, taking advantage of the Multifibre Agreement first and AGOA and EBA afterwards. Whereas these investments were aimed at enjoying duty breaks on OECD-bound exports in specific industries, the overall propensity of Chinese SOEs to co-invest in Africa and subsequently export towards OECD countries or even China seems low. Experience in its recent past has likely discouraged Beijing from delocalizing whatever high potential job, industrial processing and R&D facility it managed to acquire on its own or through its painstakingly negotiated inward FDI. Besides, China's FDI in Africa is entitled to enjoy at least the same benefits that the WTO, WB and IMF have negotiated with G90 countries mostly on behalf of OECD countries, if not better terms arising from bilateral agreements. To this extent, it is unlikely that Chinese SOEs operations in Africa will entail any economic revolution with respect to Western MNCs' policies.

4.2 People-Led Involvement

Substantial differences between OECD and China economic policies may, instead, result from the profoundly different nature of Western and Chinese migratory patterns and private investments. OECD and Chinese migratory flows to Africa are profoundly different in number, composition and finalities: while every year, Western expatriates move in the thousands to Africa on short-term stints offered by private MNCs, large SMEs, civil society organizations or diplomatic missions, Chinese move to Africa in the dozens, if not hundreds of thousands, to work as SOEs employees, contract workers, independent entrepreneurs, small farmers and petty traders.[48] Figures on the Chinese business presence in Africa vary widely: figures for 2011 go from 4600 (Shinn and Eisenman 2012, p. 129) to 1800 (Song 2011) Chinese companies in Africa, up from a 2006 ExIm Bank figure placing them at 800. While a small minority of these firms is accounted by large SOEs—only 5 % according to Song—, most of the others are small SMEs or even individual businessmen and business-women who set up shop in Africa with the intention of finding long-term opportunities. These companies and people create different sociological and market dynamics from those created by Western MNCs and major Chinese SOEs: driven by personal interests and long-term prospects, these migrants naturally seek to diversify their activities and find business opportunities in fields with lower investment thresholds than extractive industries or large-scale commercial agriculture. These are the entrepreneurs from whom larger investment diversification, import substitution industrialization and Africa-bound interests could be expected over the mid-to-long term.

Since around one million Chinese have moved to Africa, many of whom as independent economic actors, and millions more will likely follow them, the impact of Chinese SOHOs and private SMEs is of a substantially different nature from SOEs' and MNCs' brownfield or even greenfield investments. Chinese investments and migratory flows linked to small-scale manufacturing and trading are omnipresent but do not surface in most official statistics. The exact contribution that these migrants and investments will represent for Africa remains to be determined. Some hints can however be derived from the Chinese diaspora in other countries. Chinese communities in South-East Asia (Philippines, Indonesia, Malaysia) have slowly but steadily integrated with indigenous communities, often climbing the socio-economic ladder till becoming their economic and trading elites. These communities have maintained strong links with their mother country, but have nonetheless engaged in inter-ethnic marriages and contributed in nurturing a favourable business environment by integrating the hosting country's economic and financial structures. In other instances, as in several European countries, Chinese communities seem instead to have remained largely secluded, preferring intra-ethnic marriages, using parallel economic, financial and service networks, while often resorting to tax-dodging schemes. These patterns are exemplified by the high rate of business exchanges among Chinese nationals, the high number of Chinese illegal migrants, the fact that Chinese communities make little or no use of local banking, insurance and financial services, as well as a tendency to avoid education and health services, except from those provided through publicly sponsored welfare programmes. The integration pattern that will be followed by increasingly larger Chinese communities in Africa will determine the extent to which China could represent itself as a truly innovative actor in Africa's international relations.

Notes

1. For an historic review of China–Africa relations, see Shinn and Eisenman (2012) and Alden (2007).
2. When in 1904, "the Anglo-Chinese Labour Convention and the Transvaal Labour Importation Ordinance permitted the introduction of indentured labour to work in the gold mines [...] The European mining companies recruited 63,695 Chinese indentured laborers to work in the Transvaal gold mines under a contract that limited their stay to three years [...] At the beginning of 1907, there were nearly 54,000 Chinese in the Witwatersrand fields. They constituted almost 35 percent of the total unskilled work force" (Shinn and Eisenman 2012, p. 24).
3. The only two agreements that the ROC signed with African countries in this period were a 1930 exchange of notes on most-favoured nation treatment of goods traded between semi-independent Egypt and the ROC, which remained in effect for less than a year; and a treaty of friendship between independent Liberia and the ROC, which constituted China's first treaty with a fully independent African country. China also maintained an interest in the Arab world and Egypt, in particular, because of China's own minority Muslim community (Shinn and Eisenman 2012, pp. 26–28).
4. South–South cooperation is a fairly recent concept in International Relations (IR), indirectly testifying the limited scope of international exchanges between the biggest developing nation and the rest of the developing world.
5. As Abyssinia in those same years, Chinese sovereign integrity was sacrificed by the League of Nation in an effort to appease nationalist powers: in 1932, Beijing protested to no avail against the Manchurian invasion by the Japanese who, bolstered by the lack of retaliation from the West, proceeded to a full scale invasion of China in 1937.
6. Between 1970 and 1975, Canada's population stood at 21–23 million, with a nominal GDP comprised between 863 and 1706 billion USD; China had a population of roughly 850 million people and a nominal GDP comprised between 915 and 1616 billion USD. Source: World Bank.
7. Even today, China has 4 % of the IMF quota, punching below countries with smaller economies, including Germany, France and

the UK. The same happens within the WB and regional development banks controlled by lenders linked to the Bretton Woods structure, such as the Asian Development Bank, where Japan has 15.7 % of the shares; USA 15.6 % and; China 6.5 %. This phenomenon has led Beijing to promote alternative financial institutions, including the New Development Bank with BRICS states and the Asian Infrastructure Investment Bank (AIIB).

8. China was one of the 23 original signatories of the General Agreement on Tariffs and Trade (GATT) in 1948; however, after China's revolution in 1949, the government in Taiwan announced that China would leave the GATT system. Although the government in Beijing never recognized this withdrawal decision, it was only in 1986 that Beijing notified the GATT of its wish to resume its status as a contracting party. Negotiations between China and the WTO were successfully concluded on 17 September 2001.
9. Since the 1990s, Chinese senior government officials had already been paying an impressive number of visits to Africa. In February 2007, Chinese president Hu Jintao paid the longest visit ever by a non-African leader in Africa, after Chinese high officials had toured other 21 African countries in the preceding 24 months. Since 1997, over 40 chiefs of state and heads of government from African countries have visited China.
10. The previous editions of the Indian (India–Africa Summit), Japanese (TICAD–Tokyo International Conference on African Development) and French (Sommet Afrique–France, last held in 2010) forums did not manage to reach the same attendance level or volume of agreements signed by the Chinese at their first Summit in 2006.
11. As of April 2009, the European Commission and the USA stood at 46 delegations/embassies each in Africa.
12. The Fifth Ministerial Conference of the Forum on China–Africa Cooperation Beijing Action Plan (2013–2015).
13. This phenomenon is largely documented: "Many Chinese companies are willing to take losses and support prestige projects to gain market entry or share and to support government policies" (Shinn and Eisenman 2012, p. 130). Chinese economic expansion in Africa has also coincided with the general internationalization of Chinese firms, generally characterized by high levels of approximation and reliance on trial-and-error attitudes, with many of these firms venturing abroad by leveraging state capital, sometimes

already saddled with high levels of debt and minimal international experience (Alden and Davies 2006).

14. Similarly to what Europe has done with the Europe–Africa discourse, China has also successfully built a strong and deeply-engrained rhetoric on its normative relations with Africa (Strauss 2009). According to Chris Alden and Daniel Large, this is a modality of engagement that purposefully "[…] structures relations such that they may remain asymmetrical in economic content but equal in terms of recognition of economic gains and political standing" (Alden and Large 2011, p. 28). Setting aside studies directly coming from the Chinese Ministry of Foreign Affairs and the numerous institutions that receive subvention from the government, China also suffers from a lack of freedom in journalism and academia. Tellingly, very few studies of China–Africa relations from Chinese Universities or organizations raise any of the problems that have been put forward, not only by the West, but also by African countries themselves. Among the few recorded exceptions, an assessment of the Chinese Academy of Social Sciences on Corporate Social Responsibility in Mali, Ethiopia and Sudan, concluded that the Government should pay more attention to a variety of problems (Shinn and Eisenman 2012, p. 131).
15. According to the Chinese State Council, in February 2013, China roughly had 100 Million people living below the poverty line of 1.25 USD/day purchasing power parity (6.3 RMB/day) (Economist 2013); this figure roughly corresponded to 7.38 % of the 2013 Chinese population. According to the World Bank, 438 Million people in Africa, e.g. 46.8 % of its population, were below that same poverty threshold in 2013 http://povertydata.worldbank.org/poverty/home/. In OECD countries, no one falls below the 1.25 USD/day poverty threshold.
16. Among other accounts, see Alden and Large (2011), Alden (2007), Ampiah and Naidu (2008). A counter-argument on the relevance of African agency in Sino–African relations is, instead, developed by Mohan and Lampert (2013).
17. One of such practices is the Chinese Ministry of Foreign Affairs' (MOFA) habit of calling African Ambassadors in the middle of the night for "urgent" meetings, as reported by the South African Consul General to Hong Kong in 2013.
18. See, for example, the fracture between the two continental powers—Nigeria and South Africa—created by the competition over

the position of the African Union Commission chairperson, eventually won by South Africa with the election of Nkosazana Dlamini-Zuma in July 2012.

19. Won Kidane, for example, notices that while China–Africa Bilateral Investment Treaties (BITs) are outdated and lack uniformity, also "[…] because of China's fundamental and enduring doctrinal dilemma on the role of ownership of the means of production and the level of its protection", there are signs that China's latest treaties, including with Madagascar, "[…] contain the hallmarks of North–South BITs in many areas, including the definition of 'investment', 'treatment', and 'dispute settlement'" (Kidane 2013).
20. See Chap. 5. Among the most relevant figures: the sum of 47 African state budgets stands at 450 billion USD in 2011 (hence, 21.6 % of the 2013 Chinese budget); the 2011 QS World University Rankings only placed four African Universities among the top 500 worldwide; most African states have limited or irrelevant diplomatic representation in IOs and IFIs.
21. OECD, PISA 2009 Results: What students know and can do.
22. The China Export Import Bank (ExIm Bank) is a fully state-owned financial institution aimed at supporting Chinese overseas investments by offering financial products—including export credits, foreign exchange guarantees, concessional and non-concessional loans—both to Chinese companies and foreign governments. In 2011, Fitch Ratings estimated that ExIm lent about 67.2 billion USD to Sub-Saharan Africa between 2001 and 2010 (compared with the World Bank's 54.7 billion USD), mostly used in infrastructural projects. The China Development Bank (CDB) is a largely privatized Chinese bank with vast assets in China and overseas; albeit less engaged in Africa than the ExIm Bank, it runs its own special loan programme with Africa: by 2011, it helped funding, according to the CDB, more than 1000 projects in more than 25 African countries. The China–Africa Development Fund (CADF) is managed by the CDB and tasked with supporting Chinese private investments in Africa through single-project loans of small entities (5–50 million USD). The China Investment Corporation (CIC) is one of the world's largest sovereign funds, being tasked with managing part of China's foreign exchange reserves. The China–Africa Business Council (CABC) is a public–private partnership among the UN Development Programme (UNDP), the Chinese Ministry of Commerce and the China

Society for the Promotion of the Guangcai programme; it is tasked with informing and connecting interested investors and helping them in finding partners in China and Africa.

23. As a matter of example, Huawei Technologies is technically private but maintains close ties with the government, cooperates closely with the militaries and other state actors, and receives lines of credit from state banks, as well as funding for research and development. With 2500 people employed across 40 African countries, Huawei Technologies is also an example of Chinese state intervention in Africa via formally private ventures (Shinn and Eisenman 2012).
24. As a matter of example, writing about China's special economic zones in Africa, it was noted that "some of their most basic aspects are still unclear to many people, even the most obvious question as to which of the many media stories about Chinese zones are about the "official" zones that enjoy Chinese government support" (Bräutigam and Xiaoyang 2011, p. 29).
25. Chinese illegal gold diggers in Ghana, for example, have posed China–Ghana diplomatic relations under strain. After a July 2013 crackdown on more than 200 Chinese diggers illegally staying in Ghana, their relatives have requested Chinese authorities to provide stronger assistance and consular protection.
26. The agreements usually entail a Chinese upfront cash payment, an engagement of the receiving government to set aside a determined amount of commodities per year and Chinese payments for these commodities through an escrow account used to repay the debt. Technically, this arrangement has been defined as a forward contract with payments back loaded into later years. See Lee and Shalmon in Rotberg (2009, p. 119).
27. Africa was already seen as a strong diplomatic partner of China since it gave its massive support to Beijing's bid to the UNSC in 1971. Diplomatic support was further confirmed by the apologetic attitude of African capitals towards the Chinese crackdown in Tiananmen Square in 1989. Since then, political analysts agree that Beijing's diplomatic leverage on the continent has been growing steadily.
28. From a theoretical perspective, Kaplinsky suggests that Beijing is today replicating what the West was doing during the colonial period, when trade, FDI, financial flows and ODA were naturally seen as complementing each other: "[…] British colonies were seen as providers of traded commodities for UK consumers, involving FDI from UK firms (for example, producing tea in Kenya),

with infrastructures to support this trade provided by the UK Colonial Office (roads and ports to transport the tea to the UK)" (Kaplinsky and Morris 2009, p. 9). Among the reasons that brought the demise of this system, Kaplinsky also individuates a growing opposition among the OECD public opinion to a system that was seen as exploitative of low income countries.

29. Trade dumping of Chinese products is common practice in Africa, but few African states have the institutional capacity to take measures against it. The International Trade Administration Commission of South Africa (ITAC) is among the few African regulatory bodies that have been active on this, having subjected Chinese exports to several anti-dumping investigations and trade remedies. It is interesting noting that even an editorial published by the PRC Embassy to South Africa admits that "[...] at present China is dumping huge quantities of cheap imports [sic] to the severe detriment of the manufacturing sectors in Africa". At http://za.china-embassy.org/eng/zt/thirdeye/t282965.htm
30. "Local manufacturers that we interviewed in Ghana and Nigeria often argued that it is these African traders in China, rather than Chinese traders in Africa, who have been primarily responsible for the massive influx of cheap Chinese goods in recent years" (Mohan and Lampert 2013, p. 100).
31. The China International Fund Ltd (HK) has extended direct credit lines to the *Gabinete de Reconstrução Nacional* (GRN), an office under the Minister in Chief of the Angolan President's cabinet. There is much opacity around the figures (between 2.9 and 9 billion USD) and finalities (reportedly linked to vast construction projects, including Luanda's airport and drainage system) of these credit lines (Corkin 2011, p. 172).
32. ExIm Bank is the sole agency for the provision of Chinese Government concessional loans; key recipients of Exim bank loans in Africa include Angola, Equatorial Guinea, Congo Brazzaville, Ethiopia, Guinea, Nigeria, Sudan and Zimbabwe (Power et al. 2012, p. 77). A report of the World Bank, which has a Memorandum of Understanding with the ExIm Bank, defines these loans as "marginally concessional, although significantly less so than those associated with ODA". The same report, notices however that the first 2 billion USD tranche payment had a 50.3 % grant element, whereas the threshold to qualify for ODA is as low as 25 % (Corkin 2011, p. 173). It should be noted that lack of clarity on the com-

pliancy of these loans with OECD ODA criteria also emerges from the fact that neither China nor Angola are interested in having a seal of approval from the OECD DAC. In the case of Angola, the loans are repayable at Libor plus 1.5 % over 17 years, including a grace period of five years; the loan is covered by the Angolan Finance Ministry's sovereign guarantee.

33. Although oil is a commodity with internationally defined prices, it is clear that there are many other negotiation areas on which the parties can try leveraging their respective interests, including, *inter alia*, oil quality, processing levels at export, export markets aside from China, shipping conditions and operators etc.
34. It is interesting noticing that the Chinese and Angolans could not reach a compromise on the setting up of a 200,000 barrels-per-day oil refinery in Lobito, which was originally part of a "complete package". Shortly after calling off the deal in March 2007, Sinopec withdrew from its stakes in Angola's blocks 15, 17 and 18 (Corkin 2011, p. 175).
35. For example, the 2008 agreement between China and the DRC allegedly established that only one in five workers can be Chinese; 0.5 % of the investment must be spent on transfer of technology and on training Congolese staff; 1 % has to be spent on social activities in the region; 3 % to cover environmental costs; and that 10–12 % of the work has to be sub–contracted to Congolese companies (Vandaele 2008).
36. The term "off-budget" identifies spending financed through foreign flows of money (grants/loans) that do not go through the state budget and is therefore not controlled through the beneficiary's Ministry of Finance.
37. As a matter of example, in Angola's 2005 deal, China pushed to avoid the setting up of refinery capacities in Africa; these efforts are in line with China's general policy of avoiding importing refined oil. Similarly, the DRC Katanga province eventually had to recur to a legislation prohibiting the export of cobalt ore to avoid that all value-adding processing was exclusively carried out in China, while leaving relatively little profits in the DRC.
38. "China's eight-measure economic policy on Africa well implemented, says Chinese minister", People's daily on-line, 20 January 2009 http://english.peopledaily.com.cn/90001/90776/90883/6577120.html
39. In Angola, for example, Sinopec's 2004 successful bid to several oil concessions has been seen as directly attached to a 2-billion line of

credit that was opened shortly before by the Chinese government. Similarly, the Democratic Republic of Congo 2008 Socomin's maxi-deal seems to have materialized thanks to China's ability to mobilize strong financial resources (9 billion USD) and involve several SOEs (operating in water, electricity, education, health, and transport) in an extremely short time span (few months) and under no scrutiny from the Chinese civil society.

40. Concerning the Chinese government's declaration on aid to Africa, Paul Hubbard remarks that "Although the Chinese like to pledge billions of dollars worth of aid [...] loans sizes suggest that the actual volume of loans disbursed is significantly lower than that" (Rotberg 2009, p. 222).
41. This paragraph analyses financial flows defined in 4.2.1 as ODA-like and quantified in a range comprised between 0.5 and 1.5 billion USD/year.
42. Data from the United Nations Peacekeeping database.
43. South Africa's stints as a UNSC non-permanent member in 2007–2008 and 2011–2012 offer a particularly rich array of cases, with China seemingly pushing Pretoria into a number of controversial positions on resolution concerning human right violations in Myanmar; Zimbabwe and Iran. In 2009 and 2011, South Africa used preposterous reasons to deny a visa to the Dalai Lama.
44. The last African countries to switch allegiance to Beijing were Lesotho (1994), Niger (1996), Guinea Bissau (1998), Liberia (2003), Senegal (2005) and Malawi (2008). As of September 2013, only four African countries still recognize the Republic of China: Burkina Faso, Gambia, São Tomé and Principe, and Swaziland.
45. ECOWAS, ECCAS, COMESA, SADC, Community of Sahel-Saharan states (CEN-SAD), Inter-governmental Authority for Development (IGAD) and Union du Maghreb Arab (UMA).
46. For example, China vetoed UN resolutions that would have imposed sanctions on Sudan (2007) and Zimbabwe (2008).
47. The projects mainly refer to mining and oil extraction, building of infrastructures likely to be used in the extractive industry (roads, railways, power plants) and service delivery (water distribution, sewage systems).
48. Sanou Mbaye, a former senior official at the African Development Bank, notices that "[...] more Chinese have come to Africa in the past ten years than Europeans in the past 400. First came Chinese

from state-owned companies, but more and more arrive solo or stay behind after finishing contract work" (Economist 2011a). Similarly, Shinn and Eisenman note that "[…] there is one unique dimension of China's business and labour practices in Africa […] [which] distinguishes China from all other expatriate national contractors […] this is the sheer number of Chinese migrants […]. Many of these are regular employees […] others are contract workers on large infrastructures projects secured by China; others again are individual, independent entrepreneurs, large and small […] but others again are very small shopkeepers, traders and farmers" (Shinn and Eisenman 2012, p. 105).

References

AERC. (2008). *Scoping studies on China Africa economic relations.* Nairobi: African Economic Research Consortium.

Alden, C. (2007). *China in Africa: Partner, competitor or hegemon?* London: Zed Books.

Alden, C., & Davies, M. (2006). A profile of the operations of Chinese multinationals in Africa. *South African Journal of International Affairs, 13*(1), 83–96.

Alden, C., & Large, D. (2011). China's exceptionalism and the challenges of delivering difference in Africa. *Journal of Contemporary China, 20*(68), 21–38.

Ampiah, K., & Naidu, S. (2008). *Crouching tiger, hidden dragon?: Africa and China*. Durban: University of KwaZulu-Natal Press.

Biao, X. (2011). A ritual economy of 'talent': China and overseas Chinese professionals. *Journal of Ethnic and Migration Studies, 37*(5), 821–838.

Bräutigam, D., & Xiaoyang, T. (2011). African Shenzhen: China's special economic zones in Africa. *The Journal of Modern African Studies, 49*(01), 27–54.

Broadman, H. G., & Isik, G. (2007). *Africa's silk road: China and India's new economic frontier.* Washington, DC: World Bank.

Cheung, Y. W., De Haan, J., Qian, X., & Yu, S. (2012). China's outward direct investment in Africa. *Review of International Economics, 20*(2), 201–220.

Corkin, L. (2011). Uneasy allies: China's evolving relations with Angola. *Journal of Contemporary African Studies, 29*(2), 169–180.

Dikötter, F. (2010). *Mao's great famine: The history of China's most devastating catastrophe, 1958–62.* London: Bloomsbury Publishing.

Economist. (2011a). Trying to pull together – Africans are asking whether China is making their lunch or eating it. *Economist.*

Economist. (2011b). A work in progress. *Economist.*

Economist. (2013). World-class poverty. *Economist.*

French, H. W. (2014). *China's second continent: How a million migrants are building a new empire in Africa.* New York: Knopf.

Henley, J., Kratzsch, S., Külür, M., & Tandogan, T. (2009). Foreign direct investment from China, India and South Africa in Sub-Saharan Africa: A new or old phenomenon? In A. U. Santos-Paulino & G. Wan (Eds.), *Southern engines of global growth and the role of FDI*. Helsinki, Finland: Oxford University Press.

Kaplinsky, R., & Morris, M. (2009). Chinese FDI in Sub-Saharan Africa: Engaging with large dragons. *European Journal of Development Research, 21*(4), 551–569.

Kidane, W. (2013). *Reflections on China – Africa BITs*. Paper presented at the Annual Meeting of the American Society of International Law.

Lu, Y. (2011). China's trade rush with Africa. *Capital Week 25.4.2011*.

Lyman, P. (2005). *China's rising role in Africa*. Presentation to the US-China Commission, 21.07.2005. Washington, DC: Council on Foreign Relations.

MOFCOM. (2008). Statistical bulletin of China's outward FDI. Beijing: MOFCOM.

Mohan, G., & Lampert, B. (2013). Negotiating China: Reinserting African agency into China–Africa relations. *African Affairs, 112*(446), 92–110.

Mohan, G., & Tan-Mullins, M. (2009). Chinese migrants in africa as new agents of development? An analytical framework. *European Journal of Development Research, 21*(4), 588–605.

OECD. (2009). *OECD benchmark definition of foreign direct investment 2008 fourth edition*. OECD Publishing.

Power, M., Mohan, G., & Tan-Mullins, M. (2012). *China's resource diplomacy in Africa: Powering development?* Houndmills: Palgrave Macmillan.

Raine, S. (2013). *China's African challenges*. Abingdon, Oxon, New York, NY: Routledge for the International Institute for Strategic Studies.

Rosefielde, S. (2011). China's perplexing foreign trade policy: Causes, consequences, and solutions. *American Foreign Policy Interests, 33*(1), 10–16.

Rotberg, R. I. (2009). *China into Africa: Trade, aid, and influence*. Washington, DC: Brookings Institution Press.

Sautman, B., & Hairong, Y. (2007). Friends and interests: China's distinctive links with Africa. *African Studies Review, 50*(03), 75–114.

Shinn, D. H., & Eisenman, J. (2012). *China and Africa: A century of engagement*. Philadelphia: University of Pennsylvania Press.

Song, H. (2011). Chinese private direct investment and overseas Chinese network in Africa. *China & World Economy, 19*(4), 109–126.

Strange, A., Parks, B., Tierney, M. J., Fuchs, A., Dreher, A., & Ramachandran, V. (2013). China's development finance to Africa: A media-based approach to data collection. *Center for Global Development Working Paper*, 323.

Strauss, J. (2009). The past and the present: Historical and rhetorical lineages in China's relations with Africa. *The China Quarterly, 199*, 777–795.

Taylor, I. (2007). *China and Africa: Engagement and compromise*. London and New York: Routledge.

Vandaele, J. (2008). China outdoes Europeans in Congo. *Asia Times Online*, 12.02.2008.

Conclusions

Fieldwork evidence and the history of state economic praxes suggest that Western ODA will not take Africa on a path of endogenous and sustainable economic growth, primarily because it is not meant to do so. This assessment represents heterodoxy in the development literature and anathema in the institutional discourse in which the ODA industry operates. As Chinese governmental policies towards Africa hardly represent a revolutionary departure from development cooperation standards set by the West in dealing with low-income countries, the book argues that the goal of an independent and self-sustainable Africa will require a new political economy agenda pushing the continent away from the international institutional economic settings in which it is currently embedded.

Following these ideas, provisional answers to the book's research questions, accessory topics and normative ethos can be grouped under five thematic headings:

Differences between Chinese and Western foreign economic policies in Africa are limited and yet relevant. Chinese, European and American trade and FDI policies towards Africa are largely similar. Pitted against the EU and USA, Chinese trade and investment flows remain relatively small—yet aggressively growing. There are little data available on primary income and portfolio investments, but anecdotal evidence and data relating to debt suggest that behavioural differences are also fairly limited on these entries. More relevant policy differences relate instead to

S. Raudino, *Development Aid and Sustainable Economic Growth in Africa*, DOI 10.1007/978-3-319-38936-3

ODA (due both to capabilities and intention) and capital flight (mainly due to the traditional attractiveness of Western markets and banks; these trends will however likely change in the future).

The single most relevant difference between West–Africa and China–Africa relations likely results from the large flows of Chinese migrants to Africa, which is having a controversial socio-economic impact upon Africa. This difference is not only a result of deliberate migratory policies: Beijing might be indirectly favouring the Chinese diaspora, but it is, by and large, a spontaneous phenomenon, arising from the large number of Chinese nationals looking for economic opportunities in low- and mid-income countries. This flow of labourers, small entrepreneurs and petty traders entails a shift of expertise and productive capacity to Africa, a phenomenon that is already visible in labour-intensive and capital-scarce sectors. This might turn to be a positive development for the hosting economies, although it raises competition with local players and it risks reiterating economic apartheid between Chinese communities and indigenous communities, similarly to what has happened, with different modalities and to a different extent, in other countries hosting large Chinese communities.

The political structure of both representative democracies and authoritarian States, as well as their relative power in the international arena, explain these States' stances in international economic, trade and financial policies. As soon as they graduate from developing status into transition and developed economies, both democratic-representative systems and authoritarian regimes face structural incentives in turning "from poachers into gamekeepers" of international business norms. That has been the case not only for OECD countries that have coupled economic development with increasing democratization, but also for many authoritarian governments, including the People's Republic of China. This clearly shows in today's relations between China and OECD countries, on the one side, and China and Africa, on the other: China is today proposing to Africa the very same policies and agreements that it did not accept from OECD countries in its own territory.

For many years, China only allowed inward FDI to be channelled towards Joint Ventures (JV), while accepting Wholly Foreign-Owned Enterprises (WFOEs) only at a later stage and under a stringent regulatory framework. Since the opening of its economy under Deng Xiaoping and until today, China has obliged foreign companies, including MNCs operating on its territory, to surrender their foreign-currency earnings to state-controlled trading companies, under terms and conditions established by the Chinese government itself. On the other side, Chinese SOEs have negotiated extremely generous terms of agreement with African countries hosting Chinese FDI and allowing Chinese SOEs to repatriate most of their earnings. Similarly, earnings from the overseas Chinese diaspora or overseas Chinese business operations, as well as funds raised by Chinese financial firms in foreign markets, largely escape foreign fiscal pressure and seldom enter overseas banking networks: these funds are instead funnelled back into Chinese financial networks. Whereas China has established extremely stringent rules on local content requirements and on the hiring of local labours in contracts signed with foreign companies, Beijing-controlled SOEs have long been reluctant to hire local workers in Africa, both for cadre and unskilled positions. Whereas China has been eager to build labour-intensive manufacturing facilities with its inward FDI—including polluting and low-value adding facilities—, it pushes invested economies to relinquish their primary commodities at the rawest possible stage, while locating all manufacturing capacity and operations within the Chinese territory.

These considerations suggest that more than one commentator has confused Chinese engagements in Africa with the expression of a development model—the "Beijing consensus"[1]—that Africa could supposedly emulate by wholeheartedly embracing Chinese economic cooperation, the line of reasoning being that Chinese economic actors operate in Africa in the same way they operate, or have operated, in their own country. This is incorrect: Chinese companies operating in China are subject to detailed economic and industrial plans (aimed at maximizing the value-adding component of their work), strict financial provisions (not allowing them to funnel money abroad), and stringent fiscal regimes (leaving little room for tax dodging). None of these conditions apply to Chinese companies in Africa; on the contrary, many Chinese SOEs remain subject to their own national provisions even when operating abroad, rather than being subject to provisions emanating from the hosting country. Misperceptions on the supposed existence of an indigenous Chinese economic development model being now applied to Africa might have been fuelled by the fact that China is sponsoring African Special Economic Zones (SEZs) allegedly following the model of Chinese SEZs. This is a misperception: Chinese zones in Africa are either totally or majority owned by China, enjoy tax holidays and waivers on import tariffs for raw materials and inputs, provide for restrictions on strike activity, and, in some cases, grant Chinese products local certificates of origin, thus taking advantage of the hosting countries' various international trade agreements (Bräutigam and Xiaoyang 2011). Chinese companies in African SEZs have little forward and backward linkages with local economies and likely enjoy favourable terms on repatriation of profits. Since none of these conditions would have been acceptable to China's own inward FDI, the Beijing Consensus' "[…] direct challenge to the Washington Consensus ideas of interventionism" and its "[…] principles, which borrowed heavily from China's traditional views of […] equality of states and mutually beneficial exchanges" (Huang 2013, p. 114) can be seen as part of a sophisticated soft-power rhetoric aimed at balancing the "benign links" narrative coming from the West.

Paradoxically, some of the recipes contained in the "Beijing Consensus"—including sustainability of economic progresses, globalization on own terms and opposition to the Washington consensus—could be embraced by African countries exactly by avoiding falling for many of the economic cooperation models and investment conditions that the Chinese themselves are trying to set up, including by exporting consumer goods and services to Africa, importing unprocessed commodities, venting abroad their excess population, and particularly unskilled male labour, setting up overseas productive capacity that remains largely isolated from the local economic context and structuring profits abroad or keeping them in Chinese parallel financial circuits. Wholeheartedly embracing Chinese foreign investment and trade deals just as an alternative to traditional Western post-colonial economic relations and as an escape to the conditionality principle of Washington-based institutions will not improve African countries' chances to embark on a process of sustainable endogenous economic development, as that would rather correspond to transitioning from an externally-engineered and dominated economic network to another one.

Neither Western nor Chinese economic and development cooperation policies will take Africa on a path of sustainable development. Western ODA in Africa and other G90 countries has existed since the 1920s at least; statistics show that there is no significant correlation between amounts of ODA disbursed and long-term GDP growth. On the contrary, long-term statistical indexes suggest that macro-regions which received less ODA per capita (including Latin America, South-East Asia and the Far East) have eventually embarked on a more successful and sustainable path of economic growth than regions (including Sub-Saharan Africa) that received exceptionally high levels of ODA per capita. Remarkably, in almost a century of foreign assistance, there has been no single country that can claim to have embarked on a path of sustainable development because of ODA or ODA-inspired policies. While some of the countries that managed economic development in the last century were until fairly recently ODA beneficiaries at their own turn (Asian NIEs and China), there is no corroborated link between their development and the role that ODA played in this process. There are, on the other side, indications that ODA policies have often been used by donor countries to promote "window-dressing" or *trompe l'oeil* activities (addressing domestic moral concerns and international criticisms by dedicating relatively small domestic resources to charitable and philanthropic activities) or even "negative" economic policies (purposefully hampering economic growth in other regions as a means to enhance the donors' own economic agenda). Since there has been no structural change in the way ODA policies are conceived and administered, there is little ground on which stronger expectations could be built for the future.

Historical examples reviewed in the book suggest that today's high-income countries reached their status because of a mixture of institutional, investment and trade measures that are little related to today's "Washington Consensus"—or, for that matter, to the so-called "Beijing Consensus". Instead, what has been defined as the "virtuous cycle" of developmental public policies includes provisions favouring specialization in activities characterized by the principles of increasing marginal returns and economy of scale, shifting resources from agriculture and extractive industries towards technology and capital-intensive sectors, a strong entrepreneurial and regulatory role played by the government, a strong normative framework regulating relations with foreign trading partners and investors in such a way to optimize the benefits of international trade and inward FDI, a set of industrial, trade and financial policies aimed at retaining and wisely investing hard currency, and well-integrated migration and human resources policies.

These conditions might not be necessary (resource-rich countries in the Middle-East achieved mid- or high-income status without complying with all these policies) or sufficient (there are certainly other variables that contribute to the economic fate of nations) to entail sustainable economic growth, but they do establish a firm common ground among countries that successfully managed to climb the ladder of economic development. When measured against this common ground—the so-called "virtuous cycle" of developmental public policies—both Chinese and Western international economic policies in Africa fail to meet required standards. On the contrary, the economic measures promoted by both are, at times, diametrically opposite to lessons learnt from OECD and NIEs' historical experiences.

To this extent, differences between Chinese and Western economic cooperation policies in Africa are not structural and do not warrant expectations that the Chinese government—the (not so) new kid on the African block[2]—will introduce radical changes in the traditional structure of Africa's international economic relations. To a large extent, it is a matter of new rhetoric injected in the same old structures. Nor Western efforts seeking cooperation with China in Africa have so far given signs of tackling the focus of much-needed reforms, being instead directed at fostering EU–China cooperation on traditional ODA items and modalities such as security, infrastructure, protection of the environment, rural development and political dialogue.[3] Structural changes, on the other hand, may arise over the mid- to long-term from the largely uncoordinated efforts of millions of Chinese settlers moving to Africa—on top of their macroeconomic impact, these migratory flows will likely entail a controversial effect also upon the sociological, political and ethnical equilibrium of African societies.

Bold action is needed on the African governments' side. If Africa wants to emulate the success stories of the Asian NIEs and of China, it has to undertake similar policy reforms on its own, as no international ODA plan will ever push its governments to seek better arrangements in a number of negotiations in which the donor countries' own economic interests are at stake. Despite the academic and normative campaigns carried out by the neoliberal school in economics, Washington-based institutions and the many actors and interests supporting them, there is empirical evidence suggesting that many aspects of international economic relations have always been subject either to zero-sum-game logics or to extremely skewed positive-sum-game logics. Among the actions that Africa should consider and which correspond to an operationalization of the "virtuous cycle" of developmental public policies, it is worth recalling some specific measures.

First: maximization of profit margins in existing trade and investment relations. These include negotiation efforts aimed at obtaining better trade and investment deals with OECD countries and China, but increasingly also with the BRICS and South-East Asia. Resource-rich African countries have different options, particularly for highly-coveted natural resources in African hands. Brutal cartel logic worked for oil in OPEC countries and there is no reason why a similar economic mechanism could not work with minerals largely concentrated in Africa. Pan-African coordination may also be sought to stir competition among international investors: Africa's soil hosts the largest proven world oil reserves after the Middle East; in the coming years, and compatibly with fluctuations of the oil market, its governments will find themselves in an increasingly strong bargaining position, which could be exploited by playing-off the many corporate and governmental players that will knock at their doors. This is what Angola has already done between the UK, the USA, France, India and China, when in 2004, it sovereignly decided to turn down Western-backed IMF loans and FDI offers to accept China as a key partner. Continent-wide coordination among oil-producing countries could ensure even better results, considering that industrial economies will soon be left with no other region in the world to turn to when looking for fresh oil sources.

Simple political and diplomatic coordination could contribute in advancing African state's bargaining power a great deal: the few examples in which this has happened, have given encouraging results.[4] On their side, Western countries and their national corporations have long used divide-and-rule tactics in Africa—including on issues relating to DDA, EPAs and the United States Africa Command (AFRICOM)—and there are signs that China has already started employing similar techniques; better coordination among African states would compensate such negotiation imbalances.

Second: African states should seek diversification away from the primary sector and specialization in activities characterized by higher value-added capacity, increasing marginal returns and economies of scale. This means that surpluses from mining and agriculture should be diverted from consumption and channelled towards industrial investments in sectors with progressively higher capital and technology inputs. While dichotomist economic debates on inwards/outwards, ISI/export-led, protectionist/liberal options offer useful insights, history shows that successful developmental states were led by pragmatic considerations rather than ideological roadmaps. For example, if the most profitable markets are domestic, then a government likely has an incentive to promote import substitution, as the benefits to national producers offset the increased costs passed to the consumers; if the domestic market is not able to pay sufficient returns, then the government will likely be better off in prioritizing foreign markets through export-led growth. Sub-Saharan Africa has heavy negative trade balances on consumer items requiring relatively low-capital and low-technology investments, including foodstuff, automotive spare parts, basic chemicals and generic drugs—national investments in these industries should be considered a matter of priority.

In this phase, it will be important for African governments to play a strong regulatory and entrepreneurial role. Inward FDI needs being regulated in such a way to incentivize capital-intensive industries, where profit and technology spillovers are likely the highest; joint ventures should be preferred to fully foreign-owned enterprises, at least in the first phases; foreign investments should create jobs at labour, mid-management and cadre levels; and framework agreements should oblige foreign investors to high levels of national procurements, backward and forward linkages to the national economy and regulated profit repatriation. There is a wealth of knowledge and international expertise on FDI and trade negotiations and African governments should invest to access this private expertise rather than exclusively relying on traditional technical assistance from ODA donors.[5]

African governments should also play an entrepreneurial role in their national economies. Whether through SOEs, state equities or simply by nurturing private national champions via fiscal protection and other forms of regulatory support, African states will need to promote national players in sectors with a strong potential for positive social fallouts over the mid-to-long term, but where there are too many short-term risks to lure the private sector's attention. Once these industries have been established, African governments should also be actively involved in promoting adequate market opportunities, including import duties, trade defence measures, export subsidies, limits on the export of technology and expertise, etc. African countries have thousands of double passport holders, professionals and PhDs who have acquired strong and relevant experiences in overseas governments, international organizations, banking institutions, financial and equity firms, international law cabinets and universities—these are the people that African governments need poaching back through an aggressive hiring campaign, along the lines of what China has been doing.[6]

Third: At a later stage, African countries will need to work towards the setting up of a higher normative and institutional framework promoting African economic interests through knowledge, soft-power and framework institutions. These measures may include financing Universities and think tanks nurturing an African breed of social and economic research compatible with African interests (along the lines of what has happened with Structuralist economics in Latin America); promoting their own development financial institutions (along the lines of the Brazilian Development Bank at national level or the New Development Bank and the Asian Infrastructure Investment Bank at international level); and exporting political (along the lines of political parties foundations such as the *Konrad Adenauer Stiftung* or civil society foundations such as the Open Society Foundation for South Africa), business (along the lines of the Trade and Law Centre at Stellenbosch) and social and developmental (along the lines of newly established ODA donor agencies, including the South African Development Partnership Agency and the Korea International Cooperation Agency) ideas and projects compatible with African interests on the international scene.

Ultimately, it should not be forgotten that healthy economic policies reflecting in healthy Balances of Payments only cover some aspects of socio-economic development and that most African states are in desperate need to improve their governance, accountability, legal and administrative standards—the alternative being protracted poverty, unsustainably high GINI coefficient levels and resource-fuelled welfare kleptocracies.

ODA suffers from a number of limitations—both within and outside the "conceptual box" described in Chap. 1; yet, in the current international situation, it works as a useful evil. ODA does not intend to create the conditions for sustainable development, in Africa or elsewhere in the developing world—it never did, at least since the British Colonial Development Act of 1929 defined its key features. Instead, ODA redistributes a tiny percentage of the wealth that is created abroad, also thanks to international norms that are promoted by ODA itself through the conditionality principle and the power balance it contributes to reiterate in the relationship between overly-powerful creditors and highly-dependent debtors. However, there is no doubt that millions of human lives have been improved and, despite the impossibility of elaborating sound statistics, that many of these same lives were outright saved from starvation, deadly illnesses or accidental death.[7]

How to intervene upon a set of policies that, while denying a holistic solution to the problem of the incidence of world poverty, still find an ineffective, unsatisfactory and, ultimately, unacceptable alternative by tackling its prevalence, remains a moral and pragmatic dilemma of our age.

Notes

1. The term "Beijing Consensus" was firstly defined by Joshua Cooper Ramo (2004) along three theorems: (1) innovation-based development, (2) economic success measured not by per capita GDP growth but by its sustainability and level of equality, and (3) self-determination for China and for other countries via-à-vis (a) the USA's opposition to the Washington Consensus, (b) globalization on their own terms, (c) Chinese influence by example, not weaponry and (d) development of asymmetric capabilities to balance against the USA.
2. The expression is mediated from Henning Melber in (Murithi 2013, p. 334).
3. The Communication from the Commission to the European Parliament, the Council, the European Economic and Social Committee and the Committee of the Regions of 17 October 2008 entitled "The EU, Africa and China: Towards trilateral dialogue and cooperation" has five priority objectives: (1) reinforcing security and support for peacekeeping operations, (2) developing affordable and sustainable infrastructures to reinforce interconnectivity and regional integration, (3) protection of the environment and management of natural resources within a context of economic and commercial growth, (4) increase in agricultural production, quality of production and food security, and (5) extending already existing political dialogue between the AU, the EU and China. Besides, EU officials report a generally dismissive attitude of the Chinese government at EU efforts in fostering dialogue on cooperation in Africa within the general framework of the EU–China Strategic Partnership (Personal discussion, Brussels, January 2015).
4. The revamp of the East African Railway network is one of such examples, with Governments pertaining to the East African Community having agreed on a budget, set aside own resources for seed investments, agreed on the setting up of a regional authority and began implementation of the 2009 East African Railway Master Plan.
5. Typically, ODA technically assistance (TA) programmes are provided to build capacity in the beneficiaries' Ministries, either on technical portfolios (e.g. agriculture, energy and water, security, etc.) or on transversal managerial and administrative issues (procurement, transparency, disbursement capacity, human resources, etc.).

TA programmes aimed at increasing the capacity of beneficiary countries in negotiating trade, FDI or portfolio investment agreements are scarce because, by encroaching on the donor community's own economic interests, they would naturally raise conflicts of interests.

6. For example, the Thousand Talents Program offers full-time and part-time positions to overseas Chinese applicants under 55 years old (40 years for the Thousand Talent Distinguished Young Scholar Programme), who have received their doctorates from a distinguished international university and work as professors or an equivalent position at accredited academic institutions. The Chinese government also engages on a number of *ad-hoc* hiring trails in American Universities aimed at attracting back Chinese overseas PhDs. Also, in 2014, the Foshan Bureau of Foreign Trade and Economic Cooperation became the first mainland government department to accept foreigners into its internal structure (Lau 2014).
7. The discussion of ODA policies and interventions did not include humanitarian assistance, which is generally considered to be of a different nature because it is aimed at saving lives by reacting in the short term to natural and man-made disasters.

References

Bräutigam, D., & Xiaoyang, T. (2011). African Shenzhen: China's special economic zones in Africa. *The Journal of Modern African Studies, 49*(01), 27–54.

Huang, X. (2013). *Modern economic development in Japan and China*. Houndmills: Palgrave MacMillan.

Lau, M. (2014). Foshan is first Chinese local government to open up to foreign talent. *South China Morning Post*, 8.6.2014.

Murithi, T. (2013). *Handbook of Africa's international relations*. London: Routledge.

Ramo, J. C. (2004). *The Beijing consensus*. London: Foreign Policy Centre.

Index

A

Acemoglu, Daron, 56, 64, 71n17, 72n24

Africa

aggregate current accounts, 63, 131–4, 140, 148, 155n1, 176, 224

regional economic communities (RECs), 15, 26, 215, 230

Sub-Saharan, 24–7, 132–4, 136, 138, 146, 150–2, 154, 155, 156n3, 157n6, 168, 209, 217, 238n22, 248, 252

Africa, Caribbean and Pacific (ACP) group of countries, 156n4. *See also* European Union (EU)

African Growth and Opportunity Acts (AGOA), 32, 40n34, 233

African Union (AU), xxixn3, 167, 215, 230, 238n18, 254n3

AGOA. *See* African Growth and Opportunity Acts (AGOA)

agriculture, 58, 61, 63, 90, 104, 107, 115, 116, 138, 183, 187–8, 194, 204n48, 228, 234, 249, 251, 254n5

Angola, 4, 9, 13, 31, 35n1, 40n29, 63, 82, 151, 156n5, 157n6, 157n11, 182, 202n31, 203n42, 203n44, 221, 222, 240–1n33, 241n39, 251

Aristotle, 57

Association of South–East Asian Nations (ASEAN)

AU. *See* African Union (AU)

B

balance of payment (BoP), xxv, xxvii, 30, 52, 129–54, 156n1, 158n14, 160n33, 168, 183, 185, 192

balance of trade, 91, 93, 120n12, 130, 224. *See also* trade

Baran, Paul A., 46

Note: Page numbers with “n” denote notes.

S. Raudino, *Development Aid and Sustainable Economic Growth in Africa*, DOI 10.1007/978-3-319-38936-3

Beijing consensus, 247–9, 254n1
benign link. *See* Bhagwati, Jagdish N.
Bhagwati, Jagdish N.
benign link, 47–51, 248
malign link, 44–7
BoP. *See* balance of payment (BoP)
brain drain, 34, 118, 123n33
Brazil, xxii, xxiii, 24, 25, 46, 47, 66, 73n30, 83, 92, 111, 152, 173, 186, 192, 194, 201n28
Brazil, Russia, India, China, South Africa (BRICS), xxiii, 173, 236n7, 250
Bretton Woods, 45, 50, 168, 169, 171, 198n4, 198n6, 236n7
BRICS. *See* Brazil, Russia, India, China, South Africa (BRICS)
budget (national)
African countries, 63, 145, 161n36, 193
European countries, 62, 172
United States, 251
Bull, Hedley, 49

C

CAP. *See* Common Agriculture Policy (CAP)
capital
accumulation, 58, 119n8, 195
flight, xxv, xxvii, 29–31, 33, 34, 129, 130, 139, 145, 153–4, 162n43, 246
repatriation, 115, 116, 148, 153, 184
capital and financial account, 147–53
Chang, Ha-Joon, 44, 65, 105, 106, 110, 122n22, 123n33, 180, 200n21
charity, 28, 40n33, 81, 159n23, 194
Chavez, Hugo, 66
China–Africa
investments, xxviii, 145, 210, 215, 217, 221, 232, 238n19, 238n22
policies, xxvi
trade, 136, 209, 219, 221, 223, 224, 232
Chinese Government
China Communist Party (CCP), 216, 217
Chinese Ministry of Commerce (MOFCOM), 213, 217, 222, 224, 229
Chinese Ministry of Foreign Affairs (MOFA), 217, 221
Export–Import Bank (ExIm), 217, 238n22
Chung-hee, Park, 105
Churchill, Winston, 39n22, 112
Colbert, Jean-Baptiste, 96, 97
Colonial Development Act 1929. *See* United Kingdom
colonies
European, 56, 72n24, 97
New World, 92
commodities
exploitation, 219, 226
price volatility, 186
Common Agriculture Policy (CAP), 111, 123n32
Cotonou Agreement, 34, 166
Current Account
African deficit, 132, 148
African trends, 141

D

debt, 8, 41n37, 48, 63, 102, 131, 132, 139–42, 147, 153, 155, 156, 159n23, 159n30, 162n43, 221, 237n13, 239n36
Democratic Peace Theory (DPT), 66

dependentist school, 46. *See also* economic theory
Development Aid Committee (DAC). *See* Organization for Economic Cooperation and Development (OECD)
development policies
  conditionalities, 191
  coordination, 35n6, 53
  sustainability, 35n6
Diamond, Jared, 56
Dos Santos, Theotonio, 46

E

East India Company, 92
econometrics, 81, 129–31, 165
economic growth, xxvi, 3, 5–8, 10, 11, 17–19, 24, 26, 37n11, 43, 47, 50, 52, 54, 55, 57–9, 61, 63–7, 67n1, 69n7, 69n9, 79–125, 130, 134, 160n34, 180, 189, 195, 196, 245, 248, 249
economic linkages
  backward, 63, 248
  forward, 63, 116, 150, 252
Economic Partnership Agreements (EPAs), 32, 166, 177, 188, 201n26, 251
economic policies
  emulation, 85
  negative, 87, 97, 102, 109–12, 249
  vicious cycle, 84, 195
  virtuous cycle, 84, 114–18, 129, 130, 138, 192, 249, 250
economic theory
  development, 11, 43, 57; big push, 63; dependentist school, 46; export-led, 117, 251, 252; linear stage, 61; structural change, 61, 193, 249, 250; unbalanced growth, 63
  general, 54, 60, 67; monetarism, 67; neoclassicism, 67; neoliberalism, 118; structuralism, 67
endogenous
  growth, 11, 53, 85, 86
  policies, 83, 186
England, 85, 89–94, 98, 99, 106, 110, 111, 120n13, 121n15, 121n18, 122n29
EPAs. *See* Economic Partnership Agreements (EPAs)
epistemology, xxii–xxvi, 59
EU. *See* European Union (EU)
Europe–Africa
  Foreign Direct Investments (FDI), xxvii
  Official development Assistance (ODA), 1–3
  trade, 133, 209
European Union (EU)
  Africa, Caribbean and Pacific (ACP) group of countries, 134–7, 158n12, 166, 177
  development cooperation policy, 17
  treaties, 111, 166
export
  ban, 183
  led growth, 117, 252
  maximization, 250
Export–Import Bank (ExIm), 217. *See also* Chinese Government
export processing zones (EPZs), 107, 196

F

FDI. *See* Foreign Direct Investments (FDI)
Flanders, 89
FOCAC. *See* Forum on China Africa Cooperation (FOCAC)

food insecurity, 81, 118n2
Foreign Direct Investments (FDI)
brownfield, 148, 149, 195
conditions, 62, 116, 148, 175, 178, 184, 228, 232, 247–9
flows, 33, 150, 151, 161n35, 165, 225
greenfield, 148, 149, 152, 195
inwards, 33, 251; Africa, 33, 251; Asian Newly Industrialized Economies (NIEs), 250
joint-ventures (JV), 116, 148, 183, 184, 226, 246, 252
merger & acquisitions (M&A), 148, 149, 151, 152
stock, 150–1, 213
Wholly-Foreign Owned Enterprises (WFOE), 148, 246
Forum on China Africa Cooperation (FOCAC), 145, 212, 221, 223, 236n12
France, 80, 85, 88, 92, 94–7, 100, 110, 112, 119n8, 122n26, 143, 167, 170, 172, 180, 198n7, 212, 235n7, 236n10, 251
Frank, Andre Gunder, 46
free trade agreements (FTAs), 177, 178, 188. *See also* trade
French West India Company, 96
Friedman, Milton, 50, 51, 65
FTAs. *See* free trade agreements (FTAs)

G
G90. *See* Group of 90 (G90)
Gaddafi, Muammar, 66
Galen of Pergamum, 80
GATT. *See* General Agreement on Tariffs and Trade (GATT)
GCC. *See* Gulf Cooperation Council (GCC)
General Agreement on Tariffs and Trade (GATT), 171, 173, 177, 181, 236n8
Gini coefficient, 83, 119n4, 122n26, 253
Global South, 88
Grants. *See* Official Development Assistance (ODA)
Great Depression 1929, 50
gross domestic product (GDP)
and development, 106, 248
growth, 24–6, 39n24, 65, 67n1, 83, 131, 248, 254n1 (*see also* economic growth)
Group of 90 (G90), xxixn4, 3, 70n10, 84, 166, 167, 170, 171, 173, 175, 176, 179, 181, 183, 192, 224, 233, 248
Gulf Cooperation Council (GCC), 146, 202n38

H
Hamilton, Alexander, 99, 101
Heckscher–Ohlin theory, 50, 69n7
Henry VII, 85, 90
historical materialism, 58
HIV, 41n37, 82
Hong Kong, 66, 85, 104, 105, 108, 119n7, 153, 161n38, 221, 237n17
human security, 81, 190

I
IFIs. *See* international financial institutions (IFIs)
IMF. *See* International Monetary Fund (IMF)
import, 32, 47, 54, 68n5, 90–3, 95, 98, 100, 101, 103, 104, 106–11, 116, 117, 133–6, 153, 155, 157n10,

158n13, 161n42, 176, 177, 190, 197, 203n47, 204n49, 220–5, 231, 234, 240n29, 247, 251, 252
import substitution industrialization (ISI), 47, 68n5, 117, 234, 251
India, xxiii, 24, 25, 47, 92, 96, 103, 111, 121n15, 152, 170, 173, 178, 196, 236n10, 251
international financial institutions (IFIs), 8, 9, 51, 64, 124n39, 143, 167–70, 173, 184, 185, 188–91, 210, 212, 238n20
International Monetary Fund (IMF)
executive board, 169, 198–9n7, 199n10
policies, 53, 114, 143, 166, 167, 188, 199n10, 211, 233
Structural Adjustment Program (SAP), 179, 183–5, 188, 189, 192, 203n40
Intolerable Acts, 99
Italy, 66, 85, 89, 90, 112, 172, 211
Italian city states, 85, 88–90

J
Japan
colonial policy, 85
founding fathers, 102
industrial conglomerate (kareitsu), 106
modernization, 102
joint-ventures (JV), 116, 148, 183, 184, 226, 246, 252. *See also* Foreign Direct Investments (FDI)

K
Kant, Immanuel, 48
Keynesianism, 50, 67
Keynes, John Maynard, 64, 91
Kohl, Helmut, 50

L
laissez-faire, 45, 59, 94
Latin America, 47, 68n4, 115, 119n7, 123n34, 150, 154, 162n43, 168, 172, 185, 248, 253
import substitution, 47
Least Developed Countries (LDCs), 3, 24, 168, 172
Lewis, Arthur W., 4, 61
liberalism, 48, 50, 65, 118
List, Friedrich, 45, 99, 110, 115
loans
business, 212
preferential, 160n32, 168, 219 (*see also* Official Development Assistance (ODA))
lobby
groups in Europe, 133
groups in Unites States, 133
legislation, 177
London club, 8, 139, 140, 191
Louis XI, 85, 94–6
Louis XIV, 96

M
Machiavelli, Niccoló, 44, 68n2
malign link. *See* Bhagwati, Jagdish N.
Malthus, Thomas, xxii, xxviiin2, 58
manufacturing, xxvii, 7, 9, 32, 45, 63, 67, 86, 87, 89, 90, 92, 93, 95–101, 104, 105, 109, 110, 112, 115, 123n36, 138, 148, 150, 158n16, 174, 176, 177, 182, 194, 196, 200n20, 224–7, 232, 234, 240n29, 247
market
access, 32, 50, 87, 93, 96, 101, 108, 111, 116, 160n34, 175, 176, 224, 226
capitalization, 152, 155
Marxism, 58, 59

Marx, Karl, xxixn6, 45, 59, 73n31
M&E. *See* monitoring & evaluation (M&E)
mercantilism, 87, 90, 91, 94, 97, 101, 105, 109, 112, 120n12
Merger & Acquisitions (M&A). *See* Foreign Direct Investments (FDI)
migration
  Africans to China, 228
  Africans to western countries, 35, 166
  Chinese to Africa, 228
  Westerners to Africa, 16
Millennium Development Goals (MDGs), 24, 166
Mill, John Stuart, 48
mining. *See* natural resources
MNCs. *See* multinational corporations (MNCs)
monitoring & evaluation (M&E), 18–20, 26, 39n23
Morgenthau, Hans J., 44
multinational corporations (MNCs), 45, 114, 153, 174, 179, 181, 182, 187, 188, 191, 195, 203n45, 224, 231, 233, 234, 246
Myrdal, Gunnar, 45, 46

N

NATO. *See* North Atlantic Treaty Organization (NATO)
natural resources
  mining, 203n47, 222, 251
  oil, 85, 151, 203n47, 204n48, 219, 221, 222, 251
Navigation Act, 92, 94
Neoclassicism. *See* economic theory
New Deal (Franklyn Delano Roosevelt), 22, 23
newly industrialized economies (NIEs), xxvi, 52, 53, 65, 67, 84, 104–9, 115, 116, 124n39, 129, 138, 150, 170, 176, 179, 195, 215, 249, 250
Nigeria, 31, 40n29, 83, 152, 156n5, 157n6, 157n11, 173, 179, 182, 202n31, 203n44, 204n47, 223, 237n18, 240n30, 240n32
North Atlantic Treaty Organization (NATO), xxii, 167, 212
Nurkse, Ragnar, 62
Nye, Joseph, 87

O

ODA. *See* Official Development Assistance (ODA)
OECD. *See* Organization for Economic Cooperation and Development (OECD)
Official Development Assistance (ODA)
  auditing, 13, 18–21, 142, 143, 228
  China to Africa, 129, 138, 145, 212, 214, 219, 221, 232, 246
  conceptual box, 10–13, 16, 29, 253
  gap, 141, 142, 144
  grants, 22, 69n10, 143–5
  preferential loans, 160n32, 219
  quantitative studies, xxixn5, 6, 21, 52, 53, 70n13
  tied, 16, 144, 145, 193
  west to Africa, 129, 165, 191, 214, 219, 232, 246
oil. *See* natural resources
OPEC. *See* Organization of the Petroleum Exporting Countries (OPEC)
Organization for Economic Cooperation and Development (OECD), xxiii, xxvi, xxviiin1, xxixn4, 3–5, 7, 22, 23, 25, 27, 30–4, 36n5, 36n6, 37n8, 37n13,

38n18, 39n26, 40n27, 40n34, 52, 53, 67, 70n10, 72n23, 79, 81, 84, 107, 111, 115, 116, 119n4, 120n10, 124n39, 129, 131, 134, 138–45, 147, 150, 152–5, 156n3, 159n26, 159n27, 166, 167, 169, 171, 172, 174–83, 188–93, 195–7, 199n13, 200n22, 202n33, 211, 212, 214–16, 221, 223, 225, 227–9, 232, 233, 237n15, 240n28, 241n32, 246, 250
Development Aid Committee (DAC), 4–5, 40n34, 140–3, 159n27, 212, 241n32
Organization of the Petroleum Exporting Countries (OPEC), xxiii, 186, 203n44, 251

P

Paris club, 139, 212
peacekeeping operation, 12, 211, 212, 230, 254n3
PISA. *See* Program for International Student Assessment (PISA)
portfolio investments, 147, 149, 151–3, 155, 245
positive-sum game, 48, 118, 250
Poverty Reduction Strategy Paper (PRSP), 4, 19, 190, 191, 196
preferential trade agreements (PTAs), 177, 178, 191, 200n23. *See also* trade
Preston, Lewis Thompson, 51, 173
primary income, 29, 131, 139–40, 231, 245
private sector development (PSD), 9, 41n37, 196, 204n53
privatisation, 121n21, 170, 183, 190, 204n49
problem solving
questions, 53
theory, 53
procurements, 13, 16, 116, 117, 172, 184, 222, 223, 227, 252, 254n5
production cycle, 2, 11–13, 17
Program for International Student Assessment (PISA), 172, 199n13, 216, 238n22. *See also* University rankings
PTAs. *See* preferential trade agreements (PTAs)
public-private Partnership (PPP), 195, 239n23

R

realism, 44
Regan, Ronald, 50
Reinert, Erik S., 106, 112, 124n36, 200n21
remittances, 34, 123n34, 130, 132, 145–6, 155, 160n33, 161n41, 165
returns on investments (RoI), 54, 61, 130, 139, 225, 227
in Africa, 54, 130, 139, 225, 227
Ricardo, David, xxviiin2, 49, 58, 59, 72n21, 94
Rostow, Walter, 61, 62, 72n22
Russia, xxiii, 65, 112, 172, 173, 185, 188, 198n5, 203n47, 211

S

secondary income, 131–3, 144, 145, 159n31
SEZs. *See* special economic zone (SEZs)
Singapore, 66, 85, 104, 105, 107, 108, 111, 119n7, 184, 201n27
Small and Medium Enterprises (SMEs), 107, 153, 174, 179,

205n56, 213, 218, 220, 225, 233, 234
Smith, Adam
invisible hand, 49
Wealth of Nations, 57, 71n20
SOEs. *See* state owned enterprise (SOEs)
soft-power, 66, 87, 112–14, 231, 248, 252
South Africa, xxii, xxiii, 1, 26, 27, 31, 35n1, 40n34, 47, 82, 83, 104, 132–4, 151–2, 156n3, 156n5, 157n11, 173, 177, 182, 202n31, 223, 237–8n18, 240n29, 242n43, 253
South Korea
foreign currency control, 106
Heavy and Chemical Industrialization (HCI), 105
industrial conglomerate (chaebol), 106
Spain, 85, 92, 96, 112, 121n19, 211
special economic zone (SEZs), 196, 239n24, 247, 248
state owned enterprise (SOEs), 21, 116, 170, 183, 184, 213, 214, 217–19, 223, 225–7, 231, 233, 234, 242n39, 247, 252
Stiglitz, Joseph E., 114
Structural Adjustment Program (SAP), 179, 183–5, 188, 189, 192, 203n40. *See also* International Monetary Fund (IMF)
Sunkel, Osvaldo, 46, 68n4

T
Taiwan, 47, 85, 103–7, 119n7, 122n27, 183, 184, 230, 236n8
tariffs
historical, 175
reductions, 223, 224
tax
average levels, 184
exemption, 116, 184
Thatcher, Margaret, 50
Thucydides, 44
tied aid, 16, 144, 145, 193. *See also* Official Development Assistance (ODA)
trade
balance of, 91, 93, 120n12, 130, 224
free trade agreements (FTAs), 177, 178, 188
goods, 30, 45, 48, 50, 89, 91–3, 96–9, 101, 103, 112, 116, 117, 133–8, 145, 155, 158n13, 176–8, 180, 190, 196, 220, 221, 224, 225, 235n3, 248
liberalization, 9, 177–80, 193, 204n49, 211, 223
preferential trade agreements (PTAs), 177, 191, 200n23
protection, 180, 204n50
services, 30, 41n37, 48, 50, 96, 133–8, 145, 155, 176, 178, 180, 181, 194, 196, 232, 248
structure, 134–6, 155, 156n3, 221, 223–5, 232
Tzu, Sun, 44

U
UNCTAD. *See* United Nations Conference on Trade and Development (UNCTAD)
UNDP. *See* United Nations Development Programme (UNDP)
unequal treaties, 45, 68n3, 102, 103, 111, 112, 116, 123n31, 123n35
UNIDO. *See* United Nations Industrial Development Organization (UNIDO)

United Kingdom
Colonial Development Act 1929, 22, 112
colonial policies, 113
United Nations (UN)
General Assembly (GA), 36n5, 168, 198n3, 230
Security Council (SC), 168, 169, 210, 216, 220, 229–31, 239n27, 242n43
United Nations Conference on Trade and Development (UNCTAD), 25, 27, 33, 39n26, 40n31, 41n34, 68n4, 122n25, 132, 133, 140, 151, 158n21, 161n37–9, 168, 184, 187, 188, 198n3, 203n45
United Nations Development Programme (UNDP), 37n13, 39n26, 71n14, 168, 198n3, 238n22
United Nations Industrial Development Organization (UNIDO), 138, 139, 152, 168, 197, 198n3, 205n56
United States, 251
University rankings, 216, 238n20
Programme for International Student Assessment (PISA), 216
Upham, Frank, 64, 65

V
value added
Manufacturing Value Added index (MVA), 138, 158n17
Value Added index (VAI), 138
Von Hayek, Ludwig, 50–1

W
Waltz, Kenneth, xxiv, xxiii, 44
Washington Consensus, 50, 51, 114, 188–92, 248, 249, 254n1
Wei-Ming, Tu, 65
Wholly-Foreign Owned Enterprises (WFOE), 148, 246. *See also* Foreign Direct Investments (FDI)
Wolfensohn, James, 51
World Bank
board of directors, 169
policies, 6, 9, 51, 124n40, 232
World Trade Organization (WTO)
Doha Development Agenda (DDA), 166
green room meetings, 171

X
Xiaoping, Deng, 211, 246

Z
Zedong, Mao, 82
zero-sum game, 46, 87, 250
Zimbabwe, 82, 157n11, 182, 188, 189, 214, 240n32, 242n43, 242n46

The manufacturer's authorised representative in the EU is Springer
Nature Customer Service Centre GmbH, Europaplatz 3, 69115 Heidelberg,
Germany. If you have any concerns regarding our products, please
contact ProductSafety@springernature.com

Printed and bound by CPI Group (UK) Ltd, Croydon, CR0 4YY
25/09/2026
02222859-0004